T0275023

THE
SALTWATER HIGHWAY

THE
SALTWATER
HIGHWAY

ONE MAN'S JOURNEY
THROUGH THE INTERNATIONAL
DRY BULK MARITIME MARKET

ANTHONY R. WHITWORTH

Post Hill
PRESS

A POST HILL PRESS BOOK
ISBN: 979-8-88845-054-3
ISBN (eBook): 979-8-88845-055-0

The Saltwater Highway:
One Man's Journey through the International Dry Bulk Maritime Market
© 2023 by Anthony R. Whitworth
All Rights Reserved

Original cover design by Harvey Hoffenberg – Propulsion. Printed cover by Conroy Accord.

This is a work of nonfiction. All people, locations, events, and situation are portrayed to the best of the author's memory.

Post Hill Press
New York • Nashville
posthillpress.com

Published in the United States of America

For Derek and Grahame

The maritime industry has several idiomatic terms that are not common outside of the industry. To help the reader better understand this terminology, I have included a glossary that can be found at the back of this book.

Words that are in bold in the text at first mention indicate they are defined in the glossary.

CONTENTS

LIST OF ABBREVIATIONS

CAVN: Compañia Anónima Venezolana de Navegación

CVC: Citigroup Venture Capital

CVG: Corporación Venezolana de Guayana

DRI: Direct Reduced Iron (Ore Pellets)

EBITDA: Earnings Before Interest, Taxes, Depreciation, and Amortization

EEA: European Emission Allowances

ESDs: Energy-Saving Devices

ETS: Emission Trading System

FMO: Ferrominera del Orinoco

GDP: Gross Domestic Product

GHG: Greenhouse Gas

IEC: Israel Electric Corporation

IFO: Intermediate Fuel Oil

IMO: International Maritime Organization

IPO: Initial Public Offering

ISE: International Shipping Enterprises

JIT: Just-in-Time (Inventory Management)

JMU: Japan Marine United

LIBOR: London Interbank Offered Rate

LNG:	Liquefied Natural Gas
MES:	Mitsui Engineering & Shipbuilding
MV:	Motor Vessel
NAV:	Net Asset Value
NCSC:	National Coal Supply Corporation (of Israel)
NHI:	Navios Handybulk Inc.
NI:	Navios International
NMH:	Navios Maritime Holdings
NOx:	Nitrogen or Nitric Oxide
NSA:	Navios Ship Agencies
OBO:	Oil-Bulk-Ore (Carrier)
OECD:	Organization for Economic Co-operation and Development
OMC:	Orinoco Mining Company
OOCL:	Orient Overseas Container Line
OPEC:	Organization of the Petroleum Exporting Countries
OSG:	Overseas Shipholding Group
OTC:	Over the Counter
PDVSA:	Petróleos de Venezuela, S.A.
QAL:	Queensland Alumina Limited
SIDOR:	Siderúrgica de Orinoco C.A.
SPAC:	Special-Purpose Acquisition Company
STH:	Sea Trade Holdings
VAR:	Value-at-Risk
VLSFO:	Very Low Sulfur Fuel Oil
WABS:	West African Bulk Shipping
WTO:	World Trade Organization

INTRODUCTION

"Success is not the key to happiness. Happiness is the key to success. If you love what you are doing, you will be successful."

ALBERT SCHWEITZER,
Alsatian-German/French humanitarian/
physician, winner of 1952 Nobel Peace Prize

It has always struck me as odd that after more than forty-five years in the business of international maritime transportation, I have yet to meet anyone who has heard of, let alone read, a book entitled *Supership* by Noël Mostert. Published in 1974, this book changed my life. It was given to me as a gift from my father during the final semester of a four-year undergraduate program at Queen's University in Kingston, Ontario.

A Canadian citizen who was born and raised in Cape Town, South Africa, Mostert is perhaps best known for his book *Frontiers*, an epic narrative history of the founding of South Africa. *Supership* is his account of a voyage he took in 1973 on the MV *Ardshiel*, a large crude oil tanker built in Japan in 1969 and owned by P&O Shipping Lines. It is a description of not only Mostert's voyage on board the *Ardshiel* from Europe to the Persian Gulf and back, but also what life at sea is like on a modern supertanker.

To this day, I have no idea why Dad read it, and, unfortunately, as he is no longer with us, I will never know. But I do have a few thoughts as to why he gave the book to me. Perhaps he was concerned I did not have a sense of direction as to what field I might enter following my studies. But I suspect the more likely reason had to do with the fact that my mother's family had for many generations been involved in the building of ships.

For a kid born and raised in Quebec City, the idea of working in the international business of maritime transport had never entered my mind… at least not until I read this book.

***

Due to the depletion of domestic woodlands in England, by the early nineteenth century, Britain was importing significant quantities of Baltic timber. When this trade was impacted by the Napoleonic Wars, the British timber merchants moved their timber-harvesting operations to North America, specifically to areas of what is today southern Ontario and Quebec.

George Taylor, a master shipbuilder who had been appointed by British merchants, arrived in Quebec in 1811 to supervise the construction of new ships that were built primarily to transport Canadian timber back to England, to feed the insatiable demand for this commodity. However, in 1817, Taylor, sensing an opportunity, decided to strike out building ships on his own. He acquired river frontage in the Canoterie section of Quebec, known today as the Old Port area next to the St. Charles River, and set about constructing ships.

The transatlantic trade in timber grew rapidly and was aided by the passage of the British Timber Act of 1821, whose protectionist policies favored Canadian timber. That same year, Allison Davie, a young master mariner, arrived in Quebec following a difficult Atlantic crossing, during which the ship he captained endured significant damage. The vessel's British owner decided to have the ship repaired at the new Taylor shipyard, and Allison stayed in Quebec to represent the owner and oversee the work. It was during this time that he met and fell in love with Elizabeth Taylor, George Taylor's only child.

Because he had no sons, George Taylor made clear he had two stipulations for anyone wishing to marry his daughter. The husband-to-be would have to become his partner in the shipyard, and he would have to perpetuate the Taylor name by giving it to any offspring of the marriage. And for Allison Davie, he had one more condition: He would have to relinquish his profession as a master mariner and come ashore. Following a year of indecision, Allison agreed to the terms set out by George Taylor, and Allison and Elizabeth were married on April 15, 1825—the same day the partnership between Allison and his father-in-law was signed.

In the years following the marriage, the Taylor-Davie partnership prospered, highlighted in 1827 by the delivery from the yard of the first-ever

British naval vessel built in Quebec. In 1829, as their shipbuilding and repair business expanded, they acquired four hundred feet of river frontage directly across the St. Lawrence River from the city of Quebec in what is known today as Lévis.

Through the nineteenth and early twentieth centuries, successive generations of the Taylor-Davie marriage managed to grow what became known as Davie Shipyards in Lévis. During this time, the shipyard successfully managed the transition from building wooden hull vessels to those of metal hulls. Davie built tugboats, paddle steamers, ferryboats, and carried out salvage and repair work. The business was sold by the family in 1915 to Vickers and Canada Steamship Lines, although George Duncan Davie, a grandson of Allison Davie, continued to manage the business for several years following the sale.

Allison Davie was my maternal great-great-great-great-grandfather.

∗∗∗

The name Quebec is derived from an Algonquin Indian word, *kébec*, meaning "the narrowing of the river." Quebec City was established in 1608 by the French explorer Samuel de Champlain on the promontory known today as Cape Diamond, just across from the small city of Lévis on the south shore of the St. Lawrence River. It is where that majestic river narrows to about one kilometer, and de Champlain viewed it as a strategic military position that would allow him to control maritime access to the St. Lawrence south of Quebec.

Three hundred years later, about ten kilometers south of Quebec City, construction began on a new bridge that took about twenty years to complete. The project, which at the time was considered one of the greatest engineering feats of the twentieth century, failed twice due to poor engineering design, with a loss of about ninety men. But in 1919, it finally opened for railway traffic. Today, with a length of one kilometer, the Quebec City Bridge is still the longest cantilevered bridge in the world, and the farthest downstream crossing over the St. Lawrence River.

In July 1958, my parents; my younger brother, aged three; and I, aged five, along with one other couple, were booked on the MV *Carinthia* for a transatlantic voyage to Liverpool. The *Carinthia* was the third of four sister passenger ships built by Cunard Lines (independent at the time, but now part of the Carnival Cruise Line empire) specifically for transatlantic crossings from Southampton to New York, and from Liverpool to Montreal. This class of ship was known as the Saxonia class after the name of the first ship in the series to deliver. Cunard Lines had a tradition of naming its ships after provinces of the Roman and Holy Roman Empires.

This was the age of **liner service** travel, which took its name from ocean passenger ships that were designed to take "line" voyages between points A and B. The purpose of the liner passenger vessel was to reach a destination by sailing across the oceans, whereas today a cruise ship is itself the destination augmented by frequent ports of call before arriving at its final destination.

The *Carinthia* was designed to carry 125 passengers in first class and about 800 passengers in tourist class. Because tourist class had to make do with shared bathroom facilities, my mother insisted that we travel first class, and the best adjective to describe these superior accommodations on this ship is "opulent." There were large staterooms, magnificent lounges, glass-enclosed promenade decks, designated smoking rooms, luxurious dining rooms, and even a cinema!

That afternoon, we boarded a tug from the Port of Quebec and headed south up the St. Lawrence River on a route that brought us under the Quebec City Bridge. The waters were calm, although the vibration from the engines of the tug could be felt as it pushed southward up the St. Lawrence River, and the propeller churned against the strong current. I could smell diesel as dark fumes escaped from the boat's **funnel**.

As we passed under the huge bridge to meet the *Carinthia*, I looked up in awe at this massive gray iron structure that soared about one hundred meters above us. I had never seen something so huge in my young life. Then I was startled by the low-sounding single blast of a horn and turned to see the massive *Carinthia* moving toward us.

It was a sight to behold for a five-year-old. The tug turned as she approached us, so that by the time the ship passed under the bridge, we were just about alongside her, moving at the same speed. We strained our necks to look up at the white **superstructure** with a massive rounded red funnel and the huge black hull plying its way through the river. I was startled a second time when the tugboat gave three short blasts from its horn, signifying that she was alongside the enormous passenger ship.

Eventually, both the ship and the tug reduced their engine speed to a slow idle to let the downstream current propel them along. I watched as the crew connected ropes from the side of the ship to the starboard bow and stern of the tug. Once the ropes were secured, a door above the waterline on the port side of the ship opened, and out came a gangway.

Because there were only six passengers joining the ship, it was more cost effective not to dock the *Carinthia* in the port of Quebec. That is why, as incredible as it may seem in this day and age, we proceeded to board the vessel from the tug along the gangway as the current of the mighty St. Lawrence River flowed beneath us.

My brother and I had the time of our lives on that Atlantic crossing. We were the only children in first class and were treated wonderfully by all the staff. We befriended one particular sailor, who spent hours showing us around the ship, including bringing us up to the **bridge deck** so that we could see the narrow bow of the ship cut through the Atlantic **rollers** as we headed east. I recall one day he took my brother and me up onto a small deck above the bridge. The winds were so fierce that day, we were able to lean vertically into them and not fall over. It was exhilarating, and a little frightening.

The memory of that voyage has stayed with me all these years. My love of all things nautical can be traced back to that experience as a young boy.

***

My goal in writing this book is to introduce a broader audience to the fascinating business of international dry bulk maritime transport, using what, I hope, are some of my compelling experiences both personal and professional over a span of nearly fifty years in this industry. What follows, therefore, is the voyage of my career in the business, centered around the forty-eight years I spent working at just three companies: Fednav Ltd. in Canada, and Navios Corporation and Sea Trade Holdings in the United States.

I have found throughout the years that very few people outside our industry know or understand anything about it. This has always surprised me because it is a business with a global reach far beyond any other industry. According to the International Chamber of Shipping, a global trade organization representing the world's national shipowner organizations, 90 percent of world trade moves via the oceans. In 2022 alone, large ocean-going ships transported over twelve billion **tonnes** of cargo around the world. The fact that so few people follow the maritime industry, or consider it an interesting career choice, is a mystery to me because it is truly one of the more fascinating work environments today.

One of the most serious challenges we had in the maritime sector during the 1980s and 1990s was the great difficulty attracting capable young people into our industry. During this period, maritime shipping experienced tremendous upheaval that caused the **dry bulk markets** to flounder for many years. Salaries were low, hours were long, and many companies were struggling. However, the financial and capital markets were exploding at the time. Enormous trading floors were being established to trade physical and futures in currencies, bonds, and commodities; all types of new derivative instruments were being promulgated; and proprietary trading desks of banks, private equity firms, and hedge funds were all becoming a force to be reckoned with. These new, exciting opportunities paid well, and the best and the brightest took advantage of them.

Fortunately, in the first decade of this century, the commodity markets entered a super cycle that helped to change the perceptions of our industry. I am happy to see more young people choosing a career path in the maritime markets, and my hope is that this book will encourage more young people to consider such a career.

I cannot stress enough the global nature of our business. All countries, even those that are landlocked, must import or export some commodity by sea. Obviously, certain countries are more reliant on seaborne trade than others, but without a doubt, every nation on Earth makes use of the high seas. Indeed, the increase in globalization we have witnessed over the past five decades could not have occurred without a very robust maritime infrastructure.

One of the most enjoyable aspects of the international maritime business has been the travel I have undertaken around the globe. To conclude business, you have got to be "at the table," and so boarding a plane to jet off to some far-flung country is part of what has made my career choice so interesting. Whether it is a marketing trip to develop new customers, visiting port sites or manufacturing facilities of prospective clients, or traveling to meet with sources of financing or with other shipowners, I have always enjoyed the excitement of traveling to new and different places. And I am not just referring to major capital cities across the globe, although I have visited many of these.

I suspect most of you reading this may recognize no more than two or three of the following locations: Puerto Ordaz, Barranquilla, Antofagasta, Nueva Palmira, Corumbá, Macapá, Conakry, Hadera, Surabaya, Busan, Qinhuangdao, Kaohsiung, Kivalina, Bellingham, Baie-Comeau, and Oban. These are a few of the out-of-the-way places I have visited over the years, some of which make up part of the story I am about to tell, and which comprise many of my richest experiences.

Needless to say, with the advent of the global pandemic, virtual meetings have taken the place of business travel, to a great degree. While it has certainly kept business functioning, I believe that meeting clients in person remains a powerful tool—and one that I am not about to give up. Fortunately, as we learn to cope with this scourge, business travel is slowly returning.

***

The past three years have been unimaginable, with a pandemic that has shown no acknowledgment of borders, fractured families across the globe, upset the livelihood of millions, and created chaos with just about everyone's social interaction. Nevertheless, it is the downtime created by the pandemic that has afforded me the time to write this book.

This is the story of my voyage that commenced in the fall of 1975 and continues today. One of the truly wonderful aspects of this endeavor is that it has allowed me to reconnect with colleagues from the past who shared with me many of the events of which you are about to read. I am very grateful to them for imparting their reminiscences with me.

It has been a fun and exciting journey.

CHAPTER 1

THE MARITIME INDUSTRY: AN OVERVIEW

"At the global level, trade occurs because resources are unevenly distributed. Some areas of the world are rich in minerals; some have the sunny conditions required to grow fruit or cotton; others have the vast plains that can grow wheat. Over time some cultures have benefited from their expertise in making pottery, textiles or manufactured goods. They make what they are good at, and then exchange the surplus with other places that are good at making or growing something else."

PHILIP COGGAN,
British business journalist, author of *More:
The 10,000-Year Rise of the World Economy*

"Maritime transportation is the backbone of global trade and the global economy."

BAN KI-MOON,
South Korean diplomat, former UN secretary general

The international maritime transportation industry has been "global" for centuries, long before "globalization" became a catchphrase of business in the late 1970s. Ships of various types and sizes have been plying the oceans for five or six millennia promoting trade across the far reaches of the world. Well before jet travel diminished the size of the modern world, commercial ships served to connect people and countries around the globe.

And yet, when most of the people I know outside the industry think about the maritime sector, it is because they have heard news of an oil spill from a tanker casualty, or read about the recent debacle of the **container ship** aground in the Suez Canal, or seen some article about globalization or challenges to the supply chain featuring a photo of a **dry bulk carrier** moored under the loading spout of a grain terminal. These isolated bits of information only scratch the surface of the vital role maritime transportation plays on the world stage.

The overall label assigned to this industry can be at times obscure. It is often referred to simply as "shipping" or "freight transport." These terms cover the gamut of the entire business of moving parcels, commodities, and cargoes: from FedEx home deliveries to the postal service, from rail service to trucks and airlines. The term "maritime transport" is more precise and best portrays the business of the movement of ships and cargoes across the world's oceans.

The dry bulk freight market is considered to be one of the best examples of pure competition in the business world. It has low barriers to entry; up until the last few decades, government and regulatory oversight had been relatively light; it operates to a great extent within a tax-free environment; the assets themselves are largely undifferentiated and are able to be moved around the world, unlike a manufacturing plant; and there are thousands of shipowners and **charterers** operating everywhere across the four corners of the globe. Because it has such a worldwide reach, no one entity has a controlling influence on the market, which means those of us working in the business of maritime transport are all price takers. It is certainly not an industry that would meet the strict investment criteria of Warren Buffett.

But it is a fascinating business in which one finds all types of characters, including swashbuckling entrepreneurs who make and lose fortunes, who build up fleets and eventually lose them, who travel the globe searching for the next commodity that might drive our markets or the more tax-efficient regime from which to operate their fleets.

One would think that since the international maritime industry is integral to all businesses, as well as the goods and services they produce, the captains of industry, both large and small that I've known, would be well acquainted with how it operates. However, much like the general consumer, they have little concrete understanding of its complexity and how it functions.

Most people do not know how much the basic elements of many of the essential items they take for granted rely upon the maritime transport industry. For instance, the production of aluminum—a key material in hundreds of things, such as cars, window frames, and soda cans—depends on bauxite, a raw mineral. Cement, which is integral to the making of infrastructures from homes to skyscrapers to sidewalks and bridges, is a complex amalgam of many raw materials mined from around the globe. Bread, cereal, and pasta are all comprised of grains from countries as far-flung as Ukraine and Argentina, Canada and Australia. Finally, the great steel mills and power plants around the world function because of the massive trade in petroleum and **thermal coal**. The dry bulk maritime transport industry delivers all of these commodities and many more that are vital to our lives and economies on a daily basis.

MV *STH Oslo* sailing from the Columbia River, having loaded a cargo of grain at Longview, Washington destined for the People's Republic of China. Credit: MarineTraffic/Mike Cullo

Few are conscious of being *directly* impacted by any of these fundamental commodities. Perhaps members of the investment community outside of shipping do look at the **Baltic Dry Index** (BDI), as they have in recent years come to consider it to be a bellwether of the global economy. But as to the nuts and bolts of this complicated industry that form the basis of the data that makes up this index, not many people take the time to understand what makes it tick.

So, when friends ask me how international shipping affects them, I always start by referring to the Panama Canal, one of the most well-known avenues of the saltwater highway, along with the Suez Canal. Then I use some metrics to show just how important this industry is to the movement of commodities around the world:

- Approximately 292 million tonnes of cargo, including grains, petroleum products, vegetable oils, refrigerated foods, steel products, chemical products, coal, lumber, machinery, automobiles, scrap, zinc concentrates, bauxite, cars, and video monitors, to offer just a very short list, transited the canal in 2021.
- About 13,342 container ships, tankers, bulk carriers (ships that are designed to carry homogeneous cargo), and cruise ships moved through the canal—about thirty-seven ships per day.
- Even with the new locks that opened in 2016, there continues to be congestion, with ships sometimes waiting up to a week before transiting through the canal.

From a sheer business standpoint, shipowners and cargo interests use the canal to save time, and therefore money, when moving vessels between the Atlantic and Pacific Oceans. Before the canal was completed, ships were forced to travel around the Cape of Good Hope, South Africa. The voyage time for a ship steaming at twelve knots that has loaded a cargo of scrap metal in Camden, New Jersey, bound for Japan via the Panama Canal, will be about thirty-four days. The distance is about 9,800 nautical miles. The same voyage via the Good Hope strait is about 15,200 nautical miles and lasts about fifty-three days—nineteen days longer. Assume the cost of repaying the debt on a ship and its daily operating costs total $10,000 per day. Add to that the fuel consumption of twenty-five tonnes per day at today's prices, or about $17,000 per day. A total of $27,000 per day over the nineteen-day shorter voyage via the canal represents a savings of about $513,000, less the $175,000 canal tolls.

MV *STH Athens* loading a cargo of bagged cement in Hong Gai, Vietnam
destined for Peru. The backhoe on top of the bags provides the reader
with a sense of the size of a ship's hold. Credit: Master STH Athens

To understand just how ubiquitous maritime traffic is, access the following website: www.marinetraffic.com. This site will provide the reader a very real sense of the staggering number of ships moving about the oceans at any given time.

***

To provide you with some context, I would like to take a moment to drill down a little and describe the world of maritime transport, with a particular emphasis on the dry bulk market. In broad terms, there are three primary sectors of the maritime transportation industry: dry bulk ships, tankers, and container ships.

DRY BULK CARRIERS

The first large sector of maritime transport in terms of the number of ships in operation is the dry bulk carrier, and this is the segment in which I have spent most of my career. Large, generally unpackaged cargoes of iron ore, coal, grain, fertilizers, bauxite, sugar, **petcoke**, cement, wood and steel products, and minerals are among the many commodities that dry bulk carriers move. Of the three sectors, the dry bulk carrier fleet is the least well-known or understood by the public. Perhaps, it is because bulk carriers, unlike tankers and container ships, move cargoes that most people never think about or very rarely encounter in their unfinished form. In terms of numbers, the dry bulk fleet is by far the largest sector, with about thirteen thousand ships of over ten-thousand-**deadweight**-tonne capacity sailing the oceans.

Total annual movements of seaborne dry bulk cargo are currently about 5.4 billion tonnes—yes, billions, which is a staggering amount of commodities—about .69 of a tonne for every living person on our planet, *every year*. This includes iron ore moving from Brazil to Rotterdam, bauxite from West Africa to the St. Lawrence River, grain from the Mississippi River to Japan, scrap metal from the U.S. East Coast to Turkey, wheat from Ukraine to Taiwan, salt from Chile to Quebec, sugar from South Africa to Hamburg, soybeans from the River Plate area in Argentina to China, thermal coal from Indonesia to India, and wind turbine blades from India to Houston. These are just a very few examples of how commodities move around the globe 24/7, 365 days a year.

TANKERS

Until recently, tankers were the ships most nonshipping people were familiar with, primarily because when they run aground or into another ship and a breach of hull occurs, there is a release of its principal cargo, oil. The result of such a discharge can be polluted waters, oily beaches, and loss of wildlife—all of which make news headlines around the world. These serious incidents, while devastating, are isolated events. The tanker sector operates very efficiently and without mishap the vast majority of the time.

The oil tanker market can be broken down into segments based on vessel size, from small five-thousand-deadweight-tonne coastal tankers to ultra large crude carriers of five hundred thousand deadweight tonnes. It can also be classified by the type of petroleum carried—unrefined crude oil or petroleum products, natural gas and its by-products and chemicals. There are about 7,400 tankers greater than ten thousand deadweight tonnes on the water today.

The market in this sector of our industry is very broadly driven by fluctuating crude oil prices, rising and falling demand for oil and its by-products, and global urbanization.

CONTAINER SHIPS

The other vitally important sector of the maritime transport industry, and one that has gained significant prominence during the COVID-19 pandemic, is the movement of containers. These standardized truck-size intermodal units are used to transport processed or manufactured commodities, from frozen beef to automobile parts, from umbrellas to the toys found on the shelves of your local store. These large units are stacked and transported across the oceans on huge container ships.

The great advantage of this mode of transport is that the commodity can be carried seamlessly from point of origin to a load port, where it is placed onto a container ship to be transported to a discharge port, and then finally moved to an inland destination using trucks and/or rail. Today the largest container vessels rival the enormous crude tankers and **capesize** dry bulk carriers as the largest commercial vessels on the oceans. Currently, there are about 5,500 container ships greater than ten thousand deadweight tonnes plying the world's oceans.

***

The dry bulk market is fundamentally a business driven by the supply and demand of physical commodities and ships, and as such, it is affected by a variety of factors.

SHIP SUPPLY

The physical availability of ships is a significant factor in the market equation of maritime transport. Simply put, the lower the number of on-the-water vessels at any given point in time, the higher the price for transport that maritime enterprises can charge for their services. As global demand for commodities increases, it becomes a challenge to service the market with the available number of ships traversing the globe at any given time.

There are three principal factors that affect the supply of ships: **newbuilding** deliveries from shipyards, scrapping of old ships, and the speed at which the fleet is operating while at sea. While port congestion, which became a significant issue during the pandemic, is another factor, it is generally a micro supply problem. It can build up and dissipate over a few months and can have a marked, but generally not long-lasting, impact on the supply of ships.

NEWBUILDING

At the end of 2022, the dry bulk fleet of ships over ten thousand deadweight tonnes totaled about 970 million tonnes, and newbuilding deliveries (known as the order book) in 2023 are forecast to be about 33 million tonnes, representing about 3.4 percent of the existing fleet. This is quite low. By comparison, in the first decade of this century, when we witnessed the super commodity cycle led by surging Chinese demand, the dry bulk fleet was about 400 million tonnes at the end of 2007, and the scheduled newbuilding deliveries in 2008 were 55 million tonnes or about 14 percent of the existing fleet.

In the past, it took about thirty-six months from the time of placing an order for a new ship to the time of its delivery on the water. Today, the delivery time is closer to twenty to twenty-four months. The actual construction time for a midsize bulk carrier is about fourteen months. Much of the steel is precut, and many of the components are purchased prior to the commencement of actual construction. The ship is then built by assembling these parts like one big Lego set.

SCRAPPING SHIPS

The average end-of-life age of a dry bulk carrier is about twenty-seven years. Once a vessel reaches this mature age, the year-over-year operating costs (see glossary, under **technical ship management**) start to increase significantly and make it difficult to keep it in service profitably. Additionally, many charterers will not charter ships that are too old.

When past their optimal service life, the ships get "scrapped." The steel is eventually sold, primarily to electric arc steelmaking facilities, to produce new steel. If the rate of scrapping exceeds the rate of newbuilding deliveries, the active supply of ships decreases.

There are two primary factors that affect the scrapping of ships: the strength of the freight market—what an owner's ship is able to earn in the marketplace—and the demand for scrap metal steel. As I write, the dry bulk markets are strong, and so owners with older ships are able to trade them very profitably because the demand from charterers is strong. This is largely the result of monetary and fiscal policies initiated across the globe to address the COVID-19 pandemic.

The market for the scrap pricing of ships fluctuates weekly. Every ship can be measured in terms of its **lightweight**, the actual number of tonnes of steel in the ship without cargo or fuel when placed on a suitably sized weigh scale. For example, a **panamax** bulk carrier has a lightweight of about fourteen thousand tonnes. Today, scrapyards are offering shipowners $600 per lightweight tonne to acquire their ships for scrap. So, the owner of a panamax might be able to obtain about $8.4 million to sell his ship for scrap. At the start of the pandemic, the scrap price was $300 per lightweight tonne, so the same owner would have sold his ship for a price 50 percent less than what he can command today.

How does a ship get scrapped? There are specialist **shipbrokers** that focus on this activity and act as intermediaries between shipowners and scrapyards. On its final voyage, a large oceangoing ship will sail empty and literally be driven up onto a beach near a scrapyard in one of three principal locations: Bangladesh, India, or Pakistan. The ship is then broken into several different parts by scores of workers, then dragged farther ashore and cut up into yet smaller parts. The actual number of dry bulk ships scrapped can change significantly from year to year. In 2015, the amount of dry bulk ships scrapped reached 30 million deadweight tonnes, compared to only 5 million deadweight tonnes in 2022.

SHIP SPEED

The third major factor affecting vessel supply is the speed at which ships sail the oceans. The average time a bulk carrier spends at sea is about 256 days (generally less for small ships and more for larger ships). The longer a ship takes to complete its voyage, the fewer the available ships there are to take on new business.

The easiest way to think about this is to visualize a ship moving a cargo of Canadian wheat from Vancouver to Rizhao, China. At fourteen knots, the trip will take fifteen days; while at ten knots, it will take twenty-one days. The slower speed means six days of vessel supply is removed from the market.

There are various elements that go into determining the speed at which a ship is ordered to proceed. A ship may be en route to a load port that is congested, and so the ship is ordered to slow-steam so as not to arrive and wait for a week prior to loading. Or the price of **bunker fuel** may have risen and a ship may be ordered to slow-steam to reduce the amount of fuel consumed on a voyage. Perhaps a ship is en route to a discharge port in the U.S. Gulf area and a hurricane warning is in effect, so the master orders the vessel to increase speed so as to pass the storm without impacting the ship and its cargo.

The time ships take to complete their voyages thus affects the overall supply of ships and the commensurate prices charged.

DEMAND FOR DRY BULK

The demand side of the dry bulk shipping market is much more complex than ship supply because there are many more variables. Among the primary factors that affect demand for dry bulk ships are: global gross domestic product (GDP); monetary and fiscal policies of developed and developing economies; population growth and urbanization; political interventions; and both natural and man-made disasters.

Within each of these elements there are what I would describe as numerous micro demand drivers or inhibitors that all come together to impact the demand for dry bulk commodities. Because the drivers of demand are so complex, the industry tends to rely on specialized shipbrokering firms to provide demand information and also to interpret what the data metrics may mean for the forward dry bulk market.

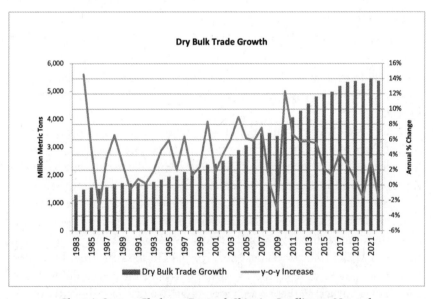

Chart A. Source: Clarksons Research Shipping Intelligence Network

As demonstrated in Chart A, dry bulk trade growth has been on a steady upward trend for the last forty years. The actual **cumulative annual growth rate** (CAGR) over this period has been about 3.5 percent. As a rule of thumb, if the annual percentage change in dry bulk trade growth is around 3 percent or more, the market is considered to be strong.

GLOBAL GDP/MONETARY AND FISCAL POLICIES:

I would estimate that as much as a quarter of my time working in the dry bulk maritime market has been spent analyzing the demand drivers of global GDP.

Central banks of sovereign nations, or associations such as the European Union (EU), have a mandate to ensure sustainable growth by managing the supply of money, known as monetary policy. Simply stated, monetary policy is what controls the amount of money circulating in an economy. If a country is in the throes of high unemployment, inflation, and/or a recession, the central bank may initiate an expansionary monetary policy to stimulate growth and create jobs.

They have three general levers to do this. They can set a limit as to how much cash banks have on hand each day, known as the "reserve requirement." They can buy securities, like treasury bonds, thereby adding to the supply of money fueling borrowing and spending, or remove money by selling securities to member banks. Finally, they can manipulate the interest rate they charge to their member banks, which flows through to the economy at large, affecting the interest rate of loans to consumers and businesses.

Fiscal policy is set by governments that utilize taxes and government borrowing and spending to manage the economic conditions of a country. Using these levers, a government can manage economic output by reducing taxes and borrowing and spending to help encourage economic growth. Or it can raise taxes and reduce expenditures to achieve the opposite result.

A recent example of how monetary and fiscal policies can affect global business are the measures taken to combat the massive downdraft to economies throughout the world caused by the COVID-19 pandemic. Unemployment soared, and business activity, except for internet-based commerce, floundered. Governments around the world established broad measures of monetary easing and expansive fiscal policies to help revive their economies. Global interest rates contracted close to zero (and in some cases turned negative) encouraging both personal consumption and corporate lending. Governments have deployed enormous fiscal stimulus to help jump-start economic growth and support groups of vulnerable people who have lost their jobs through no fault of their own.

These measures have helped world GDP growth, following the dramatic downturn in 2020. And this, in turn, increased demand for dry bulk commodities, and, by extension, increased the demand for dry bulk ships. For instance, the demand for steel around the globe has increased and the prices for steel plate and the primary ingredients used to make it, namely iron ore and **coke**, are soaring. In the summer of 2020, when I began writing this book, the daily **time charter** rate of hire for one of our **ultramax** ships was perhaps $10,000. Twenty to twenty-four months later, due to increased demand, the same ship was earning about $35,000 per day in the **spot market**.

POPULATION GROWTH AND URBANIZATION

It does not take an economist to understand that as the number of people on the planet increases, so does the demand for dry bulk and other commodities. There is a greater demand for infrastructure investments, such as housing, roads, bridges, tunnels, highways, sewer systems, chemical plants, electrical power distribution, and digital broadband. There is also demand for investment in factories that are built for manufacturing, and commercial and residential buildings. All these investments require ever-increasing amounts of dry bulk commodities and the ships to deliver them.

It is a generally accepted precept that as countries develop their economies, the percentage of their people toiling in traditional hardscrabble industries, such as agriculture or fishing or mining, declines because of productivity enhancements. New generations of people migrate into cities to find less grueling work that pays better. This is what economists call urbanization. As people's incomes go up, the demand for goods and services increases. People look to buy items they had not been able to afford previously and their diet changes, as they are better able to afford expensive protein like meat. The manufacture and delivery of these items is very much dependent on the movement of dry bulk commodities.

This trend toward urbanization started in the nineteenth century, with the introduction of industrialization, and hit its stride in the latter part of the twentieth century and early decades of the twenty-first century. The United Nations estimates that 2007 was the year when, for the first time, more people lived in urban rather than rural areas. From 1960 through today, the CAGR in urbanization is 2.5 percent versus 1.6 percent for population growth, which is why the former has such an impact on our markets.

	Population growth		Urbanization
•	1960:	3.0 billion	1.0 billion
•	1987:	5.0 billion	2.1 billion
•	1999:	6.0 billion	2.8 billion
•	2011:	7.0 billion	3.4 billion
•	2022e:	8.0 billion	4.5 billion

Source: NewGeography.com

The most pronounced example of the impact urbanization has had on the maritime transport is what happened in China over the past thirty years. Depending on which statistics you read, there has been a movement of about 300 million to 400 million Chinese from rural areas into the megacities of China in the last three decades. This massive migration over a short period of time, in both volume and pace, is unlike anything we have witnessed before in human history. As I write, the urbanization levels in China are thought to be about 60 percent, up from 30 percent in the latter part of the twentieth century.

The result has been an enormous increase in the volumes of dry bulk commodities moving into the country to service the expansion of industry and infrastructure. The CAGR for the large dry bulk movements of commodities into China over the past fifteen years has been a remarkable 9 percent.

CHINESE DRY BULK SEABORNE IMPORTS

	2005	**2013**	**2022**
Iron Ore	271	795	1087
Thermal Coal	36	205	200
Various Bulks	157	403	600
Totals	464	1403	1887

Source: Clarksons Research Shipping Intelligence Network (million tonnes)

The next big urbanization push will originate from the continent of Africa: sub-Sahara African countries currently have an overall urbanization rate of about 42 percent.

POLITICAL INTERVENTIONS

Maritime enterprises face a plethora of headwinds that impact their competitive strategies caused by external political changes occurring around the globe. New protectionist trade policies negotiated bilaterally between countries, or new regulations such as decarbonization initiatives, or wars (such as the current conflict in the Ukraine), can all impact maritime transportation.

China is dependent on Australia for two commodities, iron ore and thermal coal. Although there are six or seven countries that are responsible for global seaborne exports of iron ore, Australia and Brazil account for about 80 percent of these with the former making up about 55 percent of the global total. China imports about 75 percent of the total annual seaborne volumes of this commodity. So, the country is very dependent on supplies from Australia to support its domestic steel-making industry.

But this is not the case with thermal coal. There are six major exporters of seaborne thermal coal, and Australia, although one of the larger exporters of this commodity, only makes up about 20 percent of seaborne exports. And unlike with iron ore, Chinese imports of thermal coal are about 20 percent of global imports of this commodity.

In 2019 when China instituted a new law permitting the extradition of Hong Kong citizens to be tried under the Chinese justice in Beijing, instead of in their own courts, there was an international outcry. Huge demonstrations took place in Hong Kong and around the world. Australia supported this position against the Chinese government. This occurred at a time when Australia was initiating a strategic geopolitical shift to the West. Reacting to Australia's political decision, China announced a ban on imports of Australian-sourced consumer commodities, such as wine, beef, and lobsters. However, the ban that sent shudders through the dry bulk freight markets was the one focused on Australian-sourced thermal coal involving tens of millions of tonnes.

The initial reaction by market pundits was that demand for dry bulk ships in the Pacific basin would be significantly curtailed. But the opposite happened, for two reasons.

At the time of the ban, there were numerous ships either at anchor off the coast of China waiting to discharge or already on the water proceeding to China loaded with Australian thermal coal. By the end of 2020, there were reports of as many as 150 ships sitting off China loaded with Australian coal—they had spent months at anchor—effectively reducing the supply of ships. They were eventually rerouted to other discharge ports primarily in Asia.

China started to replace the Australian coal with imports of South Africa and U.S. coal (the latter loaded out of the West Coast), both of which involve significantly longer voyage durations than coal moving from Australia. As I have highlighted earlier in this chapter, more steaming time per voyage results in less availability of ships, thus increasing charter rates for ships.

MAN-MADE AND NATURAL DISASTERS

The transportation of dry bulk commodities is also vulnerable to interruptions in the sourcing and/or flow of commodities—at their origination point, during voyages, and even at their final discharge port. Disruptive incidents do occur, albeit infrequently, but when they do, the impact they have on supply-chain efficiencies can affect our markets dramatically.

The world's largest producer of iron ore is Vale S.A., with its primary iron ore activities centered in Brazil. Their largest export market is China, which is counterintuitive because of the distances involved––Australian seaborne iron ore is geographically much closer to mainland China, and therefore the cost of transportation is generally less. But Brazilian ore contains 67 percent iron, the most on the planet, making it more cost effective to process, which is why Vale can compete successfully with Australian iron ore sold into the Chinese market.

On January 25, 2019, a **tailings dam** at Vale's Córrego do Feijão iron ore mine in Minas Gerais, Brazil, suffered a structural failure and collapsed, releasing a tsunami of mud that destroyed hotels, houses, farms, and downstream roads, resulting in 270 deaths. Vale decided to shut down some of its iron ore mines temporarily, in order to undertake a thorough review of its operations. The net effect was to reduce its output by about a third.

Over the next six months, commodity traders around the globe watched the price of iron ore shoot up about 50 percent, whereas the freight market for large capesize vessels, which are used to transport most of Brazil's iron ore exports, declined by nearly 50 percent. As a result of this structural disaster, the six-month time charter rate for a capesize ship went from about $21,000 per day in December 2019 to about $11,000 in March 2020. Why? China, the largest importer of iron ore in the world, had to replace long-haul Brazilian iron ore with short-haul Australian iron ore, creating a significant reduction in the demand for capesize vessels.

Not a week goes by where we do not read or hear of a climatic event caused by global warming. A perfect example of this is the **draft** of the River Plate in Argentina.

Argentina is one of the world's largest exporters of grains—about 50 million to 60 million tonnes of corn, wheat, and soybeans are loaded into ships from this country every year. Vessels are loaded with grain in ports located in the Plate estuary, such as San Nicolás and Rosario, and each ship's cargo lift is determined by the prevailing water levels in the Plate. It is currently at its lowest level since 1944 due to a lack of rainfall in the northern regions of the Paraná River system in the southern part of Brazil.

A panamax vessel loading a cargo in the River Plate in the spring of 2022 will lift about forty-one thousand tonnes of grain. Because there was more depth of water available in the spring of 2021, the same vessel loading a grain cargo then would have achieved a lift of about forty-nine thousand tonnes. It should be obvious that for 2022 exports of Argentine grain to meet the same export levels as 2021, more ships will be required, each with a reduced cargo lift. This is a great example of global warming creating a climatic effect that impacts demand for ships.

***

I hope I have been able to enlighten the reader in broad terms with some of the key metrics that impact the global dry bulk freight markets. They are many and they are varied, and the transport of raw materials around the globe indirectly impacts each of us as consumers.

Of course, the average person on the street does not understand why they are paying more for their washing machine, nor does the doctor understand why a surgical scalpel is costing more. They might blame corporate greed or commodity inflation, but they are unlikely to think about increased costs of the large ships traversing the oceans transporting the raw materials that are used to make such goods.

CHAPTER 2

FEDNAV: MY MARITIME CAREER BEGINS

"If you're offered a seat on a rocket ship,
don't ask what seat! Just get on."

SHERYL SANDBERG,
American technology executive

———————

U pon graduating from Queen's University with a degree in business, with a focus on finance and economics, I did not take part in the usual spring semester ritual of attending on-campus interviews with various companies. Unlike most of my buddies, I was not interested in starting a career directly after graduation. I had a deep urge to travel the world, and so earning money to finance the trip became my priority.

I was fortunate to find summer employment at a lead and zinc mine in northwestern Ontario. The job, located near Pickle Lake, Ontario, involved heavy manual labor, seven days a week, for three continuous months. We were isolated, so there was nowhere and nothing on which to spend money. We lived in Atco trailers provided by the mine owners, and life at the mine consisted of just work—nothing else. The only distractions were the meals provided in the camp. Because the mine operated twenty-four hours a day, the cafeteria was never closed. One could arrive in the food hall in the early morning, following a night shift, and order a steak with French fries and gravy. Or you could wake up at four-thirty p.m. and walk to the food hall and order a massive plate of pancakes and bacon smothered in maple syrup.

I was paid "isolation" wages, so upon my departure, I had saved up about $9,000. That was an enormous sum of money in those days for a recent graduate. At the end of the summer, I quit and used the funds to travel throughout Europe and parts of the Middle East with various friends who joined me for different parts of my travels. I returned to Montreal penniless in the summer of 1975 to start my search for a job.

During my time at university, the one extracurricular activity I became enmeshed in was the business of rock concerts. Annually, the university funded the Queens Entertainment Agency with about $50,000, which was used to subsidize ticket sales. This was a considerable sum of money in those days, particularly for an organization that arranged concerts on campus and was managed and run by students for students. We booked singers, songwriters, and rock groups, including Canadian artists Leonard Cohen and Gordon Lightfoot, among many others, and the American bands Sha Na Na, Hall & Oates, Lou Reed, and JJ Cale, the blues guitarist who wrote "Cocaine," to name just a few. We were booking these acts through two promoters: Donald K Donald Productions out of Montreal and Michael Cohl in Toronto. And it was my intention to try and find a position with one of these two companies after my travels.

However, as often happens, life took another turn.

During my post graduation travels in Europe, I had the opportunity to board two ferries, a large Greek ferryboat in Piraeus (the port city located within the greater urban area of Athens) for the five-hour voyage to Mykonos, and a few months later, an even larger Greek ferry for the overnight voyage from Piraeus to Haifa. It left an indelible mark on me. I loved the sense of freedom that came from being on the sea, and I spent hours watching the movement of the ship as its hull plowed through the Mediterranean waters. The constant hum of the engines, the clanging of various bits of maritime equipment, and the general hustle and bustle of life on board all intrigued me. My thoughts kept returning to the book *Supership* I'd read a few years earlier.

So, upon my return to Canada, while trying to search for work in the business of concert promotions, I decided to look into job opportunities at maritime shipping companies in Quebec. Most of what I found were shipping advertisements for scheduled liner services. Not knowing much about any other aspects of the maritime industry I set my sights on these companies, eventually abandoning my plan for a career in the entertainment industry. Seeing my interest in the maritime world, my father contacted a friend who worked at a maritime transportation company called Federal Commerce & Navigation, known today as Fednav, arguably Canada's largest, most reputable international maritime shipping group.

Through my father's contact, I was able to obtain an interview with the comptroller of the company. It went well, and two weeks later, in October 1975, I joined Fednav as a voyage accountant.

***

Fednav began its operations in Canada in 1944 when Ernest Pathy, one of four brothers originally from Hungary, moved to Toronto after a sojourn in Egypt and established Federal Commerce & Navigation Company Limited. About a decade later, the company moved its headquarters to Montreal, with a focus on chartering ships into and out of the Great Lakes. The business began to expand rapidly, with the opening of the St. Lawrence Seaway System.

Map of the Great Lakes St. Lawrence Seaway System.
Credit: Great Lakes St. Lawrence Seaway System

The construction of seven new locks between Montreal and Lake Ontario was completed in 1959. Together with the eight locks of the Welland Canal, which were built in 1932 and link Lake Ontario with Lake Erie, they make up the St. Lawrence Seaway System. This system of locks effectively elevates ships about 180 meters above sea level and, along with the Soo Locks located between Lake Huron and Lake Superior, allows oceangoing ships to travel to Duluth, Minnesota, the most westerly located port in the Great Lakes.

Up until the early 1960s, Fednav operated chartered ships, and the business revolved around controlling certain cargo flows, such as steel imports from Europe into North America. During this decade, the company started owning ships; and with continuously increasing volumes in and out of the Great Lakes, enabled by the St. Lawrence Seaway, completed in 1959, Fednav's size, profits, and areas of focus increased.

It was during the 1970s that Ladi Pathy, a nephew of the founder who was now firmly in control of the company, expanded its shipowning activities by focusing on more specialized ships, such as the **roll-on/roll-off (roro)** carriers, MV *Avon Forest* and MV *Laurentian Forest*. Throughout this decade, as its economic successes continued to increase, the company invested in new areas both within the maritime sector and beyond.

It was about this time that Fednav decided to invest in a new class of bulk carriers, which came to be known as the Fednav 730s because of their length of 730 feet. These ships were designed to lift about twenty-five thousand tonnes on the prevailing Great Lakes draft, which at the time was three thousand to five thousand tonnes more than conventional oceangoing ships and therefore provided significant economies of scale. The ships were ordered from Cockerill Shipyard in Belgium because of very favorable financing from the Belgium government: an 85 percent advance rate off the price of the newbuilding order, a sixteen-year term, and 1.5 percent cost of money.

At about the time of this order, some shipyards developed a new design of bulk carrier that they described as coal carriers, but these are known today as capesize ships because they are too large to transit through the Panama Canal and must therefore sail around the Cape of Good Hope to move between the oceans. Fednav decided to convert two of the 730 orders into capesize ships, which became the MV *Federal Schelde* and the MV *Federal Skeena*, both of which ended up being built at Boelwerf Shipyard in Belgium after Cockerill went bankrupt. Later, Fednav contracted for two more capesize ships, named the MV *Amazon* and MV *Orinoco*, from Hyundai Heavy Industries in South Korea. All four of these units had a deadweight of about 138,000 tonnes, about one hundred thousand deadweight tonnes greater than the largest ships trading into the Great Lakes. They were certainly not vessels that Fednav was going to operate in their traditional trades. It was, to say the least, a big punt.

***

Fednav's offices were located on the thirty-eighth and thirty-ninth floors of a modern high-rise building called Place Victoria, which at the time was the home of the Montreal stock exchange. The first level housed the executive offices and the chartering, operations, liner, and projects departments; the accounting, insurance, human resources, and back-office staff were all located on the floor above. During my first few months at Fednav, I never set foot on the thirty-eighth floor.

Upon reflection, I believe voyage accounting proved to be a great training ground for someone with no practical experience in the maritime industry. Along with three other voyage accountants and a manager to whom we reported, I was responsible for developing the financial results for specific ship voyages. This included reviewing and posting such items as steaming time between ports, time in port, port costs, canal expenses, pilotage fees, dockage fees, and the cost of fuel. Then I would compare the actual voyage profit and loss to the estimate that was developed by the in-house chartering broker. He arranged for a fixture ("fix," to use the industry term) or contract for the freight business for each ship. So, I was able to learn how the business worked and the costs associated with operating ships.

About six months into my new career, an opportunity came up within the department to review the results of a new, dedicated roll-on/roll-off service that Fednav was developing to move cars and other wheeled equipment from Halifax, Nova Scotia to St. John's, Newfoundland. Due to my university-level educational background, the comptroller suggested that I should take a stab at it. I jumped at the opportunity, even though I had to undertake the work in addition to my daily voyage-accounting responsibilities.

I worked on this analysis for over two months, primarily by arriving at the office early in the morning or working late into the early evening hours. I concluded this new roro service was never going to turn a profit, a rather presumptuous conclusion, since I had virtually no experience in the industry. Accordingly, I set out my findings in a six-page report addressed to the comptroller of Fednav. He acknowledged its receipt and thanked me for my efforts, but other than that, I never received any feedback.

One day, about a month after I had submitted the report, a tall, distinguished-looking gentleman, who appeared to be in his late forties, burst into the accounting department, held up a paper in his hands, and in a strong British accent shouted out: "Who the hell is Anthony Whitworth?" I was not sure what to do. I leaned over to the voyage accounts supervisor who sat next to me and asked who this person was.

"That's Michael Bell, the executive vice president of Fednav," she said. "You better answer him."

Somewhat meekly, I raised my hand, and Michael Bell walked over to my desk, slammed the paper down, and in a booming voice that could be heard throughout the entire department said: "This report is complete garbage. It is clear you know nothing about our business, so why would you write it?"

I was blushing, and my heart was pounding as he continued, not waiting for me to reply.

"I want to see you in my office tomorrow at eight a.m.!"

As he turned and stormed out of the office, I had a very sick feeling in my stomach that my brief career in the maritime world was about to end.

The following morning, at seven-fifty, I arrived at the thirty-eighth-floor executive office suite of Fednav, having never before set foot there. I was ushered into Michael Bell's office at eight o'clock sharp, where, for about twenty minutes, he proceeded to take apart what I thought were my very rational thoughts on the new service. When he finished, he looked at me and said, "If you want to learn about shipping, you need to come down a floor and work in the chartering department of Fednav."

As you can imagine, I was shocked. He wasn't firing me, but rather offering me a new opportunity in the company. I was barely able to respond, then said, "Uh, I appreciate the opportunity. When would I start?"

"Well, there is no time like the present, so plan on moving down tomorrow morning."

And that is how my career in the commercial and operational aspects of international maritime transport began.

***

Ladi Pathy, the then-president of Fednav, and his second-in-command, Michael Bell, decided to search for some new employees to join the organization. The company was growing dramatically, and to meet the increasing demands of the business, Fednav needed to expand the staff. Rather than promoting from within exclusively, they decided to hire candidates from outside the company with different educational backgrounds and work experiences than many of those currently employed in the company. Given the unique aspects of the industry, it was a bold, innovative approach.

Fednav hired three individuals at a managerial level: two with experience in international shipping and one who led the outside team of auditors that prepared the company's annual financials.

Sean Day joined as an operations manager. He was a South African and a Rhodes scholar, who moved to Montreal from Hong Kong. In Asia, he had been working for Jardine Matheson, a storied corporation with deep business interests in China and around the world.

John Weale was British and came to Fednav in 1979 from Bibby Lines, a well-established shipping company based in Liverpool. John is perhaps the most intellectually brilliant person whom I have come across in my forty-eight years in shipping. He arrived as a new project manager.

John Peacock, who, as a partner at Clarkson Gordon & Co (now Ernst & Young) in Montreal was responsible for the Fednav audit, assumed the position of treasurer. All would become very close confidants of Ladi Pathy.

***

Fednav's chartering department was viewed as the real moneymaker in the organization, and it was run by an astute manager named Paul Wereley, who had a limited formal education but was a shrewd trader. He had three experienced chartering brokers reporting to him: Brian Gallimore, a British national who had migrated to Canada after having been at sea for many years with Blue Star Lines; Jean Lemay, a French Canadian with a high school education who had started as a telex operator in the Fednav communications room and who had worked his way through operations and into chartering; and Theyre Smith, who was a naturalized Canadian and probably only about six or seven years older than me. He had started work at a young age for Fednav down on the Montreal docks as a **boarding clerk** before landing a job in the company's operation department. I was the youngest in the department at the time.

My move into chartering came at exactly the right moment in Fednav's development. In the mid to late 1970s, the company was growing dramatically and management hired more people from outside the industry who could add new perspectives to the business. In those days, most individuals working ashore for maritime shipping companies had begun their careers at sea or as stevedores or working as port agents, so this was not an easy decision. More than likely, it would cause some friction within the organization.

In hindsight, I think that Bell moved me into the chartering department precisely because my report demonstrated my willingness to look outside the box—despite my lack of experience in the maritime industry.

***

My first day of work in the chartering department began on a glorious spring morning. After a long and cold Montreal winter, one of these days is always most welcome. I arrived at the office early, and the first task Paul Wereley gave me was to get him a cup of coffee…not exactly what I had expected. It quickly became clear to me that Paul was uncomfortable having a neo-phyte to the shipping industry parachuted into his small yet very import-ant department. Everyone else within the chartering and operations areas of Fednav had experience in one or more aspects of the maritime trade. A twenty-two-year-old with a double major in economics and finance from Queen's University was certainly not the type of young man Paul expected to have in his department.

I kept my head low for the first few months and spent a good deal of my time reading through all the telex traffic. In those days, communication for cargoes and ships was via telex, which was a method of sending written messages electronically between businesses. I asked a lot of questions, many of them uninformed because I simply had had no exposure to the world of chartering. I spent a considerable part of my day calculating voyage estimates for certain pieces of business that arrived into the office from shipbrokers and having Paul or Jean or Brian check them over. Because of my six months in voyage accounting, this was something I felt comfortable with, and I think Paul was impressed with my facility with numbers.

In the 1970s, Fednav had two roros dedicated to moving wood fiber from Three Rivers, Quebec and Halifax, Nova Scotia, into Avonmouth, near Bristol on the River Severn on the west coast of the United Kingdom. The ships would return to eastern Canada with cars loaded at Felixstowe on the east coast of England. One day about three months after my arrival in the chartering department, Brian walked over to tell me that one of the Fednav roro units had been delayed and was no longer in a position to load a cargo of cars from the United Kingdom. We needed to charter in another roro ship from the market to replace our vessel. He provided me with the parameters of what we required and guided me for about a week as we canvassed the market through our shipbroker networks. When we finally found a suitable vessel, he encouraged me to conclude the deal.

When one negotiates to charter a ship or to offer a ship to a charterer for their cargo, the conclusion of a successful negotiation of a fixture is codified into a **charter party** contract. Following my seventy-two-hour negotiation back and forth via telex, I concluded what would be the first of many fixtures I would do over the years.

I was ecstatic when Paul invited me to join him and the rest of the chartering team for lunch to celebrate my first fixture. After a long and somewhat boozy affair, which in those days was not at all uncommon for the chartering team, Paul presented me with the lunch bill and explained it was customary following a first fixture for the assistant chartering broker to buy the department lunch. This was not something I was expecting to do on my meager $11,000 annual salary.

I was really on a "high" at the time, but my colleagues in chartering quickly brought me back to reality by playing a joke on me to remind me that I still had much to learn.

About a week later, Fednav was desperately searching for a ship to charter in the east Mediterranean, but there were simply very few to be found. The owners with available ships knew it, and they had increased their rate indications significantly. Brian Gallimore had a shipbroker telex us the details of a ship that looked to be ideal: the right size, the right equipment, suitably outfitted to trade into the Great Lakes, available on the right dates, and offering a reasonable price indication. He walked over to my desk and said, "Here you go, Tony, this unit fits our position perfectly. She's in the Caspian Sea on our dates. Draft up a counteroffer."

I knew I had to move fast, and within twenty minutes I had put together a detailed offer to charter the ship for a period of a few months, which I had Brian review before walking it over to the telex room. I sauntered up and looked at the telex operator and said with an exaggerated air of importance, "This message is top priority, please get it out ASAP." As I turned to leave, the chartering guys were all standing there laughing themselves silly. The Caspian Sea is the world's largest body of landlocked water; no oceangoing ships move in or out of it.

One afternoon following my first ten months in chartering, Paul Wereley called me over to his desk to tell me that he had arranged for me to be placed on board a Fednav-owned ship for three to four months so I might have some hands-on experience of the saltwater highway of marine shipping. He explained that, given I had arrived at Fednav without any maritime experience, this would be a good opportunity for me to develop some knowledge of the practical activity undertaken on a ship trading into different ports.

I was skeptical of his motives, thinking that he might use this trip to hire a replacement for me. However, I took comfort from the fact that he would not arrange this without first discussing it with Michael Bell. Three weeks later, in February 1977, I boarded the MV *Federal Saguenay*, a thirty-thousand-deadweight-tonne bulk carrier that became my home away from home for the next ninety days. The ship spent her time performing Atlantic crossings from the St. Lawrence River ports of Quebec City and Three Rivers to various European ports.

This turned out to be a great learning experience for a whole host of reasons. Perhaps most importantly, I quickly came to realize that I was not prone to seasickness. Winter crossings in the north Atlantic can be notoriously brutal, and there were some crossings where we were steaming in **Beaufort Scale** 8/9 winds with sea swells of twenty to twenty-five feet. Even several of the regular crew members became ill during such crossings. Fortunately, I did not. These rough days at sea are embedded in my memory. Spray and mist hammered the windows on the bridge deck, making visibility very difficult, and gigantic waves crashed over the bow, causing the hull to shudder and the ship to slow temporarily as it plowed through one large wave after another.

My sleeping accommodation on the ship was in the "pilot's cabin," a separate bedroom used very infrequently by **marine pilots** when they have to stay on board for more than ten or twelve hours. The twin-size bed was built into the wall, and I quickly learned how to take two life jackets and place them under the mattress on the open side of the bed to prevent me from falling out of bed as the ship rolled from port to starboard and back when in heavy seas.

The aft superstructure of the ship had four tiers, the fourth being the bridge deck, and there were internal stairs leading from one deck to the next. I quickly learned that in heavy seas it was next to impossible to climb the stairs against the roll of the ship, because the stairs essentially became vertical. I would wait until the ship pitched to the opposite side and I could walk up to the next deck on almost horizontal stairs!

For a boy who grew up in Quebec City in the 1950s and 1960s, I knew virtually nothing about Asia, and when I joined the *Federal Saguenay*, with its twenty-five South Korean officers and crew, it was a strange experience. Because I was a "representative" from the owner's office, I was invited to take my meals in the officers' mess. I recall feeling apprehensive, sitting down to my first lunch at a round dining table with perhaps eight place settings. Each place had chopsticks, except for my seat, at which the steward had set a knife and fork. Not wanting to draw attention to my inexperience, I asked to be served with the same utensils as the officers. It was quite a learning curve and probably did not go unnoticed by the officers. I recall several days when the ship was rolling back and forth and I tried to pick up peas using my chopsticks. When I eventually succeeded, I knew I had mastered the art.

The three months on board as an observer allowed me to follow the loading and discharging of various types of cargo, primarily **break-bulk** commodities, such as steel and various pieces of equipment that had to be stored very carefully in the ship's holds using enormous amounts of **dunnage**. In some ports, the ship's cranes were used to carry out the loading and/or discharging; while in others, it was the shoreside equipment. I was also able to get a good sense of the various officer and crew responsibilities as they related not just to the navigation and running of the ship, but also to the loading and discharging of cargo and the maintenance and upkeep of the ship.

During my time in the Fednav voyage accounting department, I had become familiar with many of the cost items that were expensed during a voyage, and it was therefore very useful for me to witness firsthand how these costs were incurred. When in port, I took the time to sit with the **shipping agent** to better understand what it is they do. It was also especially instructive for me to observe how a large ship arrives and departs from a port, and the use of local pilots and tugs to help the ship maneuver into and out of harbors.

As much as I enjoyed my time aboard the *Federal Saguenay*, after three months I was ready to disembark and return to the office. A ship may spend anywhere from 50 to 80 percent of its time at sea, depending on its size and trade routes. So, the time between port calls quickly became monotonous for me, and I was anxious to continue my education and exposure to the commercial maritime world.

CHAPTER 3

LONDON: THE CENTER OF MARITIME INDUSTRY

"I never predict freight rates; nobody can do that."

SOREN SKOU,
Danish businessman,
former CEO of A.P. Moller-Maersk

I t was less than a month following the return from my voyage, when Michael Bell called me into his office one morning to say that management wanted me to continue my maritime education by moving to London. In those days, Fednav did not have a structured trainee program for individuals who arrived in the organization without maritime experience. I, therefore, sensed that these postings were part of an experiment to educate a neophyte. I felt certain that Michael believed my limited exposure in Montreal would be greatly enhanced by working in the London market, at the time the center of the international shipbrokering business. Afterward, I would continue my training with a posting to Fednav's office in Hamburg.

At the time, there were five major capital cities in the world where the vast majority of the commercial vessel employment contracts of international shipping were negotiated: London (the largest), Oslo, Hamburg, New York, and Tokyo. But I could not have been more excited, because in those days, London was *the* commercial center of international maritime shipping.

Fednav had an exclusive arrangement with Galbraith Wrightson (today known as Ifchor Galbraiths) to broker most of its chartering activity. Founded in 1845, it was one of the premier shipbrokering firms in London, with a global reputation. This firm had three dedicated shipbrokers working exclusively on the Fednav account. The chairman of Galbraiths was a man named Gordon Parham, who happened to be a close business confidant of Ladi Pathy, and was considered one of the preeminent, if not *the* preeminent, competitive dry cargo shipbroker in the London market.

Business contracted between shipowners and charterers of cargo is normally carried out through large shipbrokering firms. These companies are specialist intermediaries that act as the go-betweens connecting shipowners searching for employment for their ships and charterers who are looking to move cargo. Shipbrokers receive a standard commission of 1.25 percent on the revenue generated by the business they conclude. (Another customary commission used widely throughout the industry is an **address commission**, expressed as a percentage of the freight or hire, normally 3.75 percent. This is paid by the shipowner to the charterer and represents a partial reimbursement to the charterer for costs it incurs arranging for the movement of its cargo.)

When I told my father, an Englishman himself, about my new London posting, he contacted his godfather and close family friend, Hamon Dickie. In his mid-sixties and a confirmed bachelor, Hamon was a senior partner at Freshfields, one of the world's largest law firms. He lived in South Kensington and kindly offered me a room in his beautiful town house there. My commute consisted of a brief three-minute walk to the South Ken tube station, a fifteen-minute ride on the Circle or District lines to Fenchurch Street station, followed by a five-minute walk to the Galbraiths office, located on Fenchurch Street.

Hamon loved the theater and ballet, and throughout my time there, he introduced me to both. He was also very well connected, and his circle of friends included successful businessmen as well as renowned authors, musicians, and politicians. I recall vividly the evening he invited me to join him for dinner at a friend's town house in Mayfair. This was a rather formal affair, with four invited couples, and Hamon and me—the five older men wore formal dinner jackets, and I was clad in my humble business suit. The hostess for the evening had invited as her partner Sir Edward Heath, the former prime minister of the United Kingdom. The average age of the gathering must have been mid-sixties; and following a formal dinner, the men excused themselves from the dining room and off we went to an adjoining room to chat over port and cigars. It was as if I had been transported into another age.

I settled into the Galbraiths office seated among a cluster of desks with the shipbrokers who worked the Fednav account, where I set out to learn the inner workings of competitive shipbrokering. It was a stark contrast to the relatively small chartering office in Montreal, where most of the overnight telex traffic came to us from Galbraiths and a few local brokers in Montreal and New York. In the London office, telexes would arrive from shipbrokers and owners around the world. I would sit down and read correspondence from contacts in Hamburg, Athens, Tokyo, Hong Kong, Karachi, Melbourne, Durban, and Rio de Janeiro, places I had only ever heard about. You had the feeling that you were at the center of the maritime universe.

While my training involved working with the shipbrokers assigned to Fednav's account, the department was huge and covered dozens of different dry bulk cargoes transported to nearly every country around the world. Not only that, but they had a large tanker department, and another for the sale and purchase of ships as well—two sectors of the business I did not know anything about. Before this, I only had exposure to international movements of cargo moving into and out of the Great Lakes in North America. It was, therefore, an exciting, fast-paced environment that enabled me to broaden my horizons considerably.

In those days, the heart and soul of commercial maritime shipping in London was the Baltic Shipping Exchange. The origins of the Baltic, as it is known, date to the seventeenth century, when merchants and ship captains conducted business in taverns and coffeehouses in London. The proprietors of such establishments circulated refreshments, as well as newspapers, along with commercial information.

During the second half of the nineteenth century, the grain merchants made up the core activity on the exchange. The London Shipping Exchange was formed in 1891 to advocate for shipowners, and the two entities merged in 1903 to form the Baltic Mercantile and Shipping Exchange. It was during the period between the two World Wars that the floor of the Baltic became focused primarily on the chartering of ships. Shipbrokers were admitted to the exchange to represent both shipowners and merchants, and gradually the floor of the Baltic became the commercial center of global seaborne activity.

The Baltic Exchange building was architecturally known for its stained-glass war memorial, as well as its cathedral-like trading room with twelve beautiful classic red marble columns that stretched up to an enormous ceiling. Sadly, it was severely damaged in an Irish Republican Army bombing in 1992. The stained-glass windows sustained only minor damages, and they were restored and can now be seen in the National Maritime Museum in Greenwich.

The Baltic Shipping Exchange trading floor circa 1970. Credit: Baltic Exchange/Getty Images

The great room of the Baltic was the heart and soul of commercial shipping. The bombing coincided with changes that were happening with communications, and it seemed to mark the end of an era. Today, the Baltic Exchange is a London-based electronic platform that provides real-time maritime shipping information to shipbrokers and traders for settling physical and **derivative contracts**. The exchange has regional offices in Singapore, Shanghai, and Athens.

At the time, however, each day around noon, many of the London shipbrokers would congregate in the Baltic Exchange building on St. Mary Axe Street and walk about the beautiful, cavernous main hall passing out flyers to their counterparts listing the commercial positions they had "open" for ships and cargoes. It seems archaic now in the age of email and cell phones, but that was how one did business back then.

As large as the hall was, it was generally so full of shipbrokers and various other maritime personnel that it was packed to capacity and reverberated with noise. It was, therefore, often difficult to make your way through the crowded room in search of a contact. Off to one side in the middle of the hall was a raised podium on which a uniformed gentleman stood in front of a microphone. When you were trying to find a particular individual, you would approach the platform and ask the attendant to call out that individual's name, requesting him to come forward to meet you next to the podium.

My time at Galbraiths set my ambitions on fire, and it was during this period in London that I came to realize that the business of maritime commerce was going to become my profession.

Following ten hectic months, I departed London and moved to Hamburg for a few months, where Fednav had its own office with three or four employees. This proved to be a very different experience from my time in London. Perhaps the most jarring distinction was its formality. We referred to each other by our surname. In the office I would refer to my colleague Thomas Grandt, not as Thomas, but as Herr Grandt.

The Fednav office, located in a town house in a residential area of Hamburg, was used primarily to book European steel cargoes on Fednav ships to be moved into the Great Lakes. The office dealt directly with the traffic departments of various European steel mills, and it was a much slower pace than the frenetic activity I had come to enjoy in the London market. But this was nevertheless important business for Fednav. There is a significant grain export market from the Great Lakes to destinations beyond North America, and most ships **ballasted** into this area to load these cargoes. But Fednav was able to position ships into the Great Lakes with inbound cargoes, thereby meaningfully reducing the ballast costs.

The time spent in Hamburg proved very useful for me because it taught me the importance of controlling "positioning" cargoes into traditional loading areas for ships. This was an operating philosophy that would be most valuable to me later in my career.

CHAPTER 4

MY FIRST BIG BREAK

"Opportunities don't happen, you create them."

CHRIS GROSSER,
American Photographer

returned to Montreal in the summer of 1977 and settled into my desk in the chartering department ready to light the world on fire. But Paul Wereley had me back in the same routine—reading telex traffic, running numbers, and other entry-level duties—certainly in no way acting as a mentor.

Fednav owned and operated **handysize/handymax** dry bulk ships that traded internationally, but they were designed and equipped to trade into the St. Lawrence River and through the St. Lawrence Seaway into the Great Lakes to benefit from the large movement of outbound grain cargoes destined primarily for Europe. In addition, the company loaded steel parcels and break-bulk cargo out of Asia and Europe into the Great Lakes and carried cargoes of bulk sugar from South Africa to receivers in Montreal and Toronto. So the chartering team was constantly looking to fix cargo that served to position the ships into the Great Lakes or ports in the St. Lawrence River to take advantage of the outbound cargoes.

One day, I saw a communication come in from Galbraiths for the movement of a new commodity called direct reduced iron ore pellets (DRI) from the Orinoco River in Venezuela into Hamilton, Ontario. DRI is a product of iron ore that does not require the use of a blast furnace in the production of steel. It eliminates the need for the fossil fuel required by the furnace and is therefore a major savings for steel mills. The receiver was Stelco, a well-known Canadian steel company. The charterer, a company called Siderúrgica de Orinoco C.A. (SIDOR) located in Ciudad Guayana, up the Orinoco River, was looking to move two cargoes. The rest of the chartering team ignored the business, as they were completely unfamiliar with the commodity and with the trade, and they thought it looked "flighty."

I approached Paul and suggested I would like to try and develop this movement. He asked me to put together some numbers and come up with a rate per tonne to quote to the charterers. I reached out to a ship's agent in Venezuela asking for information on the Orinoco River draft, port costs, and loading speed at the berth in Puerto Ordaz, the port facility that was in Ciudad Guayana. Hamilton was a well-known port for Fednav, and so we had a good deal of in-house information on the arrival facility there.

The other attractive aspect of the business was that it was being quoted with **SHINC** terms, meaning that Sundays and holidays (when the port might not be operational) counted in the calculation of **laytime**, as opposed to **SHEX** terms, where Sundays and holidays were not to be included in the calculation of laytime, even if activity took place on the weekends. SHINC terms are therefore more attractive for a shipowner.

Most inbound voyages at the time earned $2,000 to $3,000 per day on the Fednav ships. Because this was business that we were unfamiliar with, I suggested to Paul that we send out a freight indication that would earn one of our units about $5,500 per day, starting from Europe, ballasting down to the Orinoco River to load, and then on up to Hamilton to discharge. After he reviewed and approved my notes for a firm offer—thinking, of course, that no charterer in his right mind would pay a freight rate that resulted in earnings of about $5,500 per day for inbound Great Lakes business—I walked over to the telex room and asked the operator to send it. I could not have been more excited as I stood there and watched her type my notes into the machine.

The following morning, I arrived in the office before anyone else on the team to see a telex from SIDOR with their counteroffer. Within the next few days, I had fixed two cargoes of DRI that returned $5,200 per day positioning one of Fednav's 730 ships into the Great Lakes, almost double the daily earnings of other inbound cargoes. Even Ladi Pathy walked out to the chartering area to speak with me about it, and I had my ex-boss in voyage accounting come down to ask me if the estimate she had seen for the business was correct.

The cargoes were loaded over the next few months and the voyages proceeded very smoothly: no hiccups and the turnaround time at the load and discharge ports was very quick. As a result of this deal, Michael Bell had me set up a meeting with SIDOR in Venezuela to find out more about this new DRI commodity and to investigate potential future business with them.

I had arrived.

***

Up until that time I had only ever traveled to Europe, so flying from Montreal to New York to Caracas to Ciudad Guayana was an entirely new challenge. In 1979, I was, a twenty-six-year-old, and I did not even have a credit card; all my previous trips had been organized and paid for by the company. Therefore, before I departed, I applied for and received my first credit card: the American Express green card.

I flew into New York's JFK International Airport and connected on an American Airlines flight down to Simón Bolívar Airport, the main passenger gateway into Venezuela, located along the coast outside the town of Maiquetía. I spent my first night in a seedy, run-down hotel not far from the airport and caught an early morning flight to Ciudad Guayana.

The port agency firm that I had reached out to a few months earlier to get port information was called Lloyd Sudamericano. It was owned by a colorful character, Theodoros "Rudy" Pascalides, who met me at the airport and drove me to my meeting with SIDOR. Rudy, a resourceful Greek expat who had spent years as a chief mate on board ships, had arrived in Venezuela years before and found a job in a small ship agency company that happened to be located on the Orinoco River, in what would become the heartland of industrial Venezuela. With the rapid industrial development of the Orinoco River belt region, he very quickly saw the opportunity to start his own ship agency and built up a reputation as the go-to man for anything to do with the movement of ships in and out of the Orinoco River. He was known locally as "Mr. Orinoco."

Ciudad Guayana—or Puerto Ordaz, as most people call it—was established in the 1960s through the 1970s, around the time that many of the country's prime industries, such as iron ore and bauxite mining, and steel and aluminum production, were developed in this region. As we drove around, I could see residential neighborhoods that resembled U.S. suburbs, with housing and landscaping that looked similar to what one would find in any middle-class community in the United States and Canada. This reflected the fact that United States Steel Corporation (U.S. Steel, known today as USX), which had developed much of the mining industry in the area for decades, had invested in housing for hundreds of its expat workers and their families. For the most part, however, locals did not live in these developments.

I spent the better part of the first day down at the port area being shown around the docks, the loading terminal, and commodity stockpile areas by SIDOR personnel. The second day consisted of a more formal meeting at the SIDOR offices, during which, the principals educated me on the characteristics of DRI and what it was that made it attractive to steel mills. I was given a tour of their DRI production facility, and in the evening, I was taken out for a very late, wild night on the town.

The traffic manager of SIDOR told me that the two trial cargoes of DRI had gone very well in Stelco's mill and that the Canadian company wanted to import six more cargoes the following year. I was very concerned that this freight movement might end up being quoted in the marketplace by shipbrokers other than Galbraiths. In order to prevent this, I negotiated and reached a verbal agreement on the freight price for the six cargoes, pending approval from my head office.

On arriving back to the Fednav head office, I briefed Paul Wereley about this new opportunity and the proposal I had made to SIDOR. I told him that I had made clear to SIDOR in no uncertain terms that the fixture was subject to a review by my superiors, but he was upset with me. Paul ruled the Fednav chartering department with an iron fist, and nothing—absolutely nothing—was fixed without his blessing. I had taken the initiative to fix six additional cargoes: not one, or perhaps two, but *six* cargoes. And it was freight for the following Lakes season.

However, once he reviewed the details of what I had negotiated with SIDOR, Paul approved the fixture, and I sent a telex confirmation to them, incorporating all the details we had negotiated while I was in Puerto Ordaz. Although he never said so, probably not wanting to step on Paul's toes, I had the sense that Michael Bell liked the initiative that I had shown. He, Paul, and the rest of the chartering team could not believe that this young, inexperienced junior broker had managed to fix some of the best new business the company had seen in years. For the first time, I felt I was contributing to the success of the organization.

In early March 1980, we positioned the first of our six ships into the Orinoco to load the first DRI cargo to arrive in the St. Lawrence River, once the Seaway opened after its normal winter closure caused by accumulation of ice. This voyage went very smoothly, and SIDOR requested two more ship nominations from us in quick succession. The second ship arrived, and instead of loading within a few days, she spent over three weeks waiting at anchor for the berth while the third nominated ship arrived within ten days of the arrival of the second ship. We were accumulating large **demurrage** receivables, which do not get paid until after a voyage finishes.

As this was business that I had developed and brought into Fednav, for the first time in my short career, I felt stressed. The company depended on me to ensure that the contract was fulfilled. I would arrive in the office each morning, desperately hoping for some positive news from our operations group about the loading activity down in Puerto Ordaz. There was no word—and worse, no reason for the delay.

Finally, one morning after no news, Michael Bell summoned me to his office. In no uncertain terms, he wanted the situation resolved as soon as possible. He told me to get myself down to Venezuela and deal with the problem. The next day, he arranged for the accounting department to give me an envelope containing $3,000 in large bills to help, as he put it, "to dislodge whatever the hell is blocking the loading of our ships." And so off I went to Venezuela for the second time, with a wad of cash I didn't know quite what to do with, and not at all sure what was to greet me on my arrival.

Rudy Pascalides was there to meet me, and we drove straight to the SIDOR office, where I had the first of several meetings to try to understand what was happening with our ships. It turned out that SIDOR had sold additional DRI cargoes to European receivers, who were paying considerably more for the commodity than they had agreed to with Stelco, even allowing for the demurrage charges SIDOR was incurring for the delay to our ships. But I made little headway with the sales manager at SIDOR. That evening, Rudy suggested it was time to go back to the InterContinental Hotel and have a drink, followed by a relaxed dinner to regroup.

Over dinner, he explained to me that things in Venezuela worked differently than in many other parts of the world. Management hierarchies that might work well in other countries did not necessarily translate well into Venezuelan companies. He suggested that instead of focusing my efforts on the sales manager at SIDOR, who had much to gain from the situation, it might be more productive to spend some time down on the docks "getting to know" the port captains, who controlled things there.

I took his advice to heart, and over the next several days, I commuted from the InterContinental Hotel to the port area, with him as my guide.

Within a week the envelope I had received was empty and I managed to get our ships moved to the front of the line. This was another great experience for me, particularly as it taught me how things worked in some of the ports in South America, and the lesson would come in very handy in the future.

CHAPTER 5

FEDNAV: EXPANSION BEYOND THE GREAT LAKES

"If you believe business is built on relationships,
make building them your business."

SCOTT STRATTEN,
Canadian author and podcast host

I n 1979 through 1980, my main area of responsibility in Fednav was the chartering of Great Lakes–suitable oceangoing ships to augment the company's owned fleet. But given that the St. Lawrence Seaway shuts its locks for the winter, the first quarter of each year was a quiet time. That is probably why late one afternoon in February 1980, Michael Bell called me into his office.

"Tony, John Weale and I are heading down to Nassau tomorrow to meet with Navios Corporation about a new opportunity. I think you should join us, so pack your bag and get to the office early tomorrow." I guessed Bell had tapped me to tag along on this trip because of my recent familiarity with Venezuela and the Orinoco River.

I knew a little bit about Navios Corporation because of the DRI fixture I'd made in Venezuela. It was a subsidiary of U.S. Steel and transported iron ore from its parent company mine located up the Orinoco River, primarily to the United States and Europe. The company also moved iron ore from Port-Cartier, Quebec, located along the north shore of the St. Lawrence River, down to the U.S. East Coast.

***

In the late nineteenth century, Andrew Carnegie, together with a few other associates, including Henry Clay Frick, consolidated some small steel mills located around Pittsburgh, Pennsylvania, which they called the Carnegie Steel Company. At about the same time, J.P. Morgan acquired the Federal Steel and National Steel companies, and in 1901, he convinced Carnegie that they should merge their two businesses to create United States Steel Corporation. For many decades it was the largest producer of steel products in the world.

The company's production activity grew enormously in the 1940s as a result of demand for war materials, and the postwar economic boom during the following decade further served to promote increased steel production to new historic highs.

Following the Second World War, U.S. Steel was one of the largest companies in the United States, and by midcentury, it reached its peak employment of about 325,000 people. At the time, the company was present in every geographic region of the United States, except the east, and in 1949, U.S. Steel management decided to build a large integrated steel plant on a 1,600-acre greenfield site in Bucks County, Pennsylvania. The mill, Fairless Works, which they named after its Chairman Benjamin Fairless, is located on the Delaware River and became operational in 1952. The strategic issues with this new steel facility were finding sufficient iron ore, the single largest commodity used in the making of blast furnace steel, to feed its production capacity; and the complexity and cost of moving vast amounts of iron ore to this new location on the eastern seaboard.

About then, the company initiated a strategy to diversify its sourcing of certain raw materials to geographic areas outside the continental United States. U.S. Steel geologists discovered a large deposit of iron ore in the Ciudad Guayana region of Venezuela, about 295 kilometers up the Orinoco River. It established the Orinoco Mining Company (OMC) in Venezuela for the development of this new immense asset. Through this subsidiary, U.S. Steel received an exclusive mining concession from the Venezuelan government and began to mine the ore. However, it still needed a way to move the ore out of the country to its mills in the U.S., specifically its new Fairless facility in Pennsylvania.

U.S. Steel had its own shipping company and owned a fleet of ships that focused on domestic movements of commodities, primarily iron ore, on the

Great Lakes. This company, though, was not equipped to service the mine in Venezuela; so, in 1954, U.S. Steel formed Navios, a new shipping subsidiary. It acquired its name from the small body of water Boca de Navios—its literal translation, "mouth of ships"—located between the islands of Chacachacare and Huevos, west of Port of Spain, Trinidad, visible from the flight route to the Orinoco River Delta.

U.S. Steel incorporated Navios as Navios Corporation in the Bahamas because of the country's proximity to its corporate offices in Pittsburgh, its tax advantages, and its friendly policies toward foreign workers that allowed expatriates to settle down on the island with ease. The headquarters was located in the capital city, Nassau.

As part of the process of incorporating the company on the island, U.S. Steel agreed with the Bahamian government to institute a corporate pol-icy of hiring and encouraging the advancement of locals within the Navios organization. Over the years, about 40 percent of the head office staff were Bahamian nationals, a few of whom occupied senior management roles in the company. Of the remaining 60 percent, about half were British expa-triates who were hired because of their backgrounds in the operations and commercial management of ships, while the remaining positions consisted of American financial and senior management personnel.

The transportation logistics within Venezuela proved to be daunting for a variety of reasons. At the time, there were only two proposed plans to transport the ore for export. The first of these was to build a rail link from the mine site overland to a purpose-built port located on the Gulf of Paria, the large inland sea located between Trinidad and eastern Venezuela. But the capital required for such an investment, as well as the time involved in con-structing the rail link, made it prohibitive.

The second plan was to use the lower three hundred kilometers of the Orinoco River as the export corridor. The river is the third largest in the world when measured by the outflow of water. It discharges water at a stag-gering monthly average rate of 22,500 cubic meters per second, creating a powerful surge that can cause difficulties for large oceangoing ships navigat-ing the river.

Another complication was that there are two seasons in Venezuela: the wet season from May to November and the dry season from December to April. In each season, there are substantial fluctuations in water levels of the Orinoco River. During the dry season, the draft fluctuates between twen-ty-eight and thirty-two feet. In the wet season, it averages about thirty-seven feet but can be as high as forty-one feet. It was a challenge to navigate a ship with these changing drafts.

However, despite these challenges, the management of U.S. Steel decided that this route would be the most cost-effective option to move their ore.

They hired an Italian hydraulic engineer named Giuseppe "Pino" Colombari to make the Orinoco River export corridor viable. He coordinated the dredging of the river to increase the overall draft and arranged to smooth out some of its sharp bends. He was also responsible for organizing the placement of navigational aids and buoys at certain strategic points in the river, and providing accurate navigational charts for the captains of ships who would be sailing the Orinoco.

Once the river route was viable, U.S. Steel had to arrange for the carriage of large quantities of iron ore out of Venezuela, up to the U.S. East Coast. To do this, they reached out to National Bulk Carriers, which was one of the largest shipowners in the world then. The company operated out of New York City and was owned by its founder, Daniel Keith "D.K." Ludwig.

Ludwig, who is considered one of the first billionaires in the United States, was a fascinating man. Born in Michigan into a large shipping family, he learned the trade from the ground up after dropping out of school at age nine. When he was nineteen, he began his own shipping business on the Great Lakes, using a barge to ship timber and molasses. In the decade before the Second World War, he negotiated a loan with Chemical Bank (now Chase Bank) to buy some small dry bulk cargo freighters, which he upgraded, converted to tankers, and chartered to Standard Oil. Ludwig also owned a small shipyard in Virginia, and in the early 1940s, it was there that he pioneered the use of welding, instead of riveting, steel plate to hulls to reduce the construction cost of ships significantly.

But after the war, the cost of building ships in the United States had become increasingly expensive, and this, together with Ludwig's intention to build larger ships to benefit from economies of scale for the growing market, led him to Japan. Mired in a postwar depression, and subject to the U.S. efforts to rebuild its economy and use its strategic position in the Far East, the Japanese government was concerned that their large naval shipyard located at Kure, along the Inland Sea of Japan, just south of Hiroshima, might be turned into a U.S. naval base.

When Ludwig, a private citizen, approached the Japanese government to lease the yard to build commercial vessels, they jumped at the opportunity. In 1949, National Bulk Carriers signed a ten-year lease, with an option for an additional five years, with the Japanese government for the former naval shipyard.

A brilliant business entrepreneur, Ludwig pioneered the financing of huge projects such as shipbuilding without using his own capital. He worked closely with Chemical Bank to arrange financing for the construction of ships using the charter contracts he had with the end user. It was typical for the loan repayment schedule to commence only upon completion of construction, and so in many instances, he had little up-front invested equity. This concept was successfully duplicated by several Greek shipowners in the 1960s and 1970s, including such well-known names as Aristotle Onassis and Stavros Niarchos, who built up large tanker fleets.

Following the start of the Second World War, the U.S. Navy placed domestic orders for many ships, which came to be called the Liberty or Victory class of cargo ships. These vessels were about ten thousand deadweight tonnes, and their accommodations, bridge, and engine were all located amidships, with a tunnel connecting the engine shaft to the propeller at the stern of the ship. In addition, the ships had a **tween deck**, and post and beam **derricks**. About two thousand of these ships survived the war, and many were acquired as replacement ships by Greek and Norwegian shipowners who had lost countless ships to U-boats while serving the Allied convoys. During the initial years of operation, Navios chartered many of these small Liberty ships to move iron ore out of the Orinoco River.

Because of their relatively small size, they were only able to transport limited quantities of iron ore, which resulted in a high **landed cost** into the U.S. market. In 1956, Ludwig presented to U.S. Steel a design for a much larger ship that generated significant cost efficiencies in the transport of iron ore. In addition, the design of these ships incorporated large engines, providing extra horsepower to enable better maneuverability in the river. Following months of detailed negotiations, Navios, whose performance was guaranteed by U.S. Steel, secured ten-year **bareboat charter** contracts for four 54,000-deadweight-tonne, Orinoco River–suitable, iron ore carriers to be built at the Kure Shipyard in Japan. Ludwig financed the construction using these long-term bareboat charter contracts. The Ore-class ships, named MV *Ore Saturn*, MV *Ore Venus*, MV *Ore Jupiter*, and MV *Ore Meridian*, were delivered in 1959 through 1960 and constituted Navios's core fleet for the next two decades. The bareboat contracts included a provision that provided Navios the option to purchase the ships at the end of their charters.

These Ore-class carriers were considered very specialized vessels designed to carry dense iron ore in small holds surrounded by a double-skinned bottom and large side-ballast wing tanks to compensate for cargo shifts in rough seas. The ore carriers were used primarily to transport iron ore into the U.S. Steel receiving facilities in Mobile, Alabama and Fairless Works in Pennsylvania. Occasionally, when OMC was able to sell iron ore into certain European steel mills, the ships would sail for destinations on the Continent. The ships were built with powerful steam turbine engines, which had the advantages of little or no vibration, reduced space requirements and maintenance costs, and, perhaps most importantly, the ability to increase speed very quickly to improve maneuverability. Navios eventually exercised its purchase options and acquired the four ships.

Other aspects of Orinoco River trading that Navios pioneered were vessel top-offs that were normally carried out in the low-water season at the mouth of the Orinoco River. Navios personnel working with Ludwig's National Bulk Carriers designed the MV *Ore Convey*, a thirty-thousand-deadweight **belt self-unloading** ore carrier that was delivered from the Kure Shipyard in 1956 and carried out the first Orinoco River top-offs during the low water season of 1957. It could arguably be labeled the ugliest ship ever built. Her engine room was built aft, but the bridge superstructure was well forward of the center of the ship. The funnel, located above the engine room at the stern of the ship, was much too short and stubby from an aesthetic perspective—Ludwig did everything he could to save on construction costs.

The premise for this ship was taken from the "lakers"—bulk carriers that were limited to trading only within the Great Lakes because they were not engineered to deal with the stresses associated with the sea forces of the open oceans. In the years prior to the Second World War, some of these lakers were converted into self-unloaders. Ludwig incorporated this design into the *Ore Convey*.

The *Ore Convey* would be loaded upriver and then proceed to the mouth of the Orinoco River, where she would anchor and await a ship that had been only partially loaded due to the upriver draft restrictions. Once there, the ore was transferred through **hopper** gates on the floor of each cargo hold onto a conveyor belt that ran the length of the ship from bow to stern. Then it went onto a secondary belt that ran forward on an incline from the stern of the ship and eventually protruded out through the **weather deck** and rose up to a point adjacent to the aft side of the superstructure. At that point, the ore would be transferred to a boom that was able to swing up and out across the side of the *Ore Convey* and "top off" the partially loaded vessel that arrived alongside her.

Another challenge was the river bar and channel used to access the loading installation up the Orinoco River. It was limited to about a twenty-five-foot draft. Navios contracted with Ludwig for the construction of a purpose-built dredger ship called the MV *ICOA*, with an enormous 250-foot boom to dredge the river bar under the supervision of Colombari. Once in service, the *ICOA* was able to remove approximately ten million cubic yards per month of soil from the bar of the Orinoco River—and smaller quantities from the river channel itself.

***

As Navios started to develop the iron ore exports from Puerto Ordaz, the company faced several operational issues intensified by its efforts to increase the size of the ships loading iron ore in the river. The first of these had to do with the water flow around five severe, critical bends in the Orinoco that required ships to reduce their speed in the water to close to zero knots and allow the current to take them.

The ability to steer a ship is created by the movement of water past the **rudder**. If left to drift with the current, once the ship makes it around a bend, it must ramp up speed very quickly. As the price of oil increased throughout the 1970s and into the 1980s, ships were designed with engines that had reduced horsepower to lower the cost of fuel consumed, and, in some cases, ships with these engines could not rapidly resume their speed in a short time, resulting in a loss of control and the occasional grounding in the river.

In open seas, there are no restrictions for water to flow around and under the hull of a ship. But in shallow or constrained waterways, such as rivers, the flow is restricted resulting in a higher flow velocity of water passing under the hull. This triggers a decrease in the underwater pressure on the hull, causing the vessel to sink deeper into the water. This maritime phenomenon is known as squat. The amount of squat is dependent on a vessel's speed and hull design, and the phenomenon has the potential to cause ships to run aground.

The faster a ship moves through restricted water, the greater the squat. Assume a ship is moving at five knots with an astern current of five knots. The ship is moving *with* the current, and so there is zero squat phenomenon because the ship is not moving *through* the water, and therefore no water is required to pass rapidly under the ship. With more speed through water, a vessel will push more water away as the bow moves forward, increasing squat, and to reduce squat, you reduce speed through the water. But this is sometimes difficult to do in a river with a strong current.

The other factor affecting the level of squat has to do with a ship's block coefficient, which is a ratio of the underwater volume of a ship to the volume of a rectangular block having the same length, width, and depth as the ship. In other words, it is a measurement of a ship's displacement compared to a box that it could fit into. Therefore, an imaginary ship that is a perfectly sized rectangular block will have a block coefficient of one, whereas a vessel that has a narrow bow and a stern that rises out of the water might have a block coefficient of .60.

So, which ship will have a higher block coefficient—the enormous, boxy twenty thousand–twenty equipment unit (TEU) container ship MV *Ever Given*, or a large cruise ship with narrow, aquiline features? The answer should be obvious: the *Ever Given*, because she will push more water as she moves through a restricted waterway, like the Suez Canal, causing her squat to be more pronounced than that of a cruise ship passing through the same canal, the net effect of which is to cause the hull to sink farther. And what happens? The *Ever Given* runs aground because of poor pilotage, heavy winds, and squat.

Captains George Skelton and Ennio Distefano were Navios employees responsible for the development of large-vessel navigation in the Orinoco River. They became experts in dealing with underpowered ships and squat phenomena, in addition to dealing with a multitude of other problems associated with the river. For instance, it was not at all uncommon for navigation aids in the river to be dragged off course with the very strong currents associated with the rainy season. And often, the light in light buoys would be out and not replaced for days. These types of river distractions occurred throughout the year.

When a ship enters a port or a river, a pilot with local experience comes on board to assist the bridge officers with navigating the waters. George and Ennio knew that certain Orinoco River pilots were more professional and honest in their duties than others. Some river pilots intentionally grounded ships to receive payments from the local tug companies that had to come out to salvage such units. So, this was another area they kept a close watch on, and quite often they would join a particular vessel's river transit to keep the pilots on track.

***

In early 1979, Israel and Egypt signed a peace treaty that was brokered by the Carter administration. A little-known part of this agreement is that Israel would give up the Alma oil field located in the southern Sinai on the Gulf of Suez. Years before, Israel had discovered and developed the field to help the country achieve energy independence. Israel was going through the first of what would be several middle-class population growth spurts, and the nation desperately needed to improve the quality, distribution, and volume of electricity within the country. The oil from this field was to provide the fuel for massive new energy plants it had planned to build.

However, without this cheap source of oil, the Israel Electric Corporation (IEC), the government-owned entity responsible for electricity distribution throughout the country, pivoted and decided to build the country's largest electricity-generating plant in the port city of Hadera, located on the coast about fifty kilometers north of Tel Aviv. This new plant would be fueled primarily by thermal coal instead of oil. IEC eventually formed a subsidiary named the National Coal Supply Corporation (NCSC) to arrange for the procurement and shipping of thermal coal into the country. The most cost-effective method to transport this cargo was the employment of large capesize ships.

In those early days, only a select few shipping companies owned the limited number of capesize ships. These companies also operated sizeable oil tankers fleets, and they did not want to enter into a **contract of affreightment** with an Israeli government entity for fear of their tanker fleets being banned by the Persian Gulf oil exporters.

At the time, U.S. Steel had business in Israel, and the man on the ground representing their interests with the government was an Israeli middleman named Ari Kaplan. He got wind of the government's requirement for capesize ships to move thermal coal and brought the opportunity to the management of U.S. Steel in Pittsburgh, and they quickly passed it on to the executives at Navios.

With the help of Ari Kaplan and the U.S. Steel ownership pedigree, Navios was able to negotiate a lucrative ten-year fixed-rate contract of affreightment with NCSC to move large volumes of thermal coal from Australia and South Africa into Hadera. But Navios had one major problem: It had no capesize ships in its fleet.

Navios was focused on transatlantic panamax trades then. Its management viewed the contract with NCSC as a strategic shift to expand its base of operation both geographically and in terms of vessel deployment. In addition, it was part of Navios's broader effort to reduce its traditional dependency on its parent's iron ore freight volumes.

Through his contacts at U.S. Steel, Gordon Parham, the managing director of Galbraith Wrightson Shipbrokers in London, learned of Navios's requirement for the charter of two capesize ships. He brought the opportunity immediately to the attention of Fednav. At the time, Fednav was one of very few shipowners that had capesize ships on order for its fleet.

That was the reason for the meeting in Nassau.

***

It was a strange sensation arriving on New Providence Island, the small island of the Bahamas in which its capital, Nassau, is located. I recall deplaning and being smothered with warm, humid sunshine, an abrupt change from the mid-February winter weather we had departed from four hours earlier. And I wasn't quite sure why I was traveling with the executive vice president of Fednav and its project manager. We took a taxi straight to the Navios head office, where we met with two commercial directors of the company, David Rose and Dudley Martinborough.

The Navios office was located in a single-story, T-shaped building located on Village Road, just a short distance from the center of Nassau. Its exterior clapboard was painted white, and it was unlike any other office I had ever set foot in. The executive and commercial staff were located at one end, accounting on the other end, and vessel operations in the larger center section.

This was yet another great experience for a twenty-six-year-old. To watch a seasoned shipping executive like Michael Bell, negotiate the time charters, while John Weale cranked out numbers and covered all the legalities, was a real eye-opener for me.

In a charter party contract, there is always a specific clause called Trading Exclusions, in which the parties negotiate the exclusion of trading the ship into certain countries and war and/or warlike areas. Countries and regions normally excluded might include Cuba, North Korea, Iran, the Republic of Yemen, and certain sea areas that are ice infested during the winter months. But Israel is not normally included in Trading Exclusions, and it was certainly not a country that had ports able to accept large capesize ships, so we never suspected the Fednav capesize ships would be used in a new commodity trade into Israel. And the Navios executives never let on about their contract with NCSC.

When we departed the country two days later, we had fixed ten-year time charters for two of Fednav's capesize ships, which were still under construction in South Korea. During the negotiation, the Navios executives did not divulge how they intended to employ the ships other than using them in the rapidly developing thermal coal markets. About a month after the charter party contract was signed, Navios announced to us that the ships were to be used for a new movement of Australian and South African thermal coal into Israel. It was not something any of us had expected, and it was another great lesson for me: In a negotiation, be careful not to divulge more than you must.

It was these charters that established the first significant commercial relationship between Fednav and Navios.

CHAPTER 6

THE OSLO CONNECTION

"Broaden your horizons. They're the only ones you'll
ever have, so make the suckers as wide as possible."

JENNIFER CRUSIE,
American contemporary author

———————

n 1980, the consummate shipbroker Gordon Parham came across what
he thought might be a good opportunity for Fednav, while earning lucrative shipbroking fees for Galbraiths. He convinced Ladi Pathy to take
the plunge into the tanker sector, and Fednav acquired a pair of fifty-thou-
sand-deadweight **product tankers** as an asset play. The senior management
of Fednav took the unusual step of placing both ships into a product tanker
pool called OSCO Carriers, operated out of Oslo by a wizened, crusty old
Norwegian shipowner named Ole Schröder. I say "unusual" because Fednav
was, and still is, known for maintaining a very tight rein on all its shipping
activities. But given that these were such unique and different ships for
Fednav to own, and Fednav had no experience operating tankers, the OSCO
pool was a good alternative.

A maritime shipping pool is a commercial entity created to market a
group of similar ships owned by different shipowners. Pools provide a higher
profile in the marketplace because they generally control a large fleet of
ships, which leads to increased chartering opportunities and greater bargaining clout. The ships are normally time chartered to the pool company, but
the shipowner continues, technically, to manage the ship, supply the crew,
and be responsible for repayment of debt.

When a ship is placed into a pool, it is allocated pool points, which are based on the ship's earning capacity relative to the other vessels in the pool. Elements such as the ship's deadweight, its speed and fuel consumption performance, the size of its holds or tanks (in the case of tankers), and its age are some of the many items that go into allocating points. The revenue derived by the pool is distributed monthly to the owners of the ships based on the points allocated to them.

Even though I continued with my responsibilities in the chartering department, since my trip to Nassau, I had been spending more time with John Weale trying to understand what his responsibilities were as a project manager. One thing he taught me was the nuts and bolts of the financial structures behind the acquisition of ships. He also introduced me to the practical applications of net present value and discounted cash flows. These concepts were generally unfamiliar to the day-to-day chartering broker, but I had studied these while at Queen's University and now saw how they were applied in the real world.

As my educational background was different from most others within the organization, I reflected on my time aboard the MV *Federal Saguenay*, my postings to London and Hamburg, and, of course, the trip down to the Bahamas. It was clear that members of senior management were grooming me for a larger role in the company.

During a dinner with Michael Bell and John that summer, they told me management was thinking it might be a good idea to have some boots on the ground in the OSCO pool office, to keep an eye on Fednav's interests, and they thought it might be a good opportunity for me. Before dessert arrived, it was decided that I would head off to Oslo that fall for at least a year.

Prior to my arrival in Oslo, all my shipping experience had been centered around the dry bulk shipping market. I knew virtually nothing about the tanker markets, the ships that transport oil and its products, or the terminology associated with this sector, some of which was quite different from that of dry bulk. During that summer, I set about reading a few books to learn as much as possible about this market to prepare for my new posting.

In Norway, the business of maritime transport is considered a mainstay of the local business community and a prestigious profession. Oslo is at the center of it and is home to many maritime-related companies, including shipowners, shipbrokers, marine money firms, maritime legal and insurance firms, and a **classification society**. Unlike London, which is an enormous city and in which the international maritime business is but one of many prominent professions, this industry looms large in Oslo, a relatively smaller city.

Many people who move to Oslo have trouble getting comfortable living there, primarily because of the climate, in particular the winter months. Since I grew up in Quebec, this was not an issue for me. Even though Oslo is located at a latitude considerably higher than Montreal, it is nowhere near as cold because of the influence of the Gulf Stream. What is difficult in winter are the short hours of daylight, which is something to which I did have to get accustomed. In the winter months, the sun rises between nine and nine-thirty in the morning and sets in the midafternoon. But I arrived in Oslo in early fall, when those dark winter months seemed far off.

OSCO arranged for a small but modern one-room apartment above a Vinmonopolet, a government-owned alcoholic beverage retailer, about a twenty-minute walk from the office. Each day, I was able to stroll back and forth to work, which was wonderful.

The OSCO team, led by a tall, middle-aged Norwegian named Paul Ranke, could not have been more welcoming and helpful in teaching me some of the vagaries of the product tanker market. Within two months they had me trading some of their positions and fixing the pool product tankers in the open markets.

Paul and I hit it off well, and he took a particular interest in my evolving education. In addition to giving me daily guidance, he also arranged to introduce me to people in the various key shipping firms across a broad spectrum of the local maritime community. One of the firms he introduced me to was the Torvald Klaveness Group, one of the preeminent Norwegian shipowners. I developed a relationship with some of the people in this company, including with Tom Erik Klaveness, a son of the founder, who would take over the reins of the company from his father in the latter 1980s.

After about fourteen months in Norway, and just a few months before my scheduled return to Montreal, I received an offer to interview for a position at Klaveness. The interview went well and I was offered a chartering position with the firm. I thought seriously about severing my ties with Fednav and settling in Oslo. After much deliberation, I decided to remain with Fednav. After all, I'd invested so much time with the company, and I felt I was moving up in my career there.

About a week before I was scheduled to move back to Montreal, I was playing tennis when I slid on a clay court to return a shot and rolled over my ankle, breaking it. By the end of the day, I was on crutches and had a large cast on my right leg, and I was not looking forward to my cramped flight back to Montreal. When he heard about my injury, John Weale, to whom I reported in Fednav's head office in Montreal while I was living in Norway, graciously upgraded me from economy to first class to afford me extra leg-room for the long flight home.

It was, therefore, with considerable trepidation that, a few days following my accident, off I went to Oslo Airport, which in those days was in Fornebu, a short five miles from the center of Oslo. It was for many years one of the best city airports in the world, as it was so easy to get to and from. I don't recall my flight from Oslo down to Heathrow, but I will never forget my flight from London to Montreal.

I was wheeled about the airport by escorts and eventually onto the British Airways flight. The flight attendant helped me into my spacious, first-class seat. Having only ever traveled economy class, I found it to be quite an experience. The seat was considerably wider than any seat I had used in the past. Although it did not fully recline, it had a little footrest that expanded outward.

The gentleman I sat beside on the flight looked to be in his mid-for-ties and he initiated a conversation by—what else—asking me about the cast on my leg. After I communicated my story, he told me he worked for the Aluminum Company of Canada (Alcan), which at the time was one of the largest and most well-recognized international companies in Canada, with headquarters in Montreal and a large, global footprint.

I knew that the process to make aluminum starts with the mining of bauxite, which is then treated with caustic soda to create alumina, and which is broken down into its components using electric power. In fact, it utilizes enormous amounts of electricity, which is why alumina facilities around the world tend to be located close to primary sources of electricity. The result is aluminum: Very simply put, about four tonnes of bauxite gets processed into two tonnes of alumina, from which about one tonne of aluminum can be made.

During this period, Alcan had a minority interest in Queensland Alumina Limited (QAL), one of Australia's largest alumina refineries. While living in Oslo and working in the OSCO Carrier pool, I had been involved in analyzing the freight component for the carriage of caustic soda, a key ingredient in the manufacture of aluminum, on our product tankers into the QAL facility in Gladstone, Queensland, located about midway between Sydney and Cairns on the eastern coast of Australia.

In addition, I learned a good deal about the movement of bauxite, the other key ingredient to aluminum production, in panamax ships, some of which was moved by Klaveness for Alcan out of Guinea, West Africa, into Port Alfred, Quebec, on the Saguenay River, which flows into the St. Lawrence River, about two hundred kilometers north of Quebec City. I therefore had a good brief on some of Alcan's ocean freight, and we talked at length about global freight movements generally and those of Alcan specifically. The gentleman I was seated next to seemed impressed by my knowledge of Alcan's seaborne shipments.

As he disembarked from the flight, he gave me his business card: PATRICK JEAN-JACQUES RICH, EXECUTIVE VICE PRESIDENT OF ALCAN'S GLOBAL OPERATIONS. As he turned to say goodbye—I was waiting for a wheelchair—he smiled and said he knew Fednav, and Ladi Pathy, the president of Fednav, and wished me well. He never let on about it during our six-hour flight, and I was glad I had acquitted myself well in the conversation.

CHAPTER 7

THE MOVE TO NAVIOS CORPORATION

"When things are bad, we take comfort in the thought that
they could always get worse. And when they are, we find hope
in the thought that things are so bad, they have to get better."

MALCOLM S. FORBES,
American entrepreneur and publisher

———————

I returned to Montreal from Oslo in the late fall of 1981 with a renewed sense of purpose. My time in Oslo had allowed me to broaden my horizons and realize just how multifaceted the maritime industry was. However, despite my experiences in Oslo, I was told to resume my limited responsibilities in the chartering department, where my primary activity was arranging short-period time charters for three to five months to supplement the Fednav fleet.

As much as I was enamored with the maritime industry and the business of chartering, I had been at Fednav for over five years at that point. Even though senior management seemed to be interested in my career, I came to realize that without further effort on my part, I might simply get stuck in the role of being an in-house chartering broker. I wanted something more.

Montreal offered so little in potential career paths in our industry. Other than a few domestic Great Lakes shipping companies, and some small, local competitive shipbroker offices and ship agency companies, there was not much of a maritime community, and by extension, limited career opportunities. It was not like London or Oslo, where you found many maritime legal firms, marine insurance companies, major banks with divisions focused on lending to the maritime industry, dozens of competitive shipbroker offices, and, of course, many, many shipowning operations, all of which provided numerous employment opportunities. So, I decided to return to university for an MBA. I thought that obtaining an advanced business degree would strengthen my career potential and provide me greater business possibilities abroad.

"You have got to be kidding, Tony," Michael Bell said when I informed him of my decision. "You've made tremendous strides here in a short time. You've spent time in some exciting shipping capitals and gained enormous exposure to our industry. We see you as having great potential. Are you telling me that you are going to throw away the real-world experience that you have had here at Fednav for two years on a university campus drowning in boring lectures and books?"

Michael had been very supportive of my career development within Fednav, but I was nevertheless stunned by the forcefulness of his reaction to my even contemplating departing. So, I agreed to put my plan on hold for a few months to see what the future held for me at Fednav.

A few months later, on Wednesday, July 7, 1982, I went out on the town with some close friends to celebrate my twenty-ninth birthday, which fell the following day. We had a lengthy dinner followed by some barhopping in downtown Montreal. This would be my last bachelor birthday party, as I was now engaged to be married that September. I did not get to bed until the early-morning hours, and I arrived in the office Thursday morning a little bleary-eyed. All I wanted to do was keep my head down, read the morning telex traffic, and get out to an early lunch as quickly as possible.

At about 8:30 a.m., Michael called me into his office. My head was pounding and a meeting with the executive vice president was the last thing I wanted that morning. I dutifully made my way in, hoping the meeting would be short.

Then he dropped a bombshell on me. He told me that later that day, Fednav would be issuing a press release announcing its acquisition of a 50 percent stake in Navios Corporation from U.S. Steel. He explained that David Roderick, who had taken over as chief executive officer of U.S. Steel in 1979, had initiated a strategic drive throughout the company to dispose of what he considered to be nonstrategic assets. This initiative became of paramount importance when U.S. Steel announced its acquisition of Marathon Oil in

November 1981 for $6.8 billion, which was at that time the second-largest merger in U.S. history. One of those assets was Navios Corporation.

I found out later that Gordon Parham, the ever-market-savvy shipbroker, had entered the picture once again for Fednav. Through his elaborate network of contacts, he discovered that Navios might be available for purchase. The first call he made was to the London-based shipowner of Hellespont Maritime named Basil Papachristidis, who back then had several ships on charter to Navios. But Basil passed on the deal, and his next call was to Ladi Pathy.

Fednav and U.S. Steel entered negotiations in February 1982. The four individuals involved in this behind-closed-doors negotiation were Ladi Pathy, Michael Bell, John Weale, and John Peacock. The latter two expressed their concerns about the acquisition because the metrics were based on optimistic forecasts in what was arguably a declining dry bulk market environment.

But Ladi and Michael, who had been on a very successful run over the prior ten years, believed this was a great opportunity to grow Fednav, and they prevailed. What they found particularly attractive about the business of Navios was that the company had a large base of contracts of affreightment and therefore controlled significant amounts of cargo movements. Of course, it did not hurt that Fednav had two of its four large capesize ships on charter to Navios. The deal whereby Fednav would become a 50 percent stakeholder in Navios was finalized that summer and announced on July 8.

In what I later surmised as his way to keep me in the company and out of academia, Michael arranged for me to take a noon flight down to their New York headquarters for an interview with the president of Navios, José Pablo Elverdin. Elverdin was the Argentine lawyer who had been instrumental in representing U.S. Steel during the nationalization of the Venezuelan iron ore industry, and he had been leading Navios for the past few years. Michael explained to me that due to the move to New York from the Bahamas and various personnel changes in Navios, the senior management of that company was actively looking to hire new commercial managers.

So, suffering from a birthday celebration hangover, with no time to pack or change, I flew down to New York City in a crumpled old suit that I would certainly not have worn, had I known I would be having a serious job interview. I took a cab from LaGuardia Airport to 65 Broadway, on the corner of Wall Street, where the company had its cramped headquarters. The interview with Elverdin lasted about ninety minutes.

What impressed me about the meeting was that Joe, as he liked to be called, did not focus on my background or education, but on my work experiences at Fednav and how comfortable and proficient I was working in a team environment. He did not show me around the offices or introduce me to anyone else. As soon as we were done, he thanked me and said he'd be in touch. Then I jumped into a cab to head back out to LaGuardia for the flight back to Montreal, thoroughly convinced that I would not get offered a job.

A week later, Michael called me into his office to tell me that I had a job with Navios in New York. He told me this would be yet another part of what was becoming an extended trainee program. When I asked about the position, he told me he was not sure, but I should not worry about it, because he believed there would be great opportunity for me. My immediate thought was how my fiancée would react to this news. Fortunately, she had spent time in New York previously, and since she was an aspiring artist, the thought of moving to Manhattan thrilled her.

A few weeks later, I flew back down to New York for a meeting with Don Szostak, the executive vice president of Navios, to negotiate the terms of my employment, which included the cost of temporary hotel accommodations in Manhattan. About two months later, in October 1982, I was sitting at a secretary's desk in Navios's Manhattan office. After stints in London, Hamburg, and Oslo, I was back in another major maritime capital.

My wife and I spent the first two months in New York living in a midtown hotel, and while I went off to work, she searched out suitable living accommodations. It was an exuberant time: We were newlyweds living in a great global metropolis, and I felt I was now playing in the big leagues of shipping.

When I first arrived at Navios, I was told that the company would likely be moving its head office out to Greenwich, Connecticut. So we rented an apartment on 32nd Street between Third & Lexington Avenues, which was perfect for my commute down to Wall Street and within walking distance of Grand Central Terminal for the commuter train to Greenwich. The commute proved to be easy, because the Navios office was located right next door to the Greenwich train station.

***

If one studies the history of hurricane activity in the Bahamas, the statistics are not encouraging. On average, the islands take a direct hit every five years, and they get "brushed" by a hurricane every two years. When these severe storms hit, island communications are prone to be shut down for multiple days and occasionally weeks, which can make operating an international business out of Nassau difficult. It was following the departure of Hurricane David, at the end of August 1979, that the senior management of Navios started contemplating relocating the head office to New York City.

In addition to its Nassau office, Navios had a technical ship management group that operated out of offices located in midtown Manhattan. This subsidiary was charged with managing the technical operations of the company's owned fleet. It was determined the most cost-effective action would be to merge the two groups into a head office located in downtown Manhattan, and, unfortunately, the company leased space that could not have been more cramped, bleak, and dreary.

The decision proved to be quite disruptive. Many of the longtime Bahamas-based employees chose not to relocate. In addition, some British expatriates with a great deal of maritime experience decided to exercise their options to have Navios relocate them back to the United Kingdom. The result was a serious talent drain, which impacted operations. Add to that the bundling of two disparate groups of employees onto two floors of cramped office space in the burrows of lower Manhattan, with few windows, little natural light, and warrens of small offices made working there difficult for both new and old staff members.

In addition to me, Ladi Pathy and Michael Bell moved John Weale down to New York into a vice president position. Sean Day, who had left Fednav a few years earlier for greener pastures in Manhattan, was also recruited to join the executive management ranks of Navios. And in those early years following Fednav's 50 percent acquisition, much of the burden in reforming the management structures of Navios fell to John and Sean, who both reported directly to Joe.

I can only describe my move to Navios as a culture shock. The initial months for me in the company were not easy. It was apparent that morale within the organization after the acquisition was low. Aside from the personnel changes and uncomfortable offices, there was a great deal of conflict regarding the internal management structure as well. Initially, I spent much of my time talking to the Navios staff, trying to learn what specific roles everyone performed in the organization. Little did I know that this honest attempt on my part to understand who did what, and why, would contribute to the general perception that I was a "Fednav man" parachuted into the offices, along with John and Sean, to evaluate and change how things were being run on the day-to-day level.

As I started to absorb more about the mechanics of how Navios worked, it became clear to me just how difficult it would be to integrate the Navios and Fednav systems. While they shared the goal of controlling certain key movements of ocean freight, their operational approaches to the business were very different. Navios was set up with a hierarchical, top-down bureaucratic management system that reflected its parent U.S. Steel. It certainly was not like those of a quick-footed, entrepreneurial shipping group like Fednav, which had to operate in a competitive, global maritime environment and, by necessity, make decisions at a moment's notice.

With the arrival of Fednav as a 50 percent shareholder in Navios, it was not long before Navios's three senior commercial directors, Dudley Martinborough, David Barnett, and David Rose, decided to depart for opportunities elsewhere. The backgrounds of all three were marketing and chartering, and they believed their career paths might be interrupted with the arrival of the Fednav team. A few months later, Joe Elverdin hired three new commercial managers: Larry Marr was brought in as chartering manager, and Philip Williams and Brian Taylor arrived as commercial directors responsible for developing new business lines and freight contracts for the company. They were all capable businesspeople in their own right.

Larry arrived from Monte Carlo, where he worked in Olympic Maritime, the Onassis shipping company that owned a medium-size fleet of bulk carriers. They operated the ships in the spot market, time chartering them at fixed daily rates of hire for short- and medium-term charters. Philip and Brian were London-based competitive shipbrokers. However, despite their maritime experience, none of them had spent time analyzing voyage freight or developing contracts of affreightment, both key activities for Navios. Nor were any of them familiar with the difficulties associated with scheduling a fleet of ships to position them into load ports in the most cost-efficient manner to transport contractually committed cargoes. Their learning curve proved to be steep.

One of the first people I befriended was Bruce Hoag, who was a manager of cost and statistics. He had grown up outside Gary, Indiana, and after graduating from university, he went to work as an accountant for U.S. Steel in their Gary Works, located on the shore of Lake Michigan. For many years, this was the world's largest steel mill, and it remains today the largest integrated steel mill in North America. Bruce had been seconded from

Gary Works to Navios and moved to New York just a few months before my arrival at the company. Coming from the command-and-control management environment of U.S. Steel, with short-, medium-, and long-term budgetary reviews of manufacturing processes, Bruce had a very steep uphill climb ahead of him to understand the complex, rough-and-tumble world of maritime shipping.

Bruce was a classic American Midwesterner: honest, hardworking, and persevering. We were kindred spirits, and we would spend time together in Bruce's little office at 65 Broadway discussing various aspects of Navios's business. More than occasionally, we would step out for lunch at one of the many tiny food stalls located in and around the Wall Street area.

"Tony," he said to me one day over lunch, "I don't understand how it is that we are paying Fednav twenty-two thousand dollars per day to charter each of their four large capesize ships for the NCSC freight contract, but when we employ them in the open market, they are only earning six thousand per day."

I explained to Bruce that the ships had been chartered from Fednav on an arm's-length basis when Navios had concluded the ten-year NCSC contract to move coal into Israel. Because the contract was negotiated at a time when the dry bulk market was very strong, the freight rates in the contract reflected the strong market. This meant that when the capesize ships were employed in the movement of coal into Israel, they earned sufficient revenue to cover the expensive cost of these time charters.

But the ships were not always in a physical position to load NCSC cargoes, so there were times when one of the capesize units had to be fixed in the open market, which had declined substantially over the three intervening years since Navios had fixed the Israeli contract. I went on to explain that when that happened, Navios would charter in a replacement ship to move the NCSC cargo at a substantial profit, because the charter rate reflected the weaker market. This profit would serve to offset the loss the expensive Fednav capesize ship incurred in the open market. I was trying to describe to Bruce the concept of having a "book" of freight business and ships that served to hedge each other out, even though the physical assets were not always in a position to be deployed into the ocean freight business one controlled.

***

In the spring of 1983, we moved offices to Greenwich, Connecticut. Our new headquarters in Greenwich were much more comfortable and designed as an open-plan office. This meant that for the first time since my arrival at Navios, the chartering department consisted of desks that were deployed up against one another, enabling the in-house brokers to communicate better and to trade ideas and suggestions for our daily chartering activity. The physical proximity led to a much-improved performance over a relatively brief period of time.

Shortly after the office moved to Greenwich, I was given the title of assistant chartering manager, reporting to Larry and working closely with Philip and Brian. It did not take long for me to realize that all three of these new executives were in over their heads. They would come to me asking for help and suggestions on how best to analyze the freight business. One activity that was particularly difficult for them was managing the art of scheduling optimization—scheduling the fleet into positions to carry certain contract cargoes versus having to charter in a market ship and arbitraging out into the dry bulk market our owned or period time-chartered vessel.

My experience at Fednav enabled me to answer these and other questions that arose, putting me in a strong position within the organization. However, the new commercial management team never seemed to rise to the occasion, and all three of them were let go within twelve months of their arrival. By the end of that year, I was promoted to chartering manager. During the next eighteen months, I was able to bring together a solid team of experienced chartering brokers by promoting some employees from the operations area whom I had come to respect, and also hiring some outside talent.

I structured the department so that we operated first as a team, and then I allocated particular contract responsibilities to individual chartering brokers. For example, one broker was responsible for our iron ore **liftings** out of the Orinoco River, another for fixing outbound cargoes from the United States, and yet another focused on our capesize business that revolved around the NCSC contract.

One of the inefficient aspects of the system at Navios was that the company employed two people who sat in a separate office and performed all the freight calculations for the organization. If you wanted to analyze any type of freight business, you would walk the terms over to this office, leave them in an inbox, and hopefully get a voyage calculation returned to you by the end of the day. This system had two serious flaws. Quite often a voyage calculation was required right away in order to quote a price for freight on a piece of business being offered in the market. Any delay might cause the business to be lost to another company. Just as important, by delegating this function, the chartering brokers and commercial directors never established a "feel" for the numbers, which was vital to enabling successful fixtures in this highly, fast-paced competitive business.

My background in voyage accounting quickly took hold, and I insisted the in-house chartering brokers become responsible for their own calculations, which unfortunately made the two people who used to perform these calculations redundant. I created templates for voyage estimate sheets from those I had used during my time at Fednav. There was a steep learning curve for the in-house brokers, but within six months, everyone was calculating their numbers, which led to a better understanding of the fundamentals underlying the business and resulted in a more successful chartering activity.

CHAPTER 8

POLITICS AND THE
MOVEMENT OF GRAIN

*"The future belongs to nations that
have grains and not guns."*

M.S. SWAMINATHAN,
Indian agronomist

———————

For most of the first half of the twentieth century, grain production and export in the Union of Soviet Socialist Republics (USSR), or Soviet Union, was centrally controlled by the state organizations that governed planting, distribution, and procurement. However, this structure did not support the competitive edge that spurs the efficient use of resources and served to make their per-acre production significantly less than that of other grain-producing countries such as the United States, Canada, and Australia. Although the USSR had some of the most fertile agricultural soil in the world, much of it located in Ukraine, by the late 1960s, the Politburo realized that the USSR would have to import grain to supplement their domestic supply.

Because of the Cold War, in the 1950s and 1960s, there was virtually no trade between the U.S. and the USSR. But from 1970 to 1979, the political climate had changed and trade between these countries increased from $200 million to about $3 billion, of which approximately 80 percent consisted of agricultural products, creating a trade balance heavily in favor of the United States.

As the name implies, Exportkhleb was a Soviet state trading organization set up in the early twentieth century to manage the country's grain *exports*. However, because this communist country had so few trade organizations dealing with the world beyond its borders, the government tasked Exportkhleb with sourcing their desperately needed *imports* of grain. In early 1972, a delegation from Exportkhleb arrived in Washington, DC, on the first of two trips for secret negotiations with Continental Grain and other grain traders such as Cargill, Louis Dreyfus, Garnac, and Cook Industries. There was little fanfare as the delegation traveled from DC to New York and then on to Memphis and Minneapolis.

Over a few weeks, the Exportkhleb team managed to purchase about $1 billion of American wheat, feed grains, and soybeans in what was then the largest grain deal in history. Perhaps most significantly, they concluded the deal at fixed prices for the commodities. Once the contracts were announced, the market price jumped considerably. The leverage the Soviets had was that, unlike Canada or Australia, where they dealt with one central agency, the U.S. grain market was much more fragmented. Before anyone caught wind of their intentions, they had managed to buy a staggering 25 percent of that year's U.S. wheat crop.

Thus, regular annual purchases and imports of U.S. grain into the USSR began.

The international grain business is opaque by nature and dominated by a small handful of public and privately owned companies. They are vertically integrated enterprises that operate globally from the farm level through to food manufacturing and distribution. These firms own large tracts of farmland; operate processing facilities; have cattle and poultry operations; and own grain silos, port terminals, and transportation infrastructure, including fleets of ships, barges, and, in some cases, railcars. Perhaps most noticeably, the grain majors control a flow of information that is without equal, enabling them to generate significant profits from the trading of grains and their by-products.

When the full extent of the sales became apparent, there was a political uproar in the U.S. government that culminated in a senatorial inquiry focusing on the country's strategic supplies of grain. As part of its rapprochement with the USSR, the Nixon administration offered preferential grain subsidies to aid sales; but as the contracts became known, the price of domestic grain rose sharply, causing a food crisis. In those days, sophisticated satellite monitoring of global agricultural acreage was in its infancy, and the United States was not aware that this was happening at a time of worldwide grain shortages.

However, this business ended abruptly when in January 1980, President Jimmy Carter stunned the world by imposing a grain embargo against the Soviets in response to their invasion of Afghanistan. The decision meant that the United States was effectively using food as a weapon. The Soviets were forced to search elsewhere for grain. As most Canadian grain was exported from the west coast of the country, and Australia was far removed from the Atlantic Ocean and thus too costly to ship, they looked all the way south to Argentina to make up for the lack of imports from the United States.

***

Because of his Argentine background, Joe Elverdin recognized this development as an opportunity for Navios. He knew that none of the few local Argentine shipowners had the depth of experience to manage the logistics that such a complex ocean freight contract required. He also knew Argentine maritime law required carriers of Argentine grain exports to have an Argentine flagged vessel under their control. Through Joe's contacts in Buenos Aires, Navios was able to form a joint venture with a small Argentine shipowner named Astromar, and later with another shipowning company called Marifran. These joint ventures eventually allowed Navios to fix what would be the first of multiple annual contracts executed with Exportkhleb to move grain from Argentina to the USSR.

Although Navios concluded these contracts in the name of the Navios/Astromar joint venture, the commercial and operational details were performed by Navios. Indeed, it was the Navios name and the depth of experience the company had in managing complicated contracts that enabled these deals to be consummated with Exportkhleb. Because we were chartering ships to perform the liftings in the name of Navios, the flow of funds was coordinated through our accounts. The business also had the strategic benefit of decreasing Navios's dependency on U.S. Steel freight by diversifying into other areas of independent, third-party business.

Grain being loaded into a Navios panamax bulk carrier in Rosario, Argentina. Credit: Author's Collection

Due to the restricted depth of water in the River Plate, in order to provide Exportkhleb with the most attractive commercial option, our contract proposal involved performing vessel top-offs in the Plate estuary. We were able to do this because of the expertise Navios developed over many years in vessel top-offs at the mouth of the Orinoco River. This enabled us to offer a pricing structure for the cost of freight on fully loaded, as opposed to partially loaded, panamax ships, essentially offering the Soviets economies of scale.

Astromar then owned a Swedish-built Argentine flagged iron ore carrier called the MV *Alianza*. The ship shuttled ore from Brazil into a large steel-making facility at San Nicolás, Argentina, just south of Rosario, about 240 kilometers up the Paraná River from Buenos Aires. Astromar sold the *Alianza* to the Navios/Astromar joint venture. The ship was retrofitted with cranes and large **clamshell buckets**, as well as starboard-side hoppers and weather-deck-mounted conveyors, and a cross conveyor to the port side of the vessel. There were two loading booms on the port side with sufficient outreach to pour grain into the holds of a panamax bulk carrier for transport to the USSR.

The *Alianza* was moored in an anchorage area called the Alpha Zone, located in the Plate estuary off the port of Montevideo, Uruguay. Barge trains (several barges tied up together) loaded with grain were moved out to the ore carrier, where they would moor alongside the starboard side of the ship. Through the use of the cranes and buckets that were retrofitted onto the ship, the cargo was discharged into the holds of the *Alianza* to await the arrival of a partially loaded panamax. The *Alianza*'s cranes would then be used to reclaim the grain from her holds, drop it into the hoppers, and reload it into a panamax moored along the port side of the *Alianza* using the conveyor booms. Although this activity added to the cost structure of our operational program, the resulting freight rates offered to Exportkhleb were lower because the ships were sailing with fully laden cargoes of grain, as opposed to being only partially loaded, as they would have been, had they sailed directly to the USSR from the upriver load ports in the River Plate.

Not only was this a challenging operation from a seamanship perspective, but it was a complicated procedure that required much coordination. So Navios arranged to station Captain Ennio Distefano, mentioned earlier as one of our most experienced marine captains and superintendents with significant experience in Orinoco River top-offs, to Buenos Aires to oversee the operation each season.

***

Although President Reagan lifted the grain embargo in 1981, the Soviets continued their purchases of Argentine grains. It was a smart strategic move on their part to reduce their dependency on grain purchases from their ideological foe.

The Exportkhleb contract involved the movement on average of four to five panamax cargoes per month, January through May, from grain-loading installations in the River Plate to Odessa and Novorossiysk in the Black Sea, and Riga and Tallin in the Baltic Sea. In those days, Ukraine, Latvia, and Estonia were still part of the USSR. Detailed negotiations each year were normally not finalized until December, with face-to-face meetings in Moscow. In the fall of 1983, John Weale suggested that I accompany the team on their trip to Moscow to help finalize the 1984 contract terms. I joined a team that included a representative from Astromar, our Argentine partner, the Swiss intermediary who had the right connections with Exportkhleb, and Joe Elverdin.

In preparation for the meetings, I crunched all the numbers and carried an accountant's briefcase, filled with the prior year's contract, as well as the actual data files on each lifting for that year, and numerous calculations made for the current negotiation, all in various heavy three-ring binders.

The contracts were complex because they included multiple variations of load and discharge ports, such as loading in the Plate without a top-off destined for a two-port discharge or loading with a top-off at the Alpha Zone to a one-port discharge. There were several variations, and each required a separate freight rate. In addition, the Soviets wanted the option to top off a vessel loaded in the Plate at an Atlantic coast port in Brazil.

I was also instructed to bring along dozens of cartons of Marlboro cigarettes, the brand most highly prized by the Soviets, very difficult to obtain in the USSR, as "tokens" of our goodwill.

We checked into the Hotel National on a dark and very cold early December evening, having flown into Moscow from Zurich on Swiss Air. In those days, one tried to avoid flying Aeroflot, as it did not have the best reputation. The hotel's prime location, across from Red Square and the Kremlin, and within walking distance of our meetings, was its only benefit.

The ornate, six-story hotel was built in the early twentieth century and had seen better days. The top floor had huge socialist realist artwork on its exterior walls. The blood-red hallway rugs were shabby and worn. The wooden floors under them creaked as you walked along the corridors. We ate all our meals in the hotel. Most of the food was abysmal, so we survived three days in Moscow on borscht, bread, caviar, and ice cream, all washed down with the occasional shots of chilled vodka.

The following morning, we were scheduled to meet Exportkhleb at ten o'clock, but about an hour before the meeting, we received a note explaining that the gathering had been put off until 5 p.m. I was told that the delay was a typical negotiating ploy by the Soviets to try to throw us off our game. Since I had time, I left my team and decided to spend the better part of the first day walking around central Moscow, despite the freezing weather, taking in all the sights.

My first impression of the city was that everything looked drab. Even the cars, primarily the Russian-made Ladas, were nondescript and all painted the same grayish color. As I walked about the city and visited some stores, I was struck by the lack of variety. There was very little choice of products. Whether it was canned peas or TVs, there was one brand available. *Period.* I recall walking through the famous GUM shopping arcade, located in an ornate two-story building in central Moscow facing Red Square, and looking at almost-empty food stalls. I wondered how people managed to get their basic foods and necessities. It was depressing, and it made me realize just how lucky I was to be living in the democratic, market-driven economy of North America.

Bear in mind, relations between the USSR and America were strained. A year before this trip, President Reagan had initiated the Star Wars missile defense system, so our movements were closely observed. At the end of each hallway in our hotel, there were two formidable floor ladies, who were brusque and sullen, assigned to watch our comings and goings. Routinely, we had been counseled by the State Department that our rooms were almost certainly bugged. I recall that to discuss strategy and prepare for the next day's session we turned on the shower full force in our room's bathroom and slouched down around the bathtub, whispering back and forth to one another.

One evening at the end of a long day of tense negotiations, I left the hotel with the Astromar representative for a brief walk. The temperature must have been -20 Celsius. There was no wind, and a very light snow was falling gently to the ground. As we walked into Red Square, the famous, multi-colored onion domes of St. Basil's Cathedral came into view, lit like candles stretching up into the night sky. It simply took my breath away. We walked about the exterior of the cathedral for about half an hour. It was a magical moment, like something out of *Dr. Zhivago*.

My role at the meetings was to support the senior team with notes about terms and rates. I was instructed to bring individual packs of Marlboro cigarettes to the meetings each day and place them on the conference table before each meeting began. The members of the Exportkhleb delegation would pocket them without comment. There were occasions when the negotiations involved minute details, and I would be asked to offer input particularly as it pertained to the level of freight rates we were advocating. This was because I was the only individual on our side of the table with the detailed knowledge of the inputs that went into the freight rate calculations.

I was surprised by and obviously unaccustomed to the Russian style of negotiation. They came across as being arrogant, at times to the point of being rude. They had a very machismo attitude that was unlike anything I had witnessed in previous negotiations with other nationalities. Whereas most negotiations are more of a collaborative effort, with each side endeavoring to maintain certain strategic positions, while conceding elements that are less important, the Russians' attitude seemed to be more of a "winner take all" approach. But once we did reach an agreement and the terms were codified in a contract, the negotiation was never reopened. In that sense, Exportkhleb proved to be an excellent counterparty.

We continued fixing contracts of affreightment with Exportkhleb until they decided in 1987 to quote their South American freight business to ship-brokers around the world and it became too competitive. In addition, some of the grain multinationals that operated their own large fleets of dry bulk ships started to sell their grain on a delivered basis into the USSR. In other words, the Soviets no longer controlled some of the freight aspect of their purchases.

CHAPTER 9

STRONG HEADWINDS

"If you're going through hell, keep going."

Sir Winston Churchill

————————

D uring the 1950s through 1970s, U.S. Steel, via its subsidiary the Orinoco Mining Company, developed and transported tens of millions of tons of iron ore under their original mining license with the Venezuelan government. However, in the mid 1970s, under the leadership of newly elected President Carlos Andrés Pérez, the country initiated a move away from free enterprise toward government ownership that culminated in the nationalization of certain industries, including the oil and mining sectors. Petróleos de Venezuela, S.A. (PDVSA) was formed to own and manage the oil sector, and Corporación Venezolana de Guayana (CVG) was set up to control the mining industries that included iron ore and bauxite. In 1975, Ferrominera del Orinoco (FMO) was established as a subsidiary of CVG specifically to acquire the mining interests of U.S. Steel.

When a sovereign state decides to nationalize a private enterprise, it does not make for an easy negotiation from the perspective of the acquired business entity. U.S. Steel nominated Joe Elverdin to lead the negotiations with the government. By all measures, Joe not only reached a satisfactory agreement on behalf of U.S. Steel, including payments over time of $84 million from the government of Venezuela; but as part of that agreement, he negotiated a ten-year contract of affreightment that commenced in 1978 for Navios to transport all exports of FMO iron ore.

As a result of the new contract of affreightment with FMO, Navios decided to design and build five 63,000-deadweight panamax ships to replace the Ore-class units. These older ships were rapidly becoming uneconomical to operate, not only because of their fuel consumption and smaller deadweight, but also because they were restricted in the open market due to their limited cargo flexibility. The company contracted with Sumitomo Heavy Industries and retained Anglo Nordic Shipping for newbuilding supervision. They, in turn, nominated Frank Caviglia, an Italian marine superintendent engineer, to oversee and direct the building of this series of ships in Japan. (Frank was eventually hired by Navios and had a career that spanned twenty years with the company.)

The rudders of these panamax ships were designed to have a surface capacity about 10 percent larger than most ships, which helped to provide better maneuverability in the Orinoco River. The vessels delivered into the Navios fleet, in 1977 through 1979, were known as the M-class ships. They were named the MV *Navios Miner*, MV *Navios Mariner*, MV *Navios Merchant*, and MV *Navios Monarch*. An additional unit was ordered on behalf of the Venezuelan government and named the MV *Cerro Bolívar*, which was delivered in 1978 and was operated by Compañia Anónima Venezolana de Navegación (CAVN), the state-owned maritime company.

***

The period from 1982 to 1987 saw one of the worst depressions to ever hit the dry bulk markets. The United States was still by far the largest economy in the world. But the rate of inflation had risen to 14 percent, and the Federal Reserve, under the chairmanship of Paul Volker, repeatedly raised the federal funds rate, eventually causing the prime lending rate to reach 21 percent. The high-interest rates reduced business activity, causing the global economy to tighten. In addition, as most ship mortgage loans were based on an interest rate spread above the London Interbank Offered Rate (LIBOR), they were floating, and the financial burdens for shipowners soared.

To add further fuel to the fire, by early 1980, the barrel price of oil reached about $125, up from $25 just seven years earlier, which contributed to a severe recession in the United States. Ships that were designed with engines built in a low-cost fuel environment quickly became uneconomical. At the same time, additional misery in the dry bulk market was caused by the delivering of a huge number of newbuilding ship orders that had been placed with Japanese and South Korean shipbuilders a few years earlier, causing the supply of on-the-water ships to increase.

All these factors caused freight rates to plummet, and profit margins disappeared.

From 1983 through 1986, it was not uncommon for us to be chartering our panamax ships at levels that earned $1,500 to $2,000 per day. I recall fixing a long-term chartered panamax costing Navios $12,000 per day for a trip from Asia back to the River Plate; the voyage duration was about fifty days. Because it was business that repositioned our ship back into the Atlantic basin, where the majority of dry bulk trade emanated back then, the charterers paid us no hire for the trip and reimbursed us only for the fuel consumed, which meant we locked in a loss of about $600,000 on that one voyage.

The market was so poor that earnings were not sufficient to cover the operating costs of ships, let alone service the debt on ships, and so the proprietors started to **lay up** their ships, taking them out of service to await a better market. Throughout the world, shipowners were ballasting their units to safe anchorages in Norwegian fjords or around the Singapore Straits or in various bays throughout Greece, decommissioning their vessels and repatriating their crews. This effectively reduced a ship's operating costs by about 90 percent, leaving the owner the cost of servicing debt on their ship and the layup costs. By 1984, there were thousands of large oceangoing cargo ships laid up at anchor throughout the world.

In addition, by the early 1980s, the implementation of just-in-time (JIT) inventory management had taken hold in the commodity markets. In the 1970s, Toyota developed a strategy to order inventory on an as-needed basis, which allowed Toyota to lower its inventory-carrying costs, thereby improving the company's return on investment. Many companies around the world followed suit, thereby enabling them to reduce the capital deployed to their inventories.

For instance, before this strategy became widely accepted, Navios would discharge a fifty-thousand-tonne cargo of iron ore for U.S. Steel at its Mobile, Alabama facility into an existing stockpile of as much as 2 million tonnes of ore. By 1985, when one of our panamax units arrived in Mobile to discharge, the iron ore was off-loaded and sent directly to its final destination, and it was in the blast furnace within the week. Stockpiles in yards and holding facilities were increasingly disappearing.

JIT inventory management was one of the most significant factors to impact the dry bulk shipping markets during my career. At that time, it was a substantial negative blow. It caused the dry bulk markets to move away from multiyear fixed-rate contracts of affreightment to multiyear contracts that covered volume requirements, with freight rates priced annually or even quarterly. This meant the option of ordering newbuilding ships against such fixed-rate contracts was no longer viable. Newbuilding ship orders became much more speculative. The whole business of ocean freight was moving in the direction of a spot market trading environment.

***

One of my first initiatives as chartering manager was to familiarize myself with the contract of affreightment Navios had with FMO, a complex agreement that came with much baggage because of U.S. Steel's original mineral rights associated with the Venezuelan ore mines. The FMO contract involved the movement of iron ore out of Puerto Ordaz and Palua in the Orinoco River into Western Europe, as well as into certain U.S. Gulf and East Coast ports. It was logistically a very difficult contract to undertake, but the level of freight was generally above-market, which incentivized us to continue fixing the business.

In the 1980s, the FMO contract made up about 25 percent of the total volume of commodity that Navios transported. However, the movement of Venezuelan ore into Mobile, Alabama and Fairless Works in Pennsylvania for U.S. Steel was notable because it positioned ships into what are loading areas for dry bulk ships. Instead of ballasting from Europe down to the U.S. Gulf to load a cargo of grain, a Navios panamax ship would ballast down to the Orinoco River to load a cargo of iron ore for discharge into the U.S. Gulf. Once discharged, the ship would proceed for a day to New Orleans to load a cargo of grain back to Europe. For those shipments into Fairless Works on the East Coast, we would load outbound coal cargoes from Hampton Roads. The net effect was one ballast passage followed by two laden passages, versus the more traditional one ballast leg followed by a loaded leg.

The freight rates for cargoes destined to the United States were developed on a ballast/return voyage calculation using the M-class panamax ship's newbuilding cost structure, which all but guaranteed built-in profitability for these voyages when chartering spot market ships into the liftings. Originally, the freight rates to various European destinations were developed along the same line—ballast/return calculations—but other shipping companies started to approach FMO with more aggressive levels of freight pricing for these cargoes, which we were forced to match, thus reducing our profits on the routes to Europe.

By 1984, Navios was transporting, on average, six to eight cargoes per month of Venezuelan iron ore to the United States and Europe, which was a large program, made more problematic because of the challenges of the Orinoco River itself. The river had a reputation, not entirely without merit, as a challenging and difficult waterway, and many shipowners tried to avoid trading there. But, because of the very poor dry bulk markets and Navios's background of having traded the river for close to three decades, we were able to charter ships for this trade. Nevertheless, it was a recurring struggle. Most shipowners would only consider a charter of their vessel to Navios for the "Venezuelan trade" as a last resort, and they tried to charge a premium for it.

Because the Orinoco dry season runs from November to May, when the river level is at its low point, the number of Venezuelan liftings in December through June was generally higher. These liftings, when combined with the Argentine grain exports to the USSR in the first half of each year, meant we required ten to fourteen panamax ships each month to cover our base contract requirements. This was a very large chartering program back in the early 1980s, when the total dry bulk fleet was about 175 million deadweight tonnes, compared to today's fleet of about 970 million deadweight tonnes.

***

I arrived at the office every morning to review our list of open cargo positions for which we required market tonnage. Some days I just felt overwhelmed. But the key was to charter in tonnage on a strictly private and confidential basis without the market knowing what we were doing. We would try to fix our positions using multiple shipbrokers so that none of them knew the extent of our chartering program. We aimed to fix ships for flexible periods of two to four or three to five months, or more, if we felt the market was moving up for a longer period. Managing this chartering program honed my trading skills and served me well later.

Discipline is the first characteristic of a strong trader. Find out what works for you and then stick with it. You are inevitably going to have losing streaks, but discipline is important because it helps you set parameters for limiting losses. Here's an example:

You have freight on your books paying you $10 per tonne on a sixty-thousand-tonne cargo that you need to relet (find another ship to perform the voyage) and the market is $12 per tonne. Do you step in and take the $120,000 "hit" now? Or do you wait? That depends on several factors. Do you believe the spot market is in a short-term blip? How many other cargoes do you have behind this one that you may have to relet into the market? If you fix the ship at $12, will you be able to keep the fixture off-market in the hopes that you can fix the next one at a breakeven? Is a 20 percent hit the trading loss limit that you normally set for yourself?

Part of this disciplined approach to trading is to keep emotion out of your decisions as much as possible. You will not succeed if you trade based on how you are "feeling" or with wishful thinking. Look at the historical numbers, consider the facts at hand, and decide on a course of action. Keep your emotions in check. In the example above, do you start to hold out hope that the short-term market is about to reverse itself, and maybe next week you will be able to relet the cargo at $9 per tonne, locking in a $60,000 profit? Do you start thinking about how your boss is not going to be happy with a $120,000 loss on the first of numerous uncovered positions? You must remain cleared eyed regarding all aspects of each situation.

Given the myriad of market factors that bombard us every day, the next important trait of a good trader is adaptability. When new facts develop, such as sudden events like natural disasters, man-made failures, or spiking costs, you have to be ready. A key to adaptability, apart from the right temperament, is having great, timely sources of information. Read, digest, comprehend, and act upon news from a variety of resources. And perhaps most strategically, try to find sources of information that your competitors do not use, but that have served *you* well in the past.

Another, if not the most important, quality of a successful trader is patience, especially when playing the long game of maritime transport. It is so easy to get caught up in the pressures of the moment, causing one to react too quickly. There is a maxim in commodity markets: The lows are generally lower, and the highs are generally higher, than anyone ever expects. And perhaps more crucially, the lows last longer than anyone expects, and the highs are shorter than traders expect. Patience is a very real virtue in maritime transport.

But as a trader, I believe it is imperative to understand that you are never going to hit the high or hit the low, and you should not aspire toward that. There is another trader's maxim: Bulls make money, bears make money, and pigs get slaughtered! It is worth remembering.

***

When I arrived at Navios, the company had a core fleet of eighteen owned ships: the four 54,000-deadweight Ore-class vessels, the four 63,000-deadweight M-class panamax vessels, two 80,000 deadweight Ghent suitable bulk carriers named MV *Navios Patriot* and MV *Navios Pioneer*, and eight 110/115,000-deadweight oil-bulk-ore (OBO) ships, which were built in the early 1970s. The company had acquired the OBOs in the very late 1970s, and within a few years, the weak market had made the purchase of these ships a mistake. In addition, **inert gas systems** had become mandatory for ships transporting oil into the United States, and the retrofit was very expensive. By the end of 1983, all but one of the OBOs was in layup.

The idea behind the OBO design was to alternate between transporting dry and oil cargoes, reducing the amount of time spent in ballast. But as with many concepts, what happened in practice impeded the success of this design. The Navios OBO-class vessels were acquired to develop consecutive trades of North Sea oil into the United States, followed by grain back to Europe, and they were part of the ongoing strategy for Navios to decrease its dependency on U.S. Steel for cargoes.

Many times, following a discharge of grain in, say, Rotterdam, an OBO would present to load at a European oil facility with clean holds; but upon discharge of her oil cargo in the United States, the receivers would find sediments of grain from the previous cargo in their shoreside tank installations. Eventually the oil majors would not accept OBO tonnage unless it was trading exclusively in the wet market. Another problem with OBOs had to do with the disposal of tank residues, sludge, and soiled bilge water following the discharge of oil before the loading of a dry bulk cargo, which ran contrary to the increasingly strict environmental regulations at ports.

Nevertheless, from 1983 to 1985, on the rare occasions when we did manage to trade the MV *Navios Courier*, the one OBO ship we did not have in layup, in alternate cargoes, it was a home run. The perfect trade was loading North Sea oil at Sullom Voe in the Shetland Islands bound for discharge in Portland, Maine. From there, the ship made a short two-day ballast leg up to Port-Cartier, Quebec, during which time she would be cleaned of the oil residue in preparation to load a cargo of iron ore for discharge in Mobile, Alabama. Following a further two- or three-day hold-clean there, she would load grain in New Orleans bound for Rotterdam. Three laden legs and two short ballast legs: It did not happen often, but when it did, the results were highly profitable.

Five of the OBOs were sold for scrap, and the remaining three were sold to Orient Overseas Line (the C.Y. Tung controlled company in Hong Kong now called Orient Overseas Container Line, OOCL) and chartered back at high rates that reflected an inflated sale price.

The company also had five long-term time-chartered ships: three 54,000-deadweight Polish-built ships named the MV *Konista*, the MV *Molista*, and the MV *Serrai* on charter from Hellespont Maritime, and two 61,000-deadweight units named MV *Chrismir* and MV *Saturn* on charter from another shipowner named Overseas Shipholding Group (OSG). In addition to the owned and long-term chartered fleet, on any given day Navios had a short-term (often under a year) time-chartered fleet of a further ten to fifteen ships.

By the time I took over as chartering manager of Navios, the dry bulk markets were in free fall, and despite the contracts of affreightment that Navios had on its books, the company started to hemorrhage cash. To raise desperately needed capital, the company began selling off portions of its owned fleet. The four Ore-class units were the first to go because of their high consumption of heavy fuel oil, which had quadrupled in cost making them too costly to operate.

All four ships, which were well into their third decade of service, were loaded with a final cargo of iron ore from the Orinoco River bound for discharge in Japan. They were then sent to South Korea in ballast, where they were sold for scrap. The charters of the three Polish-built ships from Hellespont Maritime and the two ships on charter from OSG were terminated. The four M-class ships were sold to Hellespont Maritime for an inflated price and chartered back at high time charter rates for about seven years.

The sales provided an infusion of cash into the company, while management held on to the hope that the markets might turn a corner. By 1985, it became apparent that Navios would not be able to continue operations without restructuring, and the company took the drastic step of informing the shipowners of the long-term chartered ships that, without some intervention, it would have to file for Chapter 11 bankruptcy.

The result was a negotiated agreement in which U.S. Steel and Fednav agreed to pay large lump-sum settlements to OOCL, Hellespont, and OSG, the owners of the long-term charters, in exchange for the termination of their charters. The net effect was to leave the company with no owned or long-term chartered fleet to service a large book of freight business.

Fortunately, these negotiations were kept strictly private among the parties involved, and they did not in any way impact Navios's ability to operate in the maritime freight market. But it was not without some painful reductions, particularly in the area of the company's technical ship management personnel.

As part of this settlement, Fednav acquired the remaining 50 percent of Navios for a nominal sum. The panamax and capesize operations of Navios were now a fully owned subsidiary of the largest shipowner and operator of small oceangoing ships trading into and out of the Great Lakes.

It was about this time that Joe Elverdin departed Navios, and Michael Bell was nominated to lead the company, while maintaining his position as executive vice president of Fednav.

CHAPTER 10

NEW MARKETS, NEW OPPORTUNITIES

"Every problem is a gift—without problems, we would not grow."

TONY ROBBINS,
American author and personal empowerment coach

I n 1984, while on a trip to the United Kingdom, Michael Bell was introduced to and befriended a gentleman named John Yeoman, who owned
and operated Foster Yeoman in England, one of the largest rock quarry
businesses in the EU. As fate would have it, they met just as Yeoman was
about to make the largest investment in his business's history, which would
require maritime transport.

The Yeoman family can trace their history back to the late nineteenth
century. In this era, they were shipowners operating out of Hartlepool, a
city located about halfway up the east coast of England. Their ships serviced
the various towns and cities located along the northeast coast of England.
Toward the end of World War I, the German U-boat fleet's strategy moved
from targeting just British naval vessels to merchant ships as well and all
the family's ships were sunk. John Yeoman's father, Foster Yeoman, sought
a new career direction, and he established a small stone-quarrying business
and eventually built it into one of the largest aggregate quarrying businesses
in England.

Stone aggregate is one of the most significant commodities used on our
planet. It is rock that is mined and then pounded into crushed stone, gravel,

and sand. The largest consumers of aggregates are the commercial and residential construction industries, which use it in cement and concrete manufacturing, as well as companies involved in transport infrastructure, where it is used for railway ballast and road base. Because aggregates are so plentiful, they have a low product value. Quarries are normally located in areas where the stone can be processed and transported cheaply by truck and/or rail. Only a very small percentage of it moves by sea.

Foster Yeoman's primary quarry, known as Torr Works, was in Somerset, England and over the years it had developed into one of the largest quarry mines in Europe. But the company faced increasing difficulties in expanding it due to decades of real estate development around the mine itself and environmental issues with local planning commissions. So Yeoman decided to buy a granite mountain in a pristine and undeveloped part of Scotland, along the north shore of Loch Linnhe, about 160 kilometers north of Glasgow. There he established the Glensanda Quarry, which derived its name from the ancient Viking Glensanda settlement, near the mouth of the Glen Sanda River. Because of its remote location, he knew the company would be able to develop the new quarry in a much less constrained manner.

From the outset, he recognized there were two key hurdles to overcome for the project to be a success. He would have to build an environmentally friendly quarry, which was expensive. Plus, due to its location far from any rail link or roadways, he would need to move his aggregate by sea in sufficiently large ships to reduce the transport cost.

As Michael Bell learned about this new venture, he recognized its potential for Navios, especially in the troubled maritime market. It was a new, niche commodity movement, and Navios needed it. We had time, as the quarry would not be up and running for at least a year, maybe two. The problem, of course, was that since aggregate is a low-priced commodity, for it to be successfully marketed, it was imperative to offer low transportation costs. But it was difficult to put together a serious proposal without more information, such as the volumes to be transported, the infrastructure that would support the loading of the ships, and the ultimate destination of the cargo. Foster Yeoman had not yet established any of these parameters, as this was an entirely new direction for the company.

On one of my frequent trips to London, I took the time to arrange a visit to Foster Yeoman. In 1985, when I first called on their main office in Frome, Somerset, Kurt Lawson, an American mining engineer who had married

John Yeoman's daughter, was the marketing manager for the new quarry. Together we headed up to Glensanda, by way of Oban, where we spent the night before taking a small boat across Loch Linnhe to the quarry site.

To placate the local authorities, the motivation behind the design development of the mine was to ensure that the open pit located at the top of a mountain could not be seen. A vertical shaft, known as a "glory hole," was dug from the mine itself, about three hundred meters down, through the heart of the mountain. There, it would connect with a tunnel bored underground, about one and a half kilometers from the shores of Loch Linnhe. The rock would be crushed at the mine site with a primary crusher and then dropped down the shaft and moved via the one-and-a-half-kilometer conveyor to the Glensanda port site, where it would undergo additional crushing before being stored for shipment. The principal challenge I noted was that even though a **radial telescopic ship loader** was in place ashore, there was no port infrastructure for a ship to attach lines to **bollards** so as to secure her alongside to take on the cargo.

I recall returning from that trip and explaining this problem to Michael, but he brushed it off. In no uncertain terms, he made clear to me that Navios had to get in on the ground floor of this new commodity movement. He was right. It was a new direction for Navios that could open other maritime possibilities for the company. His single-mindedness and enthusiasm were infectious.

We arranged to have Geoff Riches, one of our senior port captains and our fleet operations manager, visit Glensanda. He scouted the area to assess exactly how we might be able to get a panamax bulk carrier sufficiently close to the loading site to permit the shoreside radial ship-loading boom to load the cargo. The problem was, there was no quayside face along which a ship could berth. This meant that there was no surface with **fenders** for a ship to come up against and extend mooring ropes to hold her steady and close enough for the ship loader to pour the cargo into the holds.

The main issue was how to keep a large bulk carrier in a position close enough to be loaded, while not getting too close to shore. Fortunately, Loch Linnhe was well protected from weather, and as a deep-water fjord, it had little current. Geoff came up with a solution. We would charter a tugboat from Liverpool to transport two enormous anchors with extra-long anchor chains, then drop them in the fjord not far offshore. The tug would then slowly drag the anchors along the sea bottom until they held. We attached a large mooring buoy to the top of each chain. Three additional buoys were placed at a position just off the shoreline to mark the point beyond which the ship's hull should proceed no farther.

When a panamax arrived, it would pick up the buoys and attach bow and stern lines to each. Then a local tug would slowly push the panamax into a position parallel to the three smaller buoys along the shore as the ropes attached to the buoys were splayed out from the ship. The tug would remain beside the ship on standby to hold its position. In addition, piano wire was attached to the bow and stern of the ship and run to a fixed point along the shore, equipped with bright red bunting so our port captains could keep an eye on any movement of the ship. The cargo could then be loaded using the radial ship loader with a telescopic boom.

This relatively inexpensive but complex solution avoided the cost of building port infrastructure for the initial cargoes and kept the transport cost down, allowing us to move ahead with a deal. Yeoman had found a new client in Houston, Texas, so I had all the costs and operational information we needed to put together a proposal, and the contract was concluded in early 1986.

In August 1986, the MV *Hellespont Monarch*, one of the M-class panamax ships that Navios had sold to Basil Papachristidis's Hellespont Maritime and chartered back, loaded the first-ever cargo of Glensanda rock bound for the state of Texas. It was the first of a half-dozen cargoes we moved into Houston over the next year, using Geoff Riches's ingenious system.

Today, the Glensanda operation is one of the largest, most efficient quarries in the world.

***

In the latter part of the 1970s, U.S. Steel had some personnel on the ground in Guinea, West Africa, because the country had one of the largest undeveloped, high-grade iron ore bodies in the world. It is known today as the Simandou Mining project and is located in the southern part of the country, near its border with Liberia.

Through its presence in the country, U.S. Steel became aware of the movement of bauxite exports loading out of Conakry, Guinea into Port Alfred on the St. Lawrence River; Point Comfort and Houston in the U.S. Gulf; and Aughinish, Ireland. At the time, Torvald Klaveness, the shipowning company based in Oslo, had managed to develop Guinomar, a fifty-fifty joint venture with the Guinean government, to transport bauxite on panamax ships.

Joe Elverdin convinced the management of U.S. Steel that Navios could benefit greatly from involvement in this movement of bauxite. He used the resources, influence, and muscle of the Pittsburgh-based steel company to persuade the Guinean government that Navios should become active in the transportation of this commodity. The government agreed to go along with this because they viewed U.S. Steel as a likely partner to help them develop the Simandou Mine for the international export markets. In 1980, this led to the formation of West African Bulk Shipping (WABS) as a fifty-fifty joint venture between Klaveness and Navios, which, in turn, partnered in a fifty-fifty joint venture with the government of Guinea.

WABS turned out to be a scheduling and market nightmare for several reasons. Guinomar's ten-year fixed-freight-rate contract reflected strong time charter rates for panamax ships in the very late 1970s. Both Navios and Klaveness had chartered expensive ships and placed them into WABS as a hedge against the contracts. These time charters protected WABS in the event the freight markets continued to surge in the 1980s. But when the dry bulk markets collapsed, the receivers of bauxite started to cut back on their contractual purchases, leaving WABS exposed to the market with its expensive time charters. The MV *Chrismir* and MV *Saturn* were the two ships that Navios chartered from OSG at $12,000 per day, with escalations each year for ten years, as a hedge for this business.

The cargoes into the U.S. Gulf area and the St. Lawrence River were the most profitable trade for WABS because they served to position ships into traditional loading areas for outbound cargoes. The movement into Aughinish, which made up about one-third of the contract volumes, was much less attractive. When Guinomar, representing the Guinean government, called for a vessel nomination to load a cargo of bauxite to Ireland, WABS was always trying to have Guinomar take responsibility for the lifting. In those instances where that failed, Navios and Klaveness were constantly trying to outfox each other to avoid the Aughinish-bound cargoes. And of course, as with any shotgun marriage, life was generally difficult between the Norwegian and U.S.-based partners.

By the mid-1980s, the relationship became untenable. In 1986, because of the severe financial condition of Navios, we sold our 50 percent interest in WABS to Klaveness to raise much-needed cash.

***

It just seemed as though the 1980s dry bulk market threw us one curveball after another. In 1983, we had just finalized a contract renegotiation with the FMO to reduce the levels of freight under our long-term contract with them into the United States, when their receiver, U.S. Steel, decided to stop shipments of iron ore into Fairless Works. The demand for steel had collapsed, and that resulted in a stockpile of about three million tonnes of iron ore at the facility.

The contract with NCSC was only about three years old when they approached us to renegotiate the freight rates on the capesize contract we had with them moving Australian and South African thermal coal into Israel. This was the contract against which Navios had chartered the two Fednav capesize ships at an initial rate of $22,000 per day for ten years mentioned earlier. By 1983, the market for capesize ships was no more than half this level and falling. So yet again, we were forced to take a loss on another freight contract.

To keep the business, we worked out new levels of freight with NCSC. Attempting to make up for the lost revenue, John Weale came up with the brilliant idea of lengthening the MV *Federal Skeena* and MV *Federal Hunter*. This involved positioning the two ships back into the Belgium shipyard where they were built, literally cutting them in two, and inserting an additional hold, which transformed them into 165,000-deadweight ships. The project was yet again aggressively financed by the Belgium government, which was desperately searching for construction contracts for its shipyards. The economies of scale offered by the additional twenty-five thousand deadweight tonnes made the net effect of the new NCSC deal much more palatable.

Force majeure is a clause normally incorporated into maritime contracts that essentially frees up parties to reevaluate or exit a contract when an extraordinary event beyond their control occurs. It is a tool that clients with contracts of affreightment used to try and wiggle out of deals priced when the market was strong. Obviously, as a shipowner we did not want to have a force majeure declared by our clients. It would halt all freight movement, while lawyers battled it out, by calling for an arbitration proceeding that might take twenty-four to thirty-six months to resolve. The mid-1980s markets were so weak that this was a constant concern, and this reality made for many painful and difficult negotiations.

***

Up until 1980, most of Navios's ocean freight was focused on panamax-size ships. However, with the NCSC contract and the arrival of Fednav as a 50 percent shareholder in 1982, Navios now had four large capesize ships as part of its chartered fleet. I thought we should try to leverage off this base to expand our operations into the large vessel category of dry bulk.

In the 1980s, Australia was rapidly developing its exports of commodities to the world markets, particularly coal and iron ore. Although our contract to move coal into Israel was with NCSC (they were buying the product ex-Australia and therefore were responsible for the ocean transportation), we developed a rapport with the sellers of Australian coal to NCSC. This caused us to focus on commodity exports from this country, and we began a marketing campaign focused on various coal producers located primarily in Brisbane and a few iron ore producers in Perth.

We had established a small one-man marketing office in Melbourne, Australia, and at least once a year I would head there to join our sales rep on marketing visits to various companies to try and negotiate small four-to-eight cargo contracts of affreightment destined primarily to Japan. (Australian exports into China were just barely beginning then.) During these years, we were able to conclude contracts with a few coal producers selling commodity on a delivered **cost/insurance/freight** (CIF) basis into Japan.

But it was difficult to build up this business with only four ships in our capesize fleet. We were capital constrained, and so we could not buy ships in what was arguably a buyer's market. In addition, the working capital required to run these ships was much more than what we needed for smaller ships. For instance, it might have cost about $400,000 to fuel a panamax ship to capacity, whereas the cost for a capesize vessel was probably double that.

It was a constant juggling act to keep this business afloat and profitable.

***

Part of the process of making steel in a blast furnace involves coke, which generates very high levels of heat with little or no smoke. It is made from heating coal or oil at very high temperatures, the result of which is a hard porous fuel with a very high carbon content that is ideal for making raw steel.

In 1988, U.S. Steel decided to shut its coke-making facility at Fairless Works, and they approached Navios, which by this time was 100 percent owned by Fednav, to see how we might help them source imports of international coke. They were looking to source coke from different regions of the world, and we provided them with freight rates from different geographic suppliers, assuming U.S. Steel was buying commodity at the point of origin, **free on board** (FOB).

At the time, there was a preponderance of dry bulk cargoes moving east from the Atlantic to the Pacific basin, and so shipowners were on a continuous hunt for **backhaul** cargoes to assist in positioning their ships back to the Atlantic. These backhaul cargoes were therefore priced very competitively. Fortunately for us, U.S. Steel decided to source their coke from Japan, a country that imports most of its large-volume dry bulk commodities, such as coal, grain, and iron ore. Japan, therefore, is a geographic area where many ships come open, looking for cargo to take to west.

U.S. Steel bought about five hundred thousand tonnes of coke annually, most of which was loaded at Sakaide, near Osaka, and Hibikinada, a port facility just north of Fukuoka on Kyūshū, the most southern of Japan's five main islands. The stowage factor of the cargo, which represents the number of cubic meters of hold space utilized by a given type of bulk cargo, became a prominent element in this trade. Coke has a high stowage factor, causing a panamax vessel's cubic capacity to be maximized before reaching her deadweight capacity of about sixty thousand tonnes. By comparison, iron ore is a heavier cargo that will reach full deadweight tonnage, but only utilize 35 percent of the ship's storage capacity.

This meant the average lift on a panamax was about forty thousand tonnes, which translated into twelve Pacific-to-Atlantic backhaul cargoes on our books each year. Most of the Navios panamax freight activity was Atlantic-based, and so we used these cargoes to time charter ships for short periods at relatively cheap levels reflected in the weaker Pacific market and position them back into the normally stronger Atlantic basin. Following discharge on the U.S. East Coast, we employed them for a few months in the Atlantic before redelivering them back to their owners. It was a money-maker for us, even though at that time the dry bulk market was still in the last throes of its deep recession.

CHAPTER 11

TRADING IN JAPAN

"I need Japanese steel."

Uma Thurman,
as "The Bride" in *Kill Bill: Volume 1*

———————

I have been very fortunate to have visited many countries around the world during the nearly five decades I have spent working in the business of international maritime transportation. Japan is possibly my favorite. It is perhaps the complete sense I feel when visiting this nation of being in a country with an ethnic population and social norms that are so very different from those we have in the West. Walking along one of the major thoroughfares in Tokyo and not seeing many other Westerners or signs in English always reminds me I am in a strange, foreign land, which makes it even more intriguing.

Although most people know Japan is an island country, what many do not realize is that it is an archipelago about three thousand kilometers long, with close to seven thousand islands. The main island of Honshū is where the city of Tokyo is located, and the second-largest island is Hokkaido, which most people will recognize because of its capital city, Sapporo. In a 2021 survey of global performance, *U.S. News & World Report* listed Japan as the number two country in the world (Canada was ranked first). The seventy-six metrics used to develop the list include climate goals, social justice, heritage, ease of business, racial equality, and levels and disparity of income.

Doing business in Japan is quite different from the way we conduct business in the West. It requires much more focus on developing a relationship with your counterparty. A Japanese businessman will want to get to know the person he is doing business with and will not commit his company to a contractual relationship until a level of trust has been developed with that counterparty. I cannot help but smile when I think back to the hundreds of formal business meetings I have had in Japan that began with stunted conversation and awkward moments of silence. There is plenty of bowing, pleasantries, exchanging of gifts, and much discussion and negotiation during which nothing seems to get concluded. It can be extremely frustrating for a first-time business visitor.

Trust is developed not in the boardroom, but in relaxed get-togethers after hours. It is these gatherings in informal settings that are vital to the process. It can be while unwinding in a hot thermal pool following a round of golf, or during a long dinner, or, as was certainly the case in the 1980s, many late nights of drinking out in the Ginza section of Tokyo, when advances in negotiations eventually happen. The Japanese businessman simply wants to get comfortable with you as a person before deciding whether to do business with you. It is a wonderful feature of their culture.

As a nation steeped in tradition, historically ethnically homogeneous, and nearly devastated by the West after World War II, it has taken decades for the older Japanese to accept foreigners—*gaijin*—as colleagues and business partners. The day after I arrived in Tokyo on one of my first trips to this country, in the mid-1980s, Shigeki Nakagawa, the president of Fednav Asia, arranged to take me to an *onsen ryokan* up in the mountains southwest of Tokyo. An *onsen ryokan* is a simple, traditional, Japanese-style country inn that normally has some hot springs nearby. We slept on tatami floors, had our meals served in our little rooms, and as we moved about the inn, we wore the traditional *yukata*, or "bathing cloth," an unlined, cotton, summer kimono normally worn in casual settings in Japan. It was a delightful way to overcome jet lag.

I awoke the first morning, jet-lagged, at about four-thirty, and decided to go sit in the hot spring. When I arrived, I noticed two very elderly Japanese men enjoying the waters and talking quietly to each other. So, as not to disturb them, I walked over to a point in the hot spring farthest away from them, disrobed, and slowly set myself down to soak in the steaming water. It could not have been more than two minutes after my arrival that both men stood up and left the waters. Old resentments were at play at this time among that generation.

Fast-forward to today when I visit Japan. I am welcomed by business associates of all ages and have relished many hours of enjoyment in their company and concluded many successful business deals. It certainly helps that economic and geopolitical integration with the North American and European economies has been facilitated in the second half of the twentieth century. In addition, North American pop culture and technology has become a mainstay of modern Japanese society as well.

Honesty and reliability and the building of long-term relationships are very highly valued in Japan. It has been my experience that once you conclude a contract with a Japanese counterparty, you can rest assured it will be honored, no matter the circumstances. You file it away and rarely, if ever, does it get looked at again. If you order a ship to be built at a Japanese shipyard at a cost of $30 million, and twelve months following the order, when construction has not yet even commenced, the newbuilding price has increased by 25 percent, there is never any question of the shipyard coming back to you to renegotiate the contract.

***

It was during the second half of 1986 that I began to think we might be coming to the end of the dry bulk recession and there could be a window of opportunity to increase the size of our fleet of ships, or as they say in the industry: "steel." Given that we were still very much capital constrained, it made sense to charter some panamax ships for multiple years to supplement Navios's diminished core-controlled fleet.

By early 1987, we concluded five panamax charters for three years, plus one optional year with a few different shipowners who operated out of Tokyo, London, and Vancouver. What struck me about these charters was how simple the process was—not much different from chartering a ship for six to twelve months. Additionally, and significantly, because of the Navios reputation in the marketplace, we were able to conclude these contracts without ever divulging our financials. These were five- or six-year-old ships that had been ordered for about $25 million apiece. Due to the terrible market, we obtained exclusive control of them for three years at an average time charter rate of $8,250 per day, without having to put up any equity.

The other interesting takeaway for me was the pricing of the option year. The fixed rates of charter hire were $8,000 per day, escalating $250 per year, and the optional fourth year was priced at $9,000. We were essentially buying an optional year at a $500-per-day premium over the third-year rate of $8,500—or $180,000—if the option was exercised. The pricing of this optionality struck me as very favorable to Navios as the charterer of these ships. It reflected an absence of the complex Black Scholes option pricing used at that time in the financial markets.

The Black Scholes pricing model is a complicated mathematical formula used to determine the pricing of a put or, in our case, a call option for a fourth year of charter. Variables that go into the model include market fundamentals, timing of the call option, and probabilities to account for the volatility of the underlying asset. The owners of these ships were simply not applying this type of metric to the pricing of the option years.

Following these deals, I began to focus more of my time on the fixing of long-term charters, because I believed Navios needed to build up a core fleet of ships. In the second half of the 1980s, we concluded a few more charters on panamax ships owned by shipowners operating out of Hong Kong. But by the early 1990s, the best deals were being sourced out of Japan, and that is where we made our mark in gaining control of Japanese "steel" without having to buy the ships outright.

As we tried to expand our capesize activity, much of it was focused on cargo movements within the Pacific arena, primarily from Australia to Japan. Although we were not successful in permanently growing this segment of our business, our efforts did enable Navios to conclude a few small contracts of affreightment with certain Japanese steel mills moving coal and iron ore into this country. These contracts proved to be a very important entrée into the maritime business circles of Japan, and it was during this time that I built up a close working relationship with Marubeni, one of the five major international trading houses in this country.

Japan has a few large domestic corporate shipowners, most of which are publicly traded companies, such as Mitsui O.S.K. (MOSK), "K" Line, and NYK. These businesses have enormous fleets spread across the three main sectors of our industry: dry bulk, tankers, and containers. But most Japanese-controlled ships are owned by small- or medium-size family companies, many of whom are based in and around the Inland Sea of Japan. They are known collectively as Shikoku owners, because they are from or near to the island of Shikoku. During the 1990s, we commenced an aggressive campaign to source modern ships from these owners.

Working closely with Marubeni and traveling to Japan at least once each year during that time, we managed to conclude many long-term charters with Shikoku owners. The Navios brand name, the credibility we had in-country because of our Japanese steel mill contract business, and our long-term track record are what enabled us to build up our core charter fleet.

As a company without strong capitalization at that point, probably the most attractive aspect of trading in Japan was that we did not have to put up any equity capital to secure the charter contracts, other than the working capital required to operate the ships once they were in our fleet. What proved to be most fortuitous, the Japanese did not place as high a value as we in the West did on the equity capital they invested in these deals. Whereas an investment thesis in the West might look for a 15 percent return on equity capital, it was probably no more than 3 percent in Japan at the time.

Most of the charters were for a period of five years at fixed time charter rates, which included an agreed escalation for each year. As an example, we might have agreed on fixed rates of $10,000 per day, escalating $250 per year, with year five at $11,000. Because we did not own the ship, this meant that we did not have any of the risks associated with the technical management of the vessel. For instance, if crew costs went up dramatically or an auxiliary motor had to be repaired, it did not impact the fixed time charter rates.

Even more astounding, these charters were almost all based on orders for newbuilding vessels. In other words, the ships were delivered into the Navios fleet straight out of the shipyard, having been built at the owner's expense. We knew the local Japanese banks financing the deals would only negotiate a debt financing package with the Shikoku owner, provided he had a multiyear charter to a well-established, international maritime named charterer. We were therefore able to obtain some attractive additional features in these new charters. In most cases, the Navios prefix was incorporated into the ship's name; and the hull, superstructure, and funnel were painted to Navios colors—a red painted hull, with a weather deck also painted red or gray, a white superstructure, and a blue funnel with a large red circle and the white letter N in the middle. This branding further reinforced our position in the industry.

On all of these charters, we were able to obtain three one-year options so that we could effectively extend the charter out to eight years at pre-agreed time charter rates. Continuing with the example above, we might have agreed on optional years at $11,250, $11,500, and $11,750 per day. In addition, on many of these deals, we negotiated U.S. dollar purchase options (the global currency for international shipping is U.S. currency) that normally commenced at the end of the fixed five-year period, but continued out on a sliding scale to eight years if the optional years were exercised. The purchase price was set at pre-agreed levels and, as with the optional charter years, was not priced at a level that reflected their potential value to the charterers.

***

One of the metrics I used to gauge the Japanese economy on each trip was the number of tower cranes that I saw on the Friendly Airport Limousine bus that I used to take from Narita Airport to downtown Tokyo. Sometimes I would count as many as one hundred such cranes. By the early 1990s, following the collapse of the fabled Japanese bubble, I counted fewer and fewer. But I started to see more of them on my travels to Beijing, Shanghai, Tianjin, and Qingdao—in fact, everywhere I went in China. The only difference was that for every tower crane I saw in Japan, by 1998 I saw five similar cranes in China.

CHAPTER 12

CHINA AND THE BELT
SELF-UNLOADERS

"机不可失，时不再来"
"Opportunity knocks but once."

ANCIENT CHINESE PROVERB

I continued to keep a close watch on the global maritime markets for new business opportunities, particularly in the Far East as the deep-sea ocean freight markets seemed to be rapidly developing in this part of the world. We had already established relations in Japan, but mainland China was the new area of focus. Following China's opening to the West through the efforts of the Nixon administration, many companies were building business connections with Beijing. I knew very little about this potential market but was anxious to learn more.

Through a family connection, I had met a gentleman named Dickie Howson, a British-born retired shipbroker based in Montreal. He had spent time living in Hong Kong as a young military attaché, and he had traveled to mainland China many times in the 1950s. He had remained in touch with a few of his contacts in the region.

In 1985, he reached out to me, inquiring if Navios had moved any commodity into or out of China. We had not. Dickie's contacts were telling him that there could be a massive opportunity developing for dry bulk trade with China, and he suggested that we hire him as a consultant to facilitate maritime trades with this country. Over the course of a few weeks, I worked out an agreement to reimburse him the costs of his travel and agreed on a success fee for any business we might conclude through his contacts. We applied for visas to visit the country and meet with government bureaucrats to discuss their potential requirements for dry bulk commodities, and together we arrived in Beijing via Hong Kong in February 1986.

While I was somewhat familiar with parts of Asia through our business in Japan and Hong Kong, China presented an entirely new experience. On my first trip to Beijing, there were so many strange sights, sounds, and smells. Perhaps it is the burning of coal that I recall most clearly; it was the fuel used to heat almost all households, and you could smell it in the air throughout the city. We stayed in a government guesthouse that had almost no heat, with small rooms and tiny hard beds. Each morning, we were served a breakfast of hot tea, a boiled egg, and some stale bread. The roads had virtually no automobiles—other than a few government-sanctioned cars, and the occasional wobbly truck. Instead, there were thousands upon thousands of people on bicycles. Goods were transported by carts drawn by mules or, at times, by people. It was as if you had walked back into the nineteenth century.

That first visit we were provided a black Volkswagen with a driver, one of the few privileges accorded to official visitors from the West. Only senior government officials rode in similar cars, shielded from view by privacy curtains. As we were being driven about, I noticed a similar lack of color to what I had seen in the Soviet Union. It seemed everyone we saw on the streets was wearing either a tan parka, with gray or black pants, or a dark-colored "Mao" suit styled to reflect those worn by the former leader, Chairman Mao Zedong, a cross between a military uniform and a Western business suit, with high neck collars that were always buttoned up. The very few billboard advertisements we saw were enormous murals of a police officer saluting you. We passed parks where people were doing what looked like stretching exercises, which we later learned was qigong, a form of breathing exercise. Most buildings were a just a few stories high, and the government buildings were drab, but not gray like the ones I had seen in Moscow. These were more of a dirty beige color.

We had a week of meetings scheduled during this first trip, which may sound like a lot, but we only averaged two a day because getting around Beijing was difficult due to traffic congestion caused by poor transportation infrastructure and bicyclists clogging all the roads.

Dickie had warned me to bring long underwear on this trip, which I wore every day because the meeting rooms were not heated. In fact, in some meetings we wore our winter coats. Our hosts in those days were all wearing ill-fitting blue or gray Mao suits. After sitting down at a conference table, we were always presented with thermoses of hot tea, but never any food. During our meetings, most people kept their hands in their pockets or wrapped around their tea mug for warmth.

When one travels throughout the world of maritime shipping, virtually everyone speaks English, some better than others. Wherever I had traveled, communication was rarely an issue. That was not the case in China at that time. Recognizing this, Dickie had arranged for a simultaneous translator named Zhang Wei Xu to attend all our meetings, as most Chinese officials did not speak English. Wim, as he liked to be called, had spent some time in Germany studying English, and so when he communicated with us, he spoke in German-accented English, which was always strange to hear as we sat in austere conference rooms in Beijing. This was my first experience doing business through a translator. It was particularly challenging because the maritime industry uses many specialized terms, and I was never quite sure if he was able to adequately explain some of the points we were trying to make.

I have always been fortunate to appear younger than my years. As a youthful-looking thirty-three-year-old in Beijing, I found it a little disquieting when I met government officials who looked thirty years older than my age. Add to that, too, the respect paid to elders in the Chinese society. It was therefore wonderful to have Dickie by my side, for even though I led most of the meetings, Dickie's white hair, good-sized paunch, slight limp, and strong English accent lent an air of authority to our side of the proceedings. And whenever we got sidetracked, Dickie would step in to get everyone refocused on the business at hand.

Our objective, on this first of what proved to be many trips to China over the next fifteen years, was twofold: to gauge what appetite the country might have for the import of bulk cargoes like coal, iron ore, and grain; and to begin the process of securing some freight with various government ministries. Invariably, in those early years, most freight business was concluded on a cost/insurance/freight (CIF) basis, and so in many cases, we ended up developing freight contracts with the suppliers/sellers of the commodity into China.

After our meetings concluded in Beijing, we traveled to Qinhuangdao and Shanghai, two of the great port cities in China. In Qinhuangdao, we met with coal receivers who took us on a visit to a new coal-discharging facility that was being built in this port. Most of what we saw were dilapidated warehouses fronting old crumbling docks, but I was struck by the size and sophistication of the new coal-receiving terminal that was under construction. It looked to be a reprieve from the past and perhaps a sign of things to come.

In Shanghai, we met with Shanghai Haixing Shipping Company, one of several domestic shipping companies that no one outside of China had ever heard of. Their office was in the center of Shanghai in an old Western-style, eight-story office building on the Bund—a famous promenade along the embankment of the Huangpu River, with some adjacent parkland. Many of the original Beaux Arts–styled buildings built by the Western banks and trading houses in the late nineteenth and early twentieth centuries, when the Bund was the major financial center in East Asia, were still in use. Today many have been destroyed to make way for the large skyscrapers that now dominate the Shanghai waterfront.

We met in a small conference room, and while Dickie and I waited to meet with our hosts, we stood looking out a window onto the Bund and Huangpu River. There were hundreds of cyclists and people walking along the promenade, and the river was a beehive of activity, with coasters (small vessels that operate around the coastline of a country, carrying primarily domestic cargoes) steaming up and down, barges pushed by tugs, floating derricks with large cranes slowly plying the waters, public ferries similar in style to Hong Kong's famous Star ferries scurrying back and forth across the river, and small, private sampan ferries weaving their way through the larger river traffic.

As we gazed out farther east to an area across the river, all you could see was tranquil farmland and some old, decrepit factories. Today this area, known as Pudong, is where Shanghai's financial district is located, and it has been transformed into a free-trade zone filled with the offices of many multinational firms. Enormous new office towers, grand boulevards, parks, and modern housing developments have replaced the farmland. At the time, neither of us, in fact no one, realized just how massive a transformation this city was about to experience within just a few years.

Our hosts treated us very graciously, and during our discussions, we learned Shanghai Haixing owned a 27,500-deadweight belt self-unloader called the MV *Nan Ji Zhou*. The ship was constructed by Mitsui Engineering & Shipbuilding (MES) in Japan and therefore was sure to be of good quality. She had been built to detailed and sophisticated specifications against a contract to move sand domestically along the Chinese coast that only kept it employed about four months of the year. Other than the Japanese shipbuilder and Shanghai Haixing, virtually no one outside China knew she existed. It goes to highlight just how closed the country was well into the 1980s.

The MV *Nan Ji Zhou*, our first time charter with the People's Republic of China, pictured during her sea trials. The large, self-discharging boom which can pivot to the port or starboard side of the ship is clearly visible resting atop the aft hatch coamings. Credit: Mitsui Engineering & Shipbuilding

To give you a sense of how unique a vessel the belt self-unloader is, at the time of our meeting, there were probably no more than twenty of these ships in the world. (I am excluding here the Great Lakes belt self-unloader fleet, which is captive to this geographic area.) They are specialized ships and therefore expensive to build. The few owners who build and operate them do so against dedicated **take or pay** contracts of affreightment. In other words, it is not the type of ship you buy speculatively and trade in the spot market. The ones that existed then, and still do today, are controlled by a very small group of select maritime companies.

During the twelve months following my trip to China, I stayed in touch with Shanghai Haixing, and in the summer of 1987, we indicated to them an interest to charter the *Nan Ji Zhou* for a few years. We needed this specialized ship because Foster Yeoman had told us it was bidding to supply Glensanda aggregate for the construction of the new Channel Tunnel linking England and France.

This project was set to begin in 1988 and required enormous amounts of aggregate to make the precast, cylindrical concrete linings for the tunnels. Because of space limitations, the factory was located on the Isle of

Grain, a peninsula of land located on the south side of the eastern Thames Estuary in Kent. Belt self-unloading ships are perfectly suited for this type of transportation because their conveyor belts are essentially an extension of the shoreside belt conveyor systems. Due to the ship's long unloading boom, the aggregate can be discharged while at anchor, dispensing with the need for a dock face. And most importantly, by 1988, the Glensanda Quarry dock had been built.

I arranged to visit Shanghai Haixing Shipping in late October of that year to try to conclude a time charter of the *Nan Ji Zhou*. Back then, a charter of this type would have been fixed between the parties using fax machines, which had replaced telex traffic exchanges as a means of communication for commercial negotiations. However, we were dealing with a company that had virtually no commercial activity beyond the country itself and was tightly controlled by the government. The practice of receiving hire payments from a foreign entity based in the United States was completely without precedent for them.

The government provided Shanghai Haixing with ships, and they were told to offer their services to various domestic end users exclusively. In these early years of China's opening, all companies were government-owned, and the financial metrics that we were accustomed to in the West simply did not exist. Who paid whom was irrelevant, just as bottom-line profit and loss were irrelevant. I recall one evening during a Chinese banquet speaking with the hosts about the concept of profit and being amazed at how alien this was to them. So, the negotiation proved to be a little more cumbersome and complicated than most I had been involved with up until then.

Part of the problem was that Shanghai Haixing had never had any contractual business with a Western company, and they were entirely unfamiliar with some of the international charter party terms that are considered normal in the maritime trades. But when I left Shanghai that fall, we had structured a deal in principle for a three-year time charter of the vessel commencing in the spring of 1988 at a fixed rate of $8,600 per day—a "steal" for a ship of this type back then.

Based on the daily rate of hire at which we chartered the ship and the freight rate we provided to Foster Yeoman, financially we probably made less than a million dollars net profit a year on this marriage. But it had other benefits. Not only did it help to cement the relationship with Foster Yeoman, but it represented a crucial new direction for Navios in both the Chinese and the belt self-unloader markets.

The ship began shuttling aggregate between Glensanda and the Isle of Grain in the summer of 1988 and remained employed in this business for the next three years. Eventually, a Norwegian firm named Fearnley & Eger muscled into the business by offering Foster Yeoman levels of freight based on a panamax belt self-unloader, with which we could simply not compete.

In the spring of 1991, a few months before the termination of our contract with Foster Yeoman, we reached out to Shanghai Haixing to see if there was an appetite on their part to extend the charter for another three years. The domestic sand business for which the ship had originally been built was now being moved on large domestic barges and they had no business of their own for the vessel back in China. Perhaps more significantly, they liked the U.S. dollar income. We concluded a new three-year time charter at a fixed rate of $8,900 per day, subject to our reconfirmation within the unusually long period of ninety days. But considering the type of ship and the country involved, this period was suited to the special situation. There was just one problem—given that we had lost out on the Foster Yeoman aggregate movement, we had no business for the ship.

In 1986, we had hired David Elsy, an Englishman and naturalized American who joined Navios with a focus on business development. He had spent several years working for Skaarup Shipping, where he had become familiar with the self-unloader trades around the U.S. East Coast. In addition to marketing, we gave him the responsibility of managing the *Nan Ji Zhou*. David was convinced that if we positioned the vessel to the East Coast of North America, we would develop business for her. I was convinced that a belt self-unloader costing us $8,900 per day was an incredible bargain. Unfortunately, Sean Day, who was the president of Navios, having rejoined the company a few years earlier following Michael Bell's departure, was not on the same wavelength.

As commercial vice president, and then executive vice president of Navios during the 1990s, I reported to Sean. We got along very well and weathered many storms together. But as with any business relationship, there were times when we disagreed on certain issues, and when we did, I was always careful to voice my disagreement with him in private.

For several weeks, we debated the risks of chartering the specialized ship without a contractual freight commitment. We simply kicked the can down the road and avoided deciding, until a few days before the ship's last voyage to the Isle of Grain, when the issue came to a head out in the bullpen area of our head office.

Sean did not think the risk of taking the ship for three years without any business prospects outweighed any potential benefit. I agreed with David and thought strongly that this was an opportunity not to be missed. After a heated discussion, I was told by Sean to go ahead and confirm the charter, but I had to accept responsibility if anything went wrong.

The gamble paid off. We ballasted her across the Atlantic, and David managed to find immediate employment for the vessel moving aggregates for Martin Marietta from Freeport, Bahamas, to the various U.S. East Coast and Gulf ports. This trade kept her substantially employed for about 250 days a year. The balance of the time, we traded her in the East Coast gypsum trades, as well as some low-sulfur South American coal into the U.S. East Coast. She was kept employed in these trades for an additional three years, made us some good money, and helped cement our reputation in China as a serious international maritime company.

***

Politics has always played a significant role in the Chinese market. In early April 1989, news spread around the world of students leading a sit-in demonstration in Tiananmen Square in central Beijing, protesting the lack of democracy, freedom of the press, and free speech. Throughout the month, the crowd grew to perhaps five hundred thousand students, many of whom went on a hunger strike. Inspired by what was happening in Beijing, students in other cities across China began protests and strikes. On June 4, the government called in the army to crush the revolt in Tiananmen Square. Although accounts vary, it is believed as many as three thousand protesters were killed.

The West was outraged at what had happened, and this created political and economic tensions with China. During this time, the paramount leader of China was Deng Xiaoping. Deng is the leader who launched the economic reforms in China in the early 1980s, all the while continuing to keep a very tight rein on political reforms. For those too young to remember him, he is the Chinese leader who famously said: "It does not matter if the cat is black or white, so long as it catches mice."

A month following the Tiananmen Square Massacre, I received a call from Dickie Howson telling me that we should get ourselves over to China as soon as possible. His reasoning was that because of the West's protest against China's brutal handling of the situation, no foreigners would be doing business there in protest, and we might be able to jump into the vacuum it created. I was skeptical, as it was a complicated environment to do business in, under the best of circumstances. But Dickie was persistent, and after consult-ing with some of my Navios colleagues, I agreed to take the trip.

Before the Tiananmen Square Massacre, I had not really given much thought to the Chinese political system. On my first two trips to China, the lens through which I viewed the country was primarily economic, focused largely on the enormous financial disparity in the lives of the country's cit-izens versus what we were accustomed to in North America. The level of poverty that I witnessed during my travels throughout the country, even in the major cities, was always striking. But the flagrant human rights atrocity that occurred in Beijing that summer caused me to reflect for the first time on the two very different political systems that existed between China and the United States.

The government of China is an authoritarian political system that is controlled and managed by the Chinese Communist Party (CCP) which plays *the* central role in managing government, the military, and people's daily lives all with very little policy debate. It is a "top-down," command and control structure. For the most part, Chinese citizens accept this structure because they have a strong belief that power emanates from the top. Those individuals who make it to the top are viewed as the most consequential and intelligent comrades who are best able to make decisions that will positively impact the best interests of the country and its people. In other words, the CCP focuses on the collective interests of society versus the individual. What the people of China give up in exchange for such a system is freedom of expression and a lack of control over their daily lives.

On the other hand, the political system in the United States starts from the ground up. It is all about the individual and freedom of expression. Every person has his or her own rights, and getting ahead in society is largely based on what you know rather than who you know. Initiative from the ground up is prized. The economic system in the United States encourages new and innovative thinking that results in the country leading global transforma-tional change across a wide range of industries. In addition, government is powered by individual voters, which leads to regular changes in administra-tions at both the State and Federal levels. This is just the opposite of what one can expect to happen in China.

As distasteful as the Tiananmen Massacre was for me, at the time, I believed the opening up of China economically was bound to assist the population at large by increasing per capita GDP, and this is what has hap-pened. When I first visited China in 1986, per capita GDP was $282. As I write today it is about $12,600, which is quite remarkable given the population size of this country.

By the end of September, we had received our travel visas, and we arrived in Beijing in early November. This time, we stayed at a new Western-style hotel in the center of Beijing, near Tiananmen Square, built specifically for Western business travelers. Even five months after the Tiananmen debacle, the hotel was eerily empty, as were the streets. Although you could see the Great Hall of the People from a distance, Tiananmen Square was completely void of people, and it was fully cordoned off with military-style police.

Dickie was right that it was a perfect time to visit the country for business. We again hired Wim as our translator, and he provided us with a wealth of information about the current political and business climate. He spent each day with us, and in between some of our meetings, he would act as our private tour guide and show us some of the sights in and around Beijing. In addition to bringing us to the famous sites like Tiananmen Square, the Forbidden City, and the Great Wall, he took us to some out-of-the-way places.

One afternoon, he walked us through a local *hutong*, an area of narrow streets and alleys where locals lived in very tight quarters, most of which have since been demolished. There were communal water pumps located indiscriminately about, and occasionally we would bump into a man squatting on a corner selling hedgehogs for food. And we would come across small billboards full of newspaper size announcements or commentaries in Mandarin characters that people would stand in front of and read. The poverty was striking. But even then, you could sense that something was afoot in this country. Just in the three years since I had first set foot in China, one could see firsthand some significant capital investments being made.

Dickie had found through his contacts yet another shipping company we had never heard of, Dalian Maritime Transport Group, and he had arranged a meeting with them. Since domestic airplane travel was very limited in China in the 1980s, Dickie and I took a train from Beijing to Dalian, which turned out to be a very long and uncomfortable twelve-hour journey around the Liaodong Bay.

It was during this meeting with Dalian Maritime Transport, we first learned that the *Nan Ji Zhou* had an identical sister vessel, the MV *Bei Ji Xing*, which was operated by Dalian Maritime in the Chinese coastal trades moving coal from northern China down to the Yangtze River. And yet again, no one outside of China seemed to know she existed. They, of course, knew that we had successfully chartered the *Nan Ji Zhou*, and they seemed open to future business with Navios.

Our second time charter with the People's Republic of China, the MV *Bei Ji Xing*, pictured during her sea trials. Credit: Mitsui Engineering & Shipbuilding

In the fall of 1991, about twenty months before the expiration of our second three-year charter of the *Nan Ji Zhou*, we were approached by a London shipbroker who told us a transportation/shipping company in Jakarta named PT Arpeni Pratama had need of a belt self-unloader for an Indonesian coastal movement of coal. We traveled to meet the principals and survey the port. Judging from the infrastructure there, we realized we would have to make some modifications to the ship's discharging boom to fit the shoreside hopper of the coal-fired receiving plant. I worked up a proposal that included these additional costs and provided Arpeni with an indication for ocean freight transport. At our next meeting, we fixed a multiyear contract of affreightment for the trade, and in 1992, we redeployed the ship to Indonesia.

Given the up-front cost of this work and the time it would take, we decided to approach Shanghai Haixing to inquire whether they might be willing to sell us the ship. The negotiation proved to be somewhat difficult, because it was not Shanghai Haixing that owned the *Nan Ji Zhou*, but rather the Bureau of Maritime Transportation of Shanghai. This was yet another government-controlled entity that no one knew existed. We eventually acquired her for $14 million. The advance rate on first mortgage ship finance was generally much higher back then than what one can expect to obtain today. With a multiyear freight contract, we were able to borrow about 80 percent of the cost of the ship, leaving us with an equity investment of just $3 million plus $500,000 for the boom modification. We renamed her the MV *Nan Ji*.

A few years into the Arpeni contract, we reached an agreement to sell them the ship for $21 million, and after paying down the outstanding debt, we netted about $10 million from the sale.

Having built up a good reputation for reliable service in the Caribbean and U.S. Gulf and East Coast with this self-unloader, some of our customers were clamoring for us to replace the *Nan Ji Zhou*. We were able to charter the *Bei Ji Xing* along very much the same terms as we had her sister, and we deployed her into the U.S. coastal aggregate trades.

CHAPTER 13

A PIECE OF THE ROCK

"Sweat equity is the most valuable equity there is."

MARK CUBAN,
American businessman

———————

Reflecting back on it today, I believe one of the things I enjoyed most about chartering was that it was essentially entrepreneurial in nature. I would seek out new opportunities, follow up with clients, and negotiate complex deals, frequently in remote parts of the world. It often felt as if I were running my own business within the larger context of Navios.

I believe I inherited this entrepreneurial drive from my maternal grandfather. He grew up in a poor French-Canadian family, one of twelve children. At a young age, he joined the Canadian armed forces and served valiantly in World War I in France and Flanders. Returning to Quebec, he apprenticed in a small stock brokerage company and eventually was quite successful, which enabled him to strike out on his own to become a small entrepreneur in Quebec City. He acquired real estate, including a few movie theaters, and, along with a few partners, established some private fishing camps north of Quebec City. His accomplishments had much to do with the fact that he was able to move easily between the French and English enclaves, which at that time remained very separate milieux within the province.

The problem was that I had no equity stake in the business. I was working hard at Navios, earning a good salary, and had success navigating the complex charter contracts. Nevertheless, I was in essence an employee. I also knew that at some point in my career I wanted to have an equity stake in a maritime enterprise. I was not going to spend my entire business life simply employed in a company, working my way up through the management ranks without owning a "piece of the rock." This thought never strayed far from my mind. In fact, it was the one theme that helped drive me through some of the more difficult periods in my career.

It wasn't just a path to wealth that drove me. It was more than that. I was not scared of putting in long hours. Plus, I knew enough about myself that I was always searching for something else to grab onto, to take hold of new challenges and attack them head-on. I did not like staying in one position for long periods of time. I was always encouraging individuals to get things done, supporting them as they, too, endeavored to develop new business, and conveying to them not to worry about missteps along the way, because they were going to happen. And I was prepared to take risks that more conservative managers were not. But ultimately, more than anything, I think it was the idea of managing my own destiny, rather than having it managed by others, that drove me.

I began to keep my eyes open for opportunities.

Enter George Campbell, a successful naval architect born and raised in Scotland. In 1941, the British Royal Navy posted him to Canada to help salvage and repair war-damaged ships. After the war, he remained in Canada, working in the maritime trade as an engineer.

In the postwar years, the international large-volume dry bulk trades had slowly started to evolve in Europe, the United States, and Japan. The original large bulk carrier ships were lakers—ships that were designed to trade and operate within the freshwater confines of the Great Lakes. These ships were not structurally designed for the stresses associated with oceangoing trading patterns. George recognized early on the potential for the migration of this design to the international markets, which is why he first established himself in Quebec. However, much like D.K. Ludwig, he was ahead of the curve in recognizing the cost advantages of building ships in Japan. In the early 1950s, George moved his ship-designing business from Montreal to Tokyo.

He became renowned for new designs of cost-effective and operationally sound bulk carriers and built up a very successful business. Working with the shipbuilder Ishikawajima-Harima Heavy Industries (IHI) over two decades, he developed a series of newbuilding vessel designs called the Freedom, the Fortune, and the Friendship, known as the "F" series, which were very well received in the marketplace and contributed to the expansion of the international dry bulk trades.

We met purely by coincidence in 1984 in Tokyo in an elevator I was taking up to a lunch meeting in the Palace Hotel, where George lived whenever he was in Japan. Out of the blue, he looked at me and asked what a young man like me was doing in the city. I replied that I worked for a maritime firm named Navios Corporation. He knew of the company, of course. He stepped off at my floor to continue our conversation, and that is what led us to a meeting for a drink at the hotel a few nights later.

George was an outgoing Scotsman who loved nothing more than to talk shop about the business of shipping. I could scarcely believe I was having a drink with the man who was one of the leading ship designers in the world. Although he was knowledgeable about engineering and the technical management of ships, he did not know much about the business side of maritime transport. He was therefore intrigued by the commercial activities of Navios and my experiences as chartering manager. He never said so, but I think he was surprised by the fact that Navios had worked so closely with Ludwig in Japan, but never with his firm.

I kept in touch with George, and every time I was in Japan, I would arrange to meet with him. We spent evenings drinking and talking about the business. Then one morning in 1986, he called me suggesting a meeting at his six-hundred-acre cattle farm near Hemmingford, Quebec to discuss a "business opportunity." Back then, Navios was in severe financial difficulty, and life in the Greenwich office was not pleasant.

We arranged to meet one weekend a few weeks later when he was back from Japan. I drove up to his farm and spent twenty-four hours with him discussing his plan for the future. He explained that because of the severe 1980s dry bulk recession, several owners who had placed orders for the "F" ships at IHI had simply not taken delivery of the finished product. They had walked away from their contracts and, of course, the equity deposits they had placed with the yard. IHI was desperately looking for a "home" for these completed newbuilding ships. Seeing an opportunity, George had arranged with IHI to take ownership of some of these units and had set up a company in Nassau to manage them. Given the fact that he knew next to nothing about how to run a maritime transport business, it was a risky decision.

His plan was to establish, as he put it, "a proper shipping company," by which he meant a commercial operation, and he wanted me to move to Nassau to run the business. I was flattered by his offer and captivated with the idea of getting in on the ground floor of a new maritime company with a half-dozen handysize ships and no legacy costs, and helping to develop it on my own. Not to mention, the thought of living in the Bahamas was intriguing.

The sticking point was the question of equity. I made clear that any move I made away from the Navios/Fednav fold would have to include some form of equity in the venture. George said the equity would "come in good time," but he would not make a firm commitment. I did not find that reassuring. We parted ways that weekend, both saying we would consider the other's position. We had some further discussions over the next few weeks, but his position on the equity question never changed.

As a result, I ultimately turned down his offer. This was an extremely difficult decision for me because I was giving up the opportunity to manage what was essentially a new shipping venture at a time when most shipping companies were on their knees. It could have been a challenging and exciting experience. More importantly, my wife was supportive of the opportunity as well. But without receiving equity in the company, it was not worth moving from my secure position at Navios.

***

The next opportunity arrived about a year later from an unlikely source: Michael Bell, who was now the president of Navios. He approached Bruce Hoag and me confidentially to say that he thought Ladi Pathy might be willing to sell Navios. Given the fact that the market was still weak, but appeared to be turning around, he felt it would be a good investment and wanted to explore buying it and proposed cutting us in. He asked if the two of us could develop some market scenarios to produce a forward cash flow against our existing fleet and contract business, which we did.

Armed with these projections, we pitched the potential acquisition to a half-dozen private investment firms that Michael had targeted, but we were unable to gain any traction. In those days, dry bulk shipping was not on the radar screen of investors outside the industry, and certainly no one associated it with commodity markets generally.

However, the market or industry wasn't the only problem. It became clear to me that although Michael was a superb salesman, he simply did not know how to address investors. In some of the meetings, he would get carried away addressing some of the industry details and projects that Navios was developing, which left the potential investors a bit bewildered, if not downright skeptical. I came to realize that a fast-talking salesman type does not sit well with professional investment advisors, and this was a great take-away that proved useful for me later in my career.

In the spring of 1988, Michael departed rather abruptly from Navios. The reasons are still unclear to this day. Perhaps it was because his attempt at buying the company had failed, and Ladi got wind of it. Or maybe he and Ladi had a falling-out over the direction Navios, and perhaps even Fednav, should be headed. But it could have been more than that. Michael and Ladi were very different people, and their management styles reflected it. Many sensed that there had been some tension between them for a long time.

Michael was charismatic. When he walked into a room, you knew he was a force to be reckoned with. He was a tall man who had the frame of a rugby player and a tremendous personality, which led people to view him as a natural leader. Ladi, on the other hand, was a short, unassuming man who shunned the limelight and led by the power of his intellect and position. However, he did not always inspire the staff.

Indeed, there were instances when I witnessed people simply assume that Michael was the owner of Fednav, and this must have grated on Ladi. The two of them working together in the 1970s transformed Fednav. It evolved from an operator of chartered oceangoing ships, into and out of the Great Lakes, into a sophisticated shipowning and chartering enterprise with investments not just in ships but in oil and gas, offshore supply vessels, and ship financing. It was a remarkable run.

Whatever the reason, Michael's departure came as quite to shock to everyone, especially me. Michael had up until then been largely responsible for steering my career. He was responsible for my position at Navios, my promotion to manager, and supporting me on dozens of projects that had taken me around the world to broaden my horizons. He had been my mentor from my early days at Fednav.

About a month after he had departed from Navios, Michael reached out and asked if I would meet him for lunch. We met at an unassuming diner in Greenwich, where he, in his usual enthusiastic tone, told me he wanted to create a start-up commercial ship operator based in Stamford, which he was prepared to finance to the tune of $3 million. He wanted me to run it and asked me to take some time to put together a business plan outlining how I would go about creating this new business. And most significantly, he proposed to offer me an equity stake up front.

Based on my belief that the dry bulk market might be turning a corner, I was excited by the project. I trusted him and his instincts about the business. So, I set up a plan to show how one might go about creating a new start-up shipping operation by chartering ships and freight and applying one to the other much like Fednav had done in the 1950s and 1960s. There were many small "operators" located primarily in the Scandinavian countries that time-chartered ships for short periods and allocated them to cargoes they fixed in the open market. However, most of them had a short lifespan because they simply did not have sufficient capital to see themselves through difficult markets.

There were, of course, some rare successes where operators went on to develop an ever-increasing fleet of ships that also involved vessel ownership. But in most of those cases, the founders had, through contacts established with industrial end users, a leg up on a certain movement of commodity, and they used this as a base to commence their enterprise.

As I prepared the plan, I realized that the principal obstacle was investment capital.

We had a couple of difficult meetings in which I pointed out to Michael the number of times small operators had tried to charter a Navios ship and we avoided them due to their poor capitalization. In the rare case where we did fix a ship to them, we would routinely require some form of bank guarantee for the performance of the charterer. Essentially, I was telling him that $3 million was simply not going to cut it. If he wanted to set up a serious operation, we needed $10 million to $15 million of seed capital. Michael was always big on ideas, but not necessarily on follow-through. He bristled at my projection and said he'd have to think about it.

Our final meeting was at a small deli in north Stamford, next to a gas station, on a bright sunny May morning. He did not agree with my projection regarding seed capital. Seeing that he would not change his position, I thanked him for considering me for this opportunity, but explained that I had to pass, given the lack of capital I thought was necessary for success. He was subdued, which for Michael was very unusual. He didn't even try to convince me to change my mind. We said our goodbyes, and we never spoke again, even though I did try to reach out a few times over the intervening years. With Michael, it was all or nothing, and, I am sad to write, I don't think he ever forgave me for this decision.

***

While Michael Bell's start-up idea was not the path for me, I started to focus on the earlier plan he had floated of trying to buy Navios from Fednav. I blue-skyed it with Bruce, who seemed to be interested. Then I reached out to Sean Day. He had departed from Navios in the middle of the 1980s dry bulk recession to join Citigroup Venture Capital (CVC). It was a smart move. Citigroup had moved from the buyout business into private equity investing and was led by a man named Bill Comfort. He has been credited as one of the first to create the industry of venture capital and private equity.

Although he seemed to be very happy at CVC, I knew Sean well enough to understand that his first love was ocean shipping. With Michael Bell's departure, there was a good possibility of Sean's returning to the company in a chief management role. I knew that he was liked by Ladi Pathy and some of the other Fednav senior executives. I explained that given market conditions, Navios might be in play. I suggested that there could be an opportunity to recapitalize the company from a venture capital perspective and gain some equity for the management partners. Sean seemed interested in the prospect.

Early that summer of 1988, I invited Sean, together with a few other personal friends, on a salmon fishing trip to a private camp on the Restigouche River in New Brunswick, one of the premier Atlantic salmon fishing rivers in eastern Canada. Over three days, we would fly fish from early morning through noon, stop for a late lunch, followed by a quiet afternoon that might include some cards, then head back out at about four-thirty for four hours of fishing, and return to a late-evening meal after dusk.

I brought with me considerable detail on Navios and its current activities, as well as general market information. During our afternoon breaks, Sean and I would sit around the camp and spend a few hours working through some forecasts that I had developed. The dry bulk markets were beginning a strong rebound, and applying low-, base-, and high-case market scenarios, and adding probabilities to each, he could see how Navios might perform in the next few years.

It all went quiet for several months after the trip, but I kept in touch with Sean. At this time, I still had the title of chartering manager, but my responsibilities were broader in scope than the title reflected. By then, Bruce Hoag was vice president of finance. Sean contacted us and suggested a get-together. He explained that he was working on a deal with Fednav to return to Navios as its new president and it would include bringing in CVC as an equity participant. In addition to Sean, the transaction would also permit Bruce and me to acquire a small equity participation.

The deal closed in July 1989, and Sean rejoined Navios as president with a carve-out mix of common equity and preferred stock for management. He kept 11 percent for himself and offered the opportunity to purchase equity stakes at $10,000 per percentage point of the company: 3 percent for me and 1 percent for Bruce. I was also promoted to the position of commercial vice president, with broad oversight of Navios's various business lines and the terminal facility Navios had in Uruguay, as well as Navios Ship Agencies.

I could not have been more excited. I finally had that "piece of the rock," albeit a modest piece, for which I had been yearning for so many years. The dry bulk market looked healthy; we had a large chartered-in fleet of panamax ships and a good book of freight business to go with it.

***

The final opportunity for a change of career path came about six years later, although it was one without the potential for an equity stake. Out of the blue, I was contacted by a headhunter from New York City who had been retained by the Schnitzer family of Portland, Oregon, to search out a CEO for their maritime transportation company, Lasco Shipping.

The Schnitzer family started their business in 1906 as scrap metal traders. During the twentieth century, they built it into a large and successful steel-manufacturing and metals-recycling business. In the 1960s, when the company needed to ship some scrap metal, the family acquired its first ship, and they slowly built up an independent maritime business. They established Lasco Shipping, which eventually owned and operated a fleet of about twenty-five handysize up to panamax-size bulk carriers based out of Portland.

The possibility of taking on the CEO position of a well-established maritime enterprise intrigued me because I was uncertain how long Sean would remain with Navios. I first met Ken Novak, the son-in-law of Leonard Schnitzer, at a meeting in the New York City offices of the headhunter. It went well, because a few weeks later I took the first of three trips out to Portland to learn more about the business and meet some of the other family members. It was a serious enough endeavor that my wife joined me on the next two trips to get a feel for what the city of Portland had to offer and to look at some housing.

Ultimately, I passed on the opportunity because of three overriding concerns: The Schnitzer family was in the throes of some generational changes, and it was not clear who would be responsible for the family's investments, going forward. The Lasco board of directors was configured with the CEO and six Schnitzer family members, who knew virtually nothing about the maritime business. I did not think this structure would work well. Perhaps most crucially, the move would involve no equity participation in the company. In addition to these professional considerations, my wife and I were enjoying our family life in Connecticut, and we were concerned about disrupting our children's schooling.

Nevertheless, the seriousness of the Lasco Shipping approach gave me confidence that I was indeed making a name for myself within the global shipping markets. It also confirmed my thinking that others outside of the Fednav/Navios fold thought my experiences, to date, were indeed at a level that made me a realistic candidate for the CEO position of an international maritime shipping company.

CHAPTER 14

SMOOTHER SEAS

"It is not the ship so much as the skillful sailing
that assures the prosperous voyage."

GEORGE WILLIAM CURTIS,
Nineteenth-century American writer

———————

Most of the 1980s were incredibly disruptive at Navios. It was such a brutal time that when I look back on it now, I am not sure why I remained in the industry. I suppose the global scope of maritime transport is what really kept me marching through these difficult years. I enjoyed the international travel and the experience of meeting and learning about new cultures. But most importantly, I thrived on the entrepreneurial and competitive nature of the dry bulk markets.

Sean Day's return in 1989 to the company he had departed three years earlier brought an air of stability to the organization that was desperately needed. The fact that he had managed to convince CVC to invest in Navios was encouraging, and for the first time in nearly a decade, the staff felt that the company was slowly able to move forward on firmer ground.

Because Navios was moving so much Venezuelan iron ore into the U.S. market, and then fixing outbound cargoes of grain from the U.S. Gulf and coal out of the U.S. East Coast, management decided to establish Navios Ship Agencies (NSA) as its own ship agency division.

A ship agent is a company that is retained by a shipowner or cargo interests to be a local representative when the owner or charterer has business in a particular port. From the perspective of a shipowner, the agent coordinates the port of call of the owner's vessel. This can include, among other responsibilities, organizing port pilots to meet the ship on her arrival or departure, tugboat assistance when berthing and unberthing, coordinating the loading activity of the ship, arranging ship's stores for the vessel when she is in port, and coordinating any arriving or departing crew to and from the ship.

When I assumed commercial oversight in the company, NSA had offices in Baltimore, Philadelphia, Tampa, Mobile, New Orleans, and Houston. It was a measure of its success that by the 1990s, just as Navios had moved away from U.S. Steel–dominated freight business, perhaps two-thirds of NSA's business consisted of third-party shipowners and cargo interests. Many of our competitors in the ocean freight markets used the services provided by NSA in all these ports. It was a testament to a well-run, mildly profitable operation.

It employed about thirty people throughout the various offices, and its president, George Duffy, was based out of the New Orleans office. George was a seasoned shipping executive who had a long history operating in the New Orleans and Mobile areas. He was very close with the traffic department of U.S. Steel and managed to build up the agency business by actively influencing the return of a substantial quantity of U.S. Steel's steel exports to the port of New Orleans.

Since the main office of NSA was located in New Orleans, Bruce and I would travel down to New Orleans two or three times a year for board meetings. George traveled up to Connecticut to attend meetings as well.

Sean supported NSA primarily because it gave added heft to the Navios name in our markets, which was important. Because the ship agency business collects funds in advance from those parties that retain it, it was virtually self-funded and did not require us to provide cash for its ongoing operations. But the business made very little money, and I never considered it core to our primary activities.

***

With Sean's encouragement, in the fall of 1995, I took a two-month leave from Navios to attend an off-site executive management course sponsored by the MBA program at Columbia University. This was a great opportunity for me to detach from the daily grind of helping to run the business, focus on some new intellectual challenges and become familiar with new business models that I could apply at Navios.

The program was run out of Arden House, a mansion with about five hundred acres of undeveloped land in Harriman, New York, donated to the university by the Harriman Foundation. It was an intense two months with lectures and meetings and team-building activities planned over six days each week. One of the underlying themes of this program was "change" and how it impacts business, which was timely, given the dramatic changes occurring in the world of dry bulk.

I learned that there are different types of change that affect businesses. Many are incremental changes that any business will experience as it moves through different phases of growth. But perhaps the most dramatic change a business can face is *disruptive change*, which is precisely what was happening to the dry bulk markets. One of the takeaways from the program was how to tackle disruptive change by initiating ideas that might lead a company into new directions it had not focused on previously.

For the maritime transport business, the transformation of commodities being sold with fixed pricing over periods of years to commodities being priced on shorter and shorter timelines was such a change. It overturned the underlying freight principles that had been governing our business for decades. It came to head as increasing volumes of freight were priced on a spot basis, moving away from long-term fixed-rate freight contracts.

As a result of the changing environment, the underlying issue for Navios became how to manage our financial risks in a market that was becoming increasingly spot focused. Although we had already established a small derivative trading team, upon my return from the short sabbatical, I sat with Sean and convinced him that we really needed to ramp up this aspect of our business.

Traditionally, Navios had two prongs to manage risk: ships and freight. We could build a ship or time charter a ship for multiple years, against which we analyzed a freight movement and provided an industrial end user a fixed-freight quotation for the term of the contract, based on the cost of the ship, while always providing for a return on the equity capital invested in the ship. The business had been effectively "hedged."

But the industry had changed. The multiyear fixed-rate contracts had all but disappeared. So, when our customers approached us to request freight indications, we would focus on the nearby market and provide a quote for, say, six cargoes of grain from the U.S. Gulf to Italy. If in the ensuing months the market headed south, we could relet the cargoes to other owners and make a profit. On the other hand, if the market traded north, we were exposed. The way to cover this exposure was to charter a physical ship for a period of time, which effectively hedged the financial exposure of the grain cargoes, even though the chartered ship never actually was scheduled to transport any of these grain liftings.

Ocean freight derivatives offered us a third leg to manage risk. In the example above, instead of chartering a ship, we could buy a freight derivative. If the cargoes were to be moved over a six-month period, from April through to September, we could buy a Q2 and Q3 derivative, which would reflect a rising spot market and effectively hedge out the physical position. This made the process of fixing freight and/or ships more manageable.

Navios's history with freight derivatives dated back to the late 1980s. This was when we started trading futures on a very modest scale, contracts on the London-based Baltic International Freight Futures Exchange (BIFFEX), the precursor to today's very well recognized Baltic Dry Index. The underlying theme for dry bulk was the tendency for freight to become priced more frequently, with more and more cargoes being traded on a spot basis. The BIFFEX, and later the BDI, provided Navios with a mechanism to manage the financial risks associated with the trading nature of our business.

But it was complicated. We expanded into this area and tapped Mike McClure, one of our seasoned commercial executives, to set up a separate derivative trading team that worked closely with our chartering brokers. We hired a few young traders, some of whom had a maritime background but also postgraduate studies in mathematics. We also retained a consultant to help us establish value-at-risk (VAR) parameters.

Early on, all our derivative trading was done to hedge certain positions that we had with ships or cargo on our books. But as we moved into the latter part of the 1990s, our derivative desk also started to become more active in establishing proprietary derivative positions—speculative trading. I tried to keep a close eye on our derivative book, but as its level of trading expanded, it became impossible for me to follow the complexities of all our positions. We had the derivative team establish an internal VAR analysis so that at the end of each day executive management would receive a report setting out the 99 percent and 95 percent probabilities of a $1 million loss over a given month. Although VAR is not foolproof, it does allow one to gauge downside financial risk, given the derivative portfolio.

At the time, derivative contracts were all traded "over the counter" (OTC), meaning they were bilaterally traded between two counterparties. The advantage of trading OTC was that there was no requirement to post collateral. But you had signature risk, and therefore, had to be comfortable with the financial standing of the counterparty. Today, ocean freight derivatives are liquid markets and exchange traded instruments with standardized contractual terms. When you trade through an exchange, you place an initial margin deposit, and if the contract turns negative, the exchange will require additional margin deposits. But there is no counterparty risk. When the derivative contract settles, you receive funds from the exchange or pay into the exchange, depending on how your position settled.

Navios became an early global leader in this emerging activity, and I am proud to say we introduced this activity to a number of other shipowning and ship-operating companies.

***

We undertook another major initiative at this time: operating smaller dry bulk ships. Up until the early 1990s, Navios was primarily an operator of panamax ships. But the arrival into our fleet of the handysize vessels *Nan Ji Zhou* and *Bei Ji Xing* caused us to search out new opportunities in the smaller deadweight sector. We found instances where customers required handymax ships, so we started to trade in this smaller segment.

This occurred when we were expanding our long-term time charters from the Japanese Shikoku market, and so we were able to conclude a number of period charters of what, during this decade, came to be called **supramax** dry bulk carriers. We established a new division called Navios Handybulk, and hired people with experience in this sector.

CHAPTER 15

NORTH TO THE ARCTIC CIRCLE

"But why Alaska?" I asked her.
"It's from an Aleut word, Alyeska. It means
'that which the sea breaks against.'"

JOHN GREEN,
American author, *Looking for Alaska*

F ednav interest in the Arctic began in the 1950s, when the company carried out resupply voyages to various Arctic communities in Canada's eastern Arctic. Nunavut, Canada's largest and most northern territory, and Nunavik, which comprises the northern third of the province of Quebec, are the primary areas where most of the voyages occur. They take place in the summer months, since there is less ice and greater freedom of navigation, and they are vital for the remote northern communities that are cut off from civilization for much of the year. The voyages are operationally difficult because it is a short marine season, and there is a general lack of port infrastructure. As a result, Fednav developed considerable expertise trading ships into the Arctic region.

In the latter part of the twentieth century, a few Canadian mining companies were engaged in northern mineral exploration, and started to develop mines for the export of high-value commodities such as nickel and lead from the Arctic region. Because of its maritime Arctic expertise, Fednav was always at the forefront, offering these companies maritime transportation options. One of them, Cominco Alaska, a subsidiary of Cominco Ltd.

(known today as Teck Resources), had developed one of the largest zinc mines in the world.

The mine site, in a remote part of northwest Alaska, about eighty kilometers inland from the coast above the Arctic Circle, is located about 140 kilometers north of the nearest town, Kotzebue, with a population of about seven hundred inhabitants. It is known today as the Red Dog Mine, named after the Red Dog Creek, which, in turn, was named after the dog of one of the original prospectors of the site. Construction of the mine and the road leading to the sea commenced in 1987. The port was developed concurrently and consists of two large concentrate warehouses, with underground conveyors that reclaim the commodity onto a conveyor belt out to a small dock, where shuttle barges are loaded for the transshipment to ocean vessels at anchor farther out in deeper waters.

The Red Dog Kivalina port site. The two concentrate storage sheds are visible in the background as well as the Foss shuttle barges and tugboats in the foreground. Credit: *Anchorage Daily News*/Bob Hallinen

Before he left the company, Michael Bell nurtured the Red Dog ocean freight contract into existence. Given that the movements were primarily in panamax ships, it was Navios that first developed the maritime operations of the trade and had the ocean freight responsibility for the first ten years of the mine's life.

In 1988, a full two years before the first loading, our operational personnel assessed how best to handle the several logistics and hurdles of this contract. Ships arriving to load at Red Dog had to sail through the Bering Strait, a body of water just eighty-eight kilometers wide that separates Russia from the United States, and then continue up into the Chukchi Sea. Ice in the Kotzebue Sound normally starts to form in October and grows through the winter months before breaking up in May (this is known as first-year ice). However, large oceangoing ships had never traded there before, and our major challenge was chartering ships willing to trade to a new port located north of the Arctic Circle.

Geoff Riches, the manager of our fleet operations, worked with the American and British Salvage Associations, as well as Hull Insurance Underwriters, to make them aware of our project. He compiled statistics on weather, wind, and ice and reviewed them with these maritime associations because they were the bodies that any shipowner would approach for insurance coverage when they were considering fixing their vessels to Navios to trade into the region.

In addition to the contract of affreightment with Navios, Cominco had separately contracted with a company called Foss Maritime, a Seattle-based tug and barge company with a long history of activity in the U.S. Northwest markets. They designed and built the two specialized six-thousand-dead-weight-tonne barges that shuttled the concentrates from the shoreside storage sheds out to the Navios ships waiting at anchor. The barges were designed with a conveyor belt that retrieved the concentrate and transferred it to a retractable, telescopic loading boom that was able to swivel vertically and horizontally and load the holds of large oceangoing ships. It was a design very similar to the belt self-unloaders described earlier, but much smaller.

The operation was complex. Due to the shallow waters around Kivalina, ships would anchor about three miles offshore, where there was about eighteen meters of water and good holding ground. The loading process was aided by twenty-four-hour daylight during the summer months in this part of the world and, provided the weather cooperated, the barges would operate 24/7. This permitted a panamax bulk carrier to be loaded with about sixty thousand tonnes of cargo in three and a half days.

Technically, it was a difficult contract, particularly because of its location north of the Bering Sea, which involved detailed coordination between the operational personnel of Foss and Navios. The contract called for the movement of about 750,000 metric tonnes of concentrates to be loaded onto ships in a one-hundred-day ice-free window between early July and late September each year.

Perhaps the most attractive feature of this cargo movement was the value of the commodity itself. In the late 1980s, a tonne of iron ore might have been worth about $20. If the cost to transport the ore was $7 per tonne, the ocean freight component of the delivered cost was about 35 percent. Whereas during the ten years that we managed the Red Dog contract, the cost for a tonne of zinc averaged about $1,000. So, there was much less focus on the cost of transportation because it only made up 2 to 4 percent of the buyer's landed cost, which allowed us to achieve very attractive levels of profit.

***

On Tuesday, August 15, 1989, I boarded a late-evening flight in Chicago for the six-and-a-half-hour journey up to Anchorage, Alaska. Captain Ennio Distefano was with me. I was heading up to Kivalina to get a better sense of the operational constraints that we might face as we chartered ships from the open market to perform liftings. Ennio was there to spend time with the Foss personnel to review exactly how the transshipment loading operation was to be coordinated between Foss and Navios the following summer, the commencement year of the contract.

In those days there was no runway up at Kivalina—a flat portion of the road extending between the mine site and port was used as a landing strip. Unfortunately, that Wednesday morning, the ground crew in Anchorage received word that a caribou herd was moving northward across the mine road—and caribou were *the* priority there. So, our departure was delayed for several hours until the herd made its leisurely way across the road and was safely distanced from the mine area.

We were provided rooms in small container-like housing very similar to what I had experienced in the summer I spent working in Pickle Lake, prior to commencing my career in maritime transport. We spent two days reviewing all the details of the operation. We were provided data on the frequency of trucks moving concentrate from the mine down to the port site. We reviewed the capacity of the concentrate shed, located at the port, where the commodity would be stored throughout the year. It would wait there for the ice to break up and the maritime transport to commence after a long, cold fall, winter, and spring.

For our purposes, we studied and discussed with the Foss representatives how the barges would load large oceangoing ships. Although Foss had designed the barges with a telescopic boom to load these types of ships, it was not just a simple matter of pouring concentrate into a vessel's holds. It had to be done in such a way that the loading sequence did not affect the stability of a ship. We had tested and developed various scenarios using the technical plans of various sizes of ships, and worked out how long we thought it would take the operation to load a panamax.

The first export cargo transported out of Kivalina was loaded in July 1990 onto the MV *Navios Enterprise*, a panamax vessel. This was one of the first ships that Navios had chartered for multiple years, in 1987, as we exited the dry bulk recession. In our first year of operation, we transported about three hundred thousand tonnes of concentrate destined for Vancouver, where it was then transported to the Cominco smelter in Trail, British Columbia, and to Cominco customers in Asia and Europe. Over the next few years, as the mining operations grew and the transport infrastructure made more robust and shipowners became more comfortable with the trade, the volumes increased up to the targeted contract volumes.

During the ten years that Navios managed the Red Dog contract of affreightment, we performed 127 voyages without any serious mishap occurring to any of the oceangoing ships that we traded into Kivalina.

What I am most proud of is that Navios was the first company to define the movement of Red Dog concentrate as an established trade for large oceangoing ships north of the Arctic Circle. The credit for much of that success is due to the tremendous efforts of the operational managers who were stationed at different times up at the Red Dog site: Captains Mukul Bhushan and Ennio Distefano, and Navios's manager of fleet operations, Geoff Riches.

CHAPTER 16

THE POWER OF COAL

"To shipbrokers, coal was black gold."

ROALD DAHL,
British author

One of the new commodity movements that Navios was instrumental in developing in the early 1990s was the movement of low-sulfur Colombian coal and Venezuelan thermal coal into the electricity facilities located on the eastern seaboard of the United States. These were generally older power plants that had traditionally bought Appalachian coal. But due to new federal and state regulations on emissions, this coal was no longer compliant because of its high-sulfur content, so they had to switch to a low-sulfur variety. The primary domestic source was the Powder River Basin in Montana and North Dakota. However, it was only available to the East Coast power plants by rail freight, which was prohibitively expensive.

David Elsy spent a good deal of time marketing Navios to many of these receivers and worked with some local shipbrokers to try and develop new import sources of coal. This occurred at a time when Colombia was developing its large deposits of thermal coal for export from its Atlantic coast. (Today it ranks number five in the export of thermal coal globally.) He was able to convince the receivers that ocean transport of foreign low-sulfur coal was a viable alternative to domestic sourcing of coal.

However, the problem faced by the power companies was how to discharge oceangoing ships carrying cargo from South America into locations normally serviced by small barges from Baltimore and Hampton Roads. The

126

discharging equipment the facilities used to unload the barges was simply not suitable for large ships. In addition, it was a learning process for these receivers who had never before had to deal with the international coal and maritime markets.

Using the *Nan Ji Zhou*, and later her sister, the *Bei Ji Xing*, Navios began delivering occasional trial cargoes of Colombian coal to some of these power plants at a cost much lower than domestic coal by rail. The receivers were impressed with the self-unloading capabilities of these ships.

In addition to Colombian coal, there were small deposits of thermal coal being developed in the north of Venezuela. What was particularly attractive about this thermal coal was that its sulfur content was even lower than that of Colombia's. The local producers were looking to export this coal out of Lake Maracaibo, a large, protected bay of water, but they had no loading infrastructure then.

Given the potential for new trades of this highly desirable commodity, we started to model the concept of what we in Navios called the "poor man's belt self-unloader." Our goal was to find a ship with a larger deadweight capacity than the Chinese ships and convert her into a customized belt self-unloader that was also able to self-load from barges. This was something that traditional belt self-unloaders were not able to do.

Although we saw the need and opportunity for a self-load/self-discharge ship for this specialized movement, neither the sellers nor the buyers of the coal were prepared to commit to multiyear fixed-rate contracts. It was all so new. Without a freight contract, it would be difficult to arrange financing to acquire and retrofit a suitable ship. So, we reached out to Marubeni in Tokyo to see if they might be able to help us source a ship for this new trade.

Fortunately, they had an IHI Future 32 ship (one of the George Campbell designs) in their fleet, and we were able to conclude a ten-year bareboat charter. She was a thirty-eight-thousand-deadweight ship (about ten thousand more deadweight than either of the two Chinese belt self-unloaders), and we named her the MV *Navios Pioneer*. As part of this agreement, we negotiated the right to modify at our expense the weather deck with additional equipment, and we put her into a Japanese dry dock, where the work was carried out and supervised by our Frank Caviglia.

The *Navios Pioneer* came equipped with four large cranes and four large clamshell buckets. We arranged to have the ship modified with two longitudinal belt conveyors built onto the starboard weather deck. We designed four large receiving hoppers to maximize the amount of cargo that could be unloaded into them by the ship's clamshell buckets. These were then welded to the deck and positioned above the belts so that the ship's cranes could discharge commodity from all five of the ship's holds into the hoppers. We had another cross-conveyor belt that transferred the commodity from the starboard side to the port side of the ship, where we built a discharging boom onto which the commodity was transferred for eventual discharge to the shore side receiving installations.

It was much simpler in design than the traditional belt self-unloaders and therefore much cheaper. Because the ship had its own cranes and clamshell buckets, we had the added benefit of being able to self-load commodity from barges directly into the ship's holds as well. Depending on the specific gravity of the commodity, we were able to discharge at an average rate of about 750 tonnes per hour versus about 1,750 tonnes per hour on the traditional belt self-unloaders. But this slower speed of discharge was more than adequate for the receiving facilities.

Using the *Navios Pioneer*, we were able to offer the U.S. receivers the option of loading Colombian coal from traditional load port installations or Venezuelan coal from barges using the *Navios Pioneer*'s own equipment. This, of course, provided them more flexibility in negotiating the offshore purchases of thermal coal, and it allowed us to build up a successful business with them. Over its eight years of service, the *Navios Pioneer* discharged thermal coal into barges or single-point receiving facilities in Bridgeport, Connecticut; Wilmington, North Carolina; and the Delaware River, as well as an electricity facility located up the Piscataqua River in Portsmouth, New Hampshire.

These were all technically difficult undertakings, and Geoff Riches and Ennio Distefano assisted in many of these operations with on-site supervision. Unlike our traditional open-market trading business, this was a good example of solving a transport requirement by developing a new type of self-discharging ship and providing the end user with competitive freight and quality service.

CHAPTER 17

THE URUGUAY TERMINAL

"Set your sail to the big world, to the big ports but
never forget your little world, your little port!"

MEHMET MURAT ILDAN,
Turkish novelist and playwright

———————

U ruguay is a wonderful country. I have been blessed to travel there
many times over three decades and have become very fond of the
country, its people, and its culture. It is a tiny country, and if you
mention it to people, you can tell quite often by their reaction that they
are not sure where it is. I suppose this is not surprising, because it is the
second-smallest country in South America, about the size of the state of
Missouri, and it lies between the two largest countries in South America,
Brazil and Argentina.

Whenever I was on an extended trip to South America visiting multiple countries, I would try to end my travels in Montevideo, the capital of
Uruguay. Corporación Navios Sociedad Anónima (Navios Uruguay) operated the largest dry bulk terminal in the country located in Nueva Palmira.
We had an office in Montevideo that was responsible for the management
of our terminal business, and so that was my excuse to stop there at the end
of my journey.

There are several reasons why I think Uruguay is so special. Perhaps
the most compelling is that unlike almost all the other countries of South
America, it has a large socioeconomic middle-class population. Most of the
well-known countries on this continent, such as Brazil, Argentina, Chile,

and Venezuela, have a large percentage of their population living in poverty, a smaller percentage that is middle class, and an upper class that controls most of the wealth. The wealth is more evenly distributed in Uruguay, and the people seemed to be happier as a result.

Uruguay ranks first in South America in democracy, peace, and freedom of the press. On a per capita basis, it contributes more troops to the United Nations peacekeeping forces than any other country in the world. About 90 percent of the country's electricity comes from renewables, mostly hydroelectric and wind power. It is a democratic republic that has the second highest per capita GDP of any country on this continent, second only to Chile. It is perhaps the most socially progressive country in South America, allowing same-sex marriage and abortions. And one more remarkable feature of this country: In 2009, Uruguay became the first country in the world to provide every schoolchild with a free laptop and Wi-Fi access, which helps to explain why Uruguay has a literacy rate of 99 percent, one of the highest in the world.

Not bad for a country that most people do not have on their radar screens.

Its capital city, Montevideo, is located on the southern coast of the country and sits on a peninsula of land at the mouth of the Plate estuary, about two hundred kilometers due east of Buenos Aires. Much of the city is surrounded by wide public beaches, and one can walk for miles from the downtown area to the eastern suburb of Carrasco, all the while seeing families out enjoying the surf and sand. The old downtown core of Montevideo, known as Ciudad Vieja, has, like many cities, gone through a gentrification process; and over the past few decades, old run-down buildings have been remodeled and turned into small boutique hotels, funky offices, and fun restaurants.

About a two-hour drive east of the city is the famous South American beach resort of Punta del Este. It is very popular in the summer months, not just with Uruguayans, but with Argentineans, who flock in droves to the area from Buenos Aires.

West/northwest from the capital to Colonia and eventually Nueva Palmira are fertile lowlands punctuated with rolling plains and bluffs of trees that remind me of the English countryside. When I first visited Uruguay, this drive took about five to six hours depending on the number of *gauchos* (skilled horsemen) we bumped into moving livestock across the route (vehicular traffic was normally quite light). The route now has many sections of highway, and the travel time has been halved, although today it is perhaps a bit less interesting.

My first trip to Uruguay was in 1985. In the 1980s, most South American countries were ruled by military dictatorships, and Uruguay was no exception. The dictatorship had come to power twelve years earlier, and during this period, about 20 percent of the population was arrested for varying durations. It is estimated that as much as 10 percent of the population emigrated, as many Uruguayans looked for political asylum abroad. Montevideo was drab, somewhat decrepit, and eerily quiet. One sensed a lack of joie de vivre, a reflection of censorship of the press and Uruguayans as a whole. People were fearful about opening themselves up to outsiders.

Since the military government relinquished control after a general uprising over human rights violations, and the country elected its first democratic leader, it has been a beacon of democracy and the rule of law on the continent ever since. I will never forget arriving in Montevideo in the fall of 1989, a few weeks before the national elections, after a seven-day trip through other parts of South America. People were out banging pots and pans; vans with large loudspeakers on their roofs were slowly roaming the streets, with people shouting out slogans for their candidates. There was generally a boisterous carnival atmosphere.

I witnessed a population coming out to embrace their newly found democratic freedom. The country's national election turnout generally averages about 92 percent, a remarkable statistic today. Many other countries that I have visited over the years—where the populations take their democracy for granted (including my country of residency, the United States)—could learn much from little Uruguay.

***

In the early 1950s, U.S. Steel was searching around the world for deposits of manganese ore, one of the key elements in the production of blast furnace steel, to support its ever-growing domestic steel production. One of the mines it developed was in the upper region of the Paraná River in southwestern Brazil. About 1,500 kilometers downriver, U.S. Steel built a small port terminal facility in the sleepy little town of Nueva Palmira, Uruguay, located at the confluence of the River Plate and the Río Uruguay. The company arranged for the shipment of the manganese ore from Brazil on small river barges down to the terminal for onward transshipment to their U.S.-based steel mills. Twenty years later, the mine was depleted, and the terminal was barely operational. In 1982, when U.S. Steel sold 50 percent of Navios to Fednav, they included this defunct terminal in the sale.

With the USSR's increasing purchases of Argentine grain in the early 1980s, Navios management decided to adapt and revive the Nueva Palmira terminal for the export of soybeans to the world markets.

I became responsible for this terminal operation when I was promoted to commercial vice president of Navios, and I would visit Uruguay and Nueva Palmira regularly. It was a fascinating business because we operated the terminal in a commercial free-trade zone. This permitted the transfer of commodities from foreign countries through our terminal for onward movement to the international export markets without any taxes being paid to the Uruguay government. The government was supportive of the port transfer facility because it wanted to promote economic development and increase employment opportunities in an economically poor region of Uruguay.

We concluded contracts primarily with some of the grain majors such as Cargill, ADM, Dreyfus, and Bunge through their local South American offices. They would source grain principally from Paraguay, and, later, as the trade developed, from the southern parts of Bolivia and Brazil, and then arrange for barges to carry the grain down to our terminal facility, where we would discharge, warehouse, and then eventually reload it onto oceangoing ships.

Aerial view of the Navios terminal facility in Nueva Palmira, Uruguay with a panamax being loaded and the Uruguay River in the background. In the foreground are trucks loaded with domestic Uruguayan soybeans waiting to discharge their commodity. Credit: Author's Collection

The terminal still had the original dock, built and designed in the late 1950s by Uruguayan civil engineers employed by U.S. Steel. Like many infrastructure investments in those days, it was overengineered and over-constructed, which resulted in a remarkably long shelf life. It consisted of eight cylindrical cement **caissons**, or large platforms, positioned parallel to the shore. These were located about ninety meters from the riverbank and permitted ships to load to the prevailing deepest portion of the river. Ships were moored and loaded on the western side of the caissons, and barges were moored and discharged on the eastern side of the caissons. Two of the caissons were much larger than the others. One of these had a conveyor belt leading to it from the shore and a loading boom through which grain was loaded into a ship's holds as the ship **warped** alongside. The other had a large crane permanently erected on it for the discharge of barges onto the same conveyor belt for storage into our single twenty-five-thousand-tonne grain silo.

On my first visit to Nueva Palmira in 1985, I was surprised to see that our twenty-five-thousand-tonne silo was made of concrete, and perhaps more intriguing, it was horizontal. Most grain silos were vertical steel bins, but this horizontal construction was quite unusual. In many parts of the world, steel silos were favored because they were less expensive to build. They could be manufactured off-site, the ground on which they are built does not need to be reinforced, and they have a better ability to aerate the commodity and therefore store grains longer term.

Cement silos are expensive, with the construction cost of labor a major contributing factor. Fortunately, labor costs in U.S. dollar terms were very reasonable in the western countryside of Uruguay. So, despite the labor-intensive nature of their construction, the cement silos were an attractive alternative to the more typical steel silos at this location.

Alfonso Soler Rocca, the civil engineer who had originally helped build the terminal facility, managed the business. He was a tall and lean Uruguayan who spoke good English, and he knew and understood the practical workings of his business. But what I loved about him was how passionate he was about the terminal and its upkeep. As a sign of respect, I used to call him Don Alfonso, and some years after he retired, when we inaugurated our first seventy-thousand-tonne silo, we named it after him.

At the naming celebration of the Navios Uruguay's first 70,000-ton silo, the Alphonso Soler Roca. Left to right: Gabriel Soler, Mike McClure, Sean Day, Alfonso Soler, John Peacock, Pablo Soler, and the author. Credit: Author's Collection

He had two sons, Gabriel and Pablo, who were both trained as engineers and whom he eventually brought into the business. Gabriel, the elder son, managed the terminal itself and lived in Nueva Palmira. Pablo became the general manager of the business after Alfonso retired in 1989. I developed a close working friendship with Pablo. I admired his down-to-earth attitude and the high level of can-do common sense that he always brought to issues, not just when we were analyzing new investment possibilities, but when we were managing the business and operational aspects of the enterprise as well.

Once or twice a year I would take a seven-to-ten-day trip with Pablo around the region to visit customers and their upriver terminal facilities, where much of the soybeans were loaded. We would search out new customers, negotiate terms for some of our contracts, and occasionally meet with certain government ministries. Pablo and I would normally start in Rio de Janeiro and travel to various other cities in the southern part of the continent such as São Paulo, Asunción, and Santiago. These stays were almost always followed by an overnight stop in Buenos Aires to meet with clients before arriving in Montevideo. But occasionally our trips took us to some remote destinations.

If you take a pin and place it into the center of a map of South America, you will be very close to the Brazilian city of Corumbá, the main upriver loading facility for Bolivian-sourced soybeans. This city's greater municipality borders the northeast corner of Paraguay and the southeast corner of Bolivia, making for some interesting trade routes, along with some interesting characters. Thirty-eight years ago, when I first started traveling there, it had the feel of a Wild West town. Many of the streets were not paved and the wind blew dust into your eyes; scrawny stray dogs seemed to roam about everywhere; and food odors wafted from most buildings you walked by.

On one of my visits, we walked into a small taverna-like restaurant and were seated next to a group of three Americans with aquiline features, strong jaws, and the oversize build you would expect to see on a Delta Force ranger. Two of them were wearing those rectangular sunglasses you see on actors in Tom Clancy movies. They were certainly not in town looking to conclude grain transshipments. I suspect they were members of the American Drug Enforcement Agency working in the region, which had a well-deserved reputation for all types of contraband smuggling.

Our competitors were other grain terminals on the Argentine side of the Paraná River. They had a distinct geographic advantage over us because the barge trains had to pass by them to reach our terminal. But they were inefficient, even those owned by the grain producers themselves, due to labor rules and union contracts that constrained their operations. So, as we developed our terminal business, we also aimed to implement operating practices that made our terminal more attractive to our customers.

For instance, we instituted 24/7/365 operations. Our competitors generally did not work on weekends—and certainly not on holidays. To the barge operators and our customers' delight, we also discharged barge trains of grain more quickly.

Unlike our competitors, who invoiced overtime charges, extraneous taxes and special terminal fees, we charged one fixed rate for our services that included the discharging of barges, the movement of grain into our silos, reclaiming the grain from the silos, and reloading it onto ocean vessels. It was clean and efficient and easy to budget for. Our customers knew their final cost for transshipment from the outset. With our competitors, it would be well after the grain had been loaded onto a ship when the sellers would receive a final price for transshipment services. Together with our enterprising, forward-thinking, great management team, these are the practices that allowed us to grow the business into the premier dry bulk transshipment operation in the Paraná-Paraguay Rivers waterway system, known as the Hidrovía.

***

The Hidrovía is perhaps the most significant commercial watercourse system on the continent. Similar in size to the Mississippi River System, although less developed, it is composed of two distinct sectors: 4,500 kilometers of upper inland navigation, which eventually feeds into the second, a three-hundred-kilometer maritime corridor in the lower estuaries of the Paraná and Plate and Uruguay Rivers. However, the Hidrovía had many logistical bottlenecks: silting and seasonal rain fluctuations leading to draft problems, very tight curvatures in upriver sections of the river, bridges with narrow spans requiring the breakup of barge trains so that they were able to transit under them, and limited night navigation. Despite these challenges, though, it served as a significant inland export corridor for grain.

In 1991, Argentina, Brazil, Paraguay, and Uruguay formed a regional free-trade bloc called Mercosur, whose mandate was to promote free trade within the region and improve infrastructure to support the movement of commodity exports. The formation of Mercosur spurred the development of grain exports leading to an increase in investments at our terminal. Before its creation, we were completely dependent on Paraguayan soybean exports; but in the 1990s, we started to see Bolivian beans come downriver, and even some beans from southern Brazil. The Brazilian beans had previously been transported overland by truck to the Atlantic coast ports, but the river corridor became more cost-efficient.

Our three 25,000-tonne silos were built parallel to one another and parallel to the shoreline. Our first one was built in 1982, followed by a second in 1987, and another in 1990; each of these cost us about $1.25 million.

As the barge trains became larger, we saw the benefit of a dedicated barge dock, and in 1992, we finished the construction of a large cement pier between the main caisson dock used to load ships and the shore. We added a new heavy-duty cycle crane, which enabled us to discharge barges—not only on the new dock, but also on the inside of the caisson dock using the old crane. This gave us much more flexibility in managing barge fleets. At $3.3 million, this investment was by far the largest investment made in the terminal at that time. But the investment paid off, as it permitted us to turn around barge trains much faster than all our competitors and increase our throughput volumes. Even though we were twelve hours farther downriver than most of the Argentine terminals, the barge owners preferred to come to our terminal because of its greater discharging efficiencies.

A panamax bulk carrier being loaded at the Uruguay terminal
while a barge loaded with grain is being discharged for storage
into the shoreside silos. *Credit: Author's Collection*

One key metric we focused on with this terminal business was through-put tonnes, as opposed to actual tonnes. Our concrete silos were not designed for long-term storage, as we did not want any of our customers to store their grain for extended periods. A quick turnover allowed more of their commodity to flow through the facility.

Our next major investment came in 1995 when, for about $1 million, we upgraded all our rubber conveyor belt systems, making them wider and faster by increasing the angle of repose of the belts on their rollers. These kinds of rubber conveyor systems can move large volumes of grain rapidly over long distances with no product degradation. The new belts allowed us to speed up the loading of ships and the discharging of barge trains. All these investments meant increasing throughput volumes, which then required more storage capacity.

In 1997, we built our largest cement silo with a capacity of seventy thousand tonnes. Costing $3.8 million, this was an even greater investment than the new dock. The silo was built perpendicular to the three smaller silos and the shoreline.

In between these silos was the original outdoor concrete stockpile area that handled the U.S. Steel manganese ore transshipments, and under the concrete pad was the old conveyor tunnel used to reclaim the ore. From the time of my first visit, it remained unused. It was large enough to store about forty-five thousand tonnes of ore, and on one of our trips, Pablo came up with the brilliant idea of building a cheap metal cover over the space. It only cost us $750,000, and because grain has a higher stowage factor than ore, it provided an additional eighteen thousand tonnes of grain storage capacity.

As volumes increased each year, we installed new hoppers, a large Weightometer for trucks arriving to discharge domestic grain into our silos, garage infrastructure, electrical upgrades, small tractors to help with grain reclamation in the silos, new push boats to assist moving the barges about our docks, a new on-site office building, dust prevention systems, and electrical upgrades.

Throughout the forty years of operation at the terminal, ships were loaded using a single conveyor that extended out from shore with a fixed conveyor loading arm that was able to articulate perhaps 30 degrees and was therefore able to distribute grain evenly into the hold of a ship. But because it was fixed, vessels had to shift alongside the dock face so that the different holds could be positioned beneath the loading spout. These interruptions reduced our effective loading speeds, which at the time averaged about four days for a panamax bulk carrier. With increasing grain volumes, we needed to upgrade our vessel loading capabilities to stay ahead of our competitors.

Designing and erecting new ship loaders at a terminal facility in the western region of Uruguay was a difficult investment to sell to the Navios board, not just because of the size of the cash outlay, which turned out to be $4.7 million, but because the new ship loaders wouldn't necessarily translate into more commodity throughput within our facility.

Nevertheless, because of my experience managing the Navios fleet, I recognized that shipowners would quote lower levels of ocean freight to a seller of grain if that seller was able to offer a faster load port turnaround time for a ship, so we pushed ahead with the project.

The investment was completed in 1999 and was unlike anything we had undertaken before. Not only were the ship loaders a completely new investment direction for us at the terminal, but they also involved work out over the water, which was bound to make things more difficult. And the work, of course, was going to effect our loading of ships which would temporarily impact our operations.

The management team in Uruguay, led by Pablo and Gabriel, came up with a design that was relatively simple, cost-effective, and operationally sound. Once the project was completed, we were able to load a panamax to the prevailing river draft in about two and a half days—a 40 percent improvement in performance—and this significantly increased customer demand for our facility.

***

The terminal business became a welcome distraction for me from the vagaries of the international freight markets, which made up the largest portion of Navios's business and took up most of my time. In the Connecticut head office, we would live and die each day based on the whims of the dry bulk market, where freight and ships, not to mention ocean freight derivatives, were all essentially fungible assets. Every day, we would establish positions to go long or short on these three elements of our business. We were asset-light, reflecting the fact that up until the early 2000s we did not own any ships. All we had on our balance sheet was one long-term bareboat charter (the MV *Navios Pioneer*) and the terminal. So, while Navios's main operational divisions were all trading businesses, our Uruguay business was something altogether quite different.

The terminal was a tangible asset with a unique position on the Uruguay River, and unlike our other trading divisions, it was a business we could invest in and grow because it had a steady revenue profile. Our contract base was a mix of annual and multiyear agreements. When we had an operational problem at the terminal, we could approach our clients and get support to work around the issue. They, too, on many occasions, would approach us with problems or needs related to production issues, or the availability of river barges, and we would do our level best to help them. In other words, it was a relationship business that was very different from the transactional nature of our other trading operations.

The fact that we were able to grow organically by investing our earnings back into the terminal was another attractive aspect of the business. The terminal's annual free cash flows were used to make the equity capital investments. In fact, we never distributed a dividend from the Uruguay operation up into Navios during my tenure, nor did we ever have any debt allocated to the business. We did not even have a line of credit.

The financial metric we used to analyze the Navios Uruguay operation was return on assets, which is something we implemented in the early 1990s as the business started to expand and we deployed more capital into it. What I like about this metric is that it takes profits and compares them to the resources or assets you use to earn them. Return on investment, on the other hand, is more of a tool that can be used to consider when planning on making investments. Our annual return on assets was consistently between 7 and 12 percent.

**

As good a business as it was, the terminal was dependent on one commodity and perhaps no more than three or four key customers. Eighty-five percent of our revenue base was derived from four subsidiaries of the global, multinational grain traders. We believed it would be a good strategy to have a second type of commodity move through our terminal. Woodchips from the abundant eucalyptus trees in the area seemed like a good possibility. Since the trees grow to maturity in just about ten years, they were therefore a renewable commodity whose volumes could ramp up quickly. Most importantly, **biomass energy** was being promulgated by various governments around the world as an environmental alternative to dependency on fossil fuels.

The government of Uruguay supported forestry development to create employment and export earnings, and new eucalyptus plantations were being developed a few hundred miles north of Nueva Palmira in the northwestern region of the country, not far from the Uruguay River. We could visualize an export corridor using barges to transport eucalyptus wood chips down to our terminal.

In the mid-1990s, Pablo and I met with all types of companies involved in eucalyptus production. In addition to the two or three largest producers in Uruguay, we visited wood chip companies based in Santiago, Chile and traveled to other countries to see large, existing wood chip export facilities. When I was in Japan, I took the time to arrange meetings with the wood chip divisions of some of the major trading houses that were involved in the global trade of wood chips. I also met with some of the Japanese shipbuilders to learn more about wood chip carriers, specially built ships with extra-large cubic capacity and special deck-mounted discharging equipment, which Japanese shipyards specialized in constructing.

It all sounded like a home run, but nothing ever came of it. In this region of the world, the economics of using the wood fiber locally in purpose-built pulp mills made more sense. The export market of this commodity just wasn't strong enough to warrant the required investments. But we certainly learned a lot, and more importantly, it got us focused on developing new movements of commodity through our terminal.

We looked into the potential of Uruguayan soybeans. I could never understand why Uruguay did not have a domestic soybean grain industry for the export markets when all the countries around it did. We learned Argentine farmers had started to acquire land holdings in the western region of Uruguay in the mid-1990s and began to plant soybeans. They did this to avoid higher taxes on grain exports implemented by the Argentine government, and because the cost of arable land in Uruguay was about half the value of equivalent Argentine farmland.

It has taken several years for this trade to develop. In 2002, we moved about sixty thousand tonnes of Uruguayan soybeans through our terminal. By 2004, the number had grown to 248,000 tonnes.

For the last fifteen years before we sold Navios, the cumulative annual growth rate of throughput volumes of Navios Uruguay was an impressive 11 percent.

CHAPTER 18

SHIFTING TIDES

"Don't say it cannot be done, rather say,
you don't know how to do it yet."

TOMAS BATA,
Czech entrepreneur

On a warm and humid June day in 1998, Sean Day called Bruce Hoag and me into his office to tell us that after much thought he had decided to leave Navios. His departure came as a complete surprise to Bruce and me. Together we'd weathered the storms of choppy dry bulk markets and successfully developed the trading desks of the company, which was significant because we were still an asset-light business.

But unknown to both of us, upon his arrival back at Navios, Sean had managed to obtain from Fednav, presumably as an inducement to have him return to the Fednav/Navios fold, a "put" option on his ownership stake in Navios. This allowed him to sell his equity to Fednav, and he decided to exercise that option and leave. This left a particularly bad taste in our mouths. For even though we were working partners, he had never divulged this arrangement to us, nor had we ever been offered such an option. Bruce and I continued as illiquid minority shareholders and were therefore completely dependent on Fednav, the majority owner of Navios. CVC also maintained its small minority interest in Navios.

All Ladi Pathy's key lieutenants in Navios had now departed. Michael Bell was gone, John Weale had returned to the Fednav head office in Montreal in 1989, and now Sean had departed for what he viewed as greener pastures. As executive vice president, I was the last remaining key individual in Navios with a Fednav pedigree. I should have been next in line to lead the company.

However, Ladi had never entrusted me with the same responsibility he had the other executives. Perhaps it was because he still viewed me as a young chartering assistant sitting in his Montreal office. Or perhaps my independent character presented too much of a challenge to his management style. Whatever the reason, I wasn't sure of what the future might hold for me.

In the early fall of 1998, a few months following Sean's departure, I received a call from Ladi saying he was planning to come down to New York from Montreal the following week and he would like to meet with me in Manhattan. I was not sure what the purpose of this meeting was about. Perhaps it was to discuss the management spot left vacant with Sean's departure. We arranged to meet at his Upper East Side hotel suite one afternoon a week later.

I reviewed with him the entire Navios portfolio: the fleet, all of which was chartered as opposed to owned; the freight contracts currently on our books; the Uruguay terminal operation, for which he showed little interest; the year-to-date financial results; and our book of derivative contracts. He plied me with some questions on each of the Navios business segments and personnel.

However, when I started to lead Ladi through some of our derivative positions and explain how they worked, it quickly became apparent to me that he felt uncomfortable with these "paper" positions. It did not help that the world of derivatives had been badly tarnished three years earlier. In 1995, Nick Leeson, a rogue trader at Barings Bank, had made unauthorized, fraudulent trades that led directly to the collapse of the bank. For the uninitiated, derivatives equated to unquantifiable risk, which, I suspect, contributed to Ladi's discomfort.

The other takeaway from this meeting was Ladi's apparent focus on the Cominco Red Dog contract. He asked me many questions about the 1998 summer season: how many liftings had Navios performed, to what destinations, and what type of chartered ships, etc. Fednav prided itself on being the dominant carrier of cargoes in and around the Canadian Arctic. It had built up a well-earned reputation for trading ships into the Arctic region during the summer months, and it was, and still is, known as a shipping company that has numerous ships rated as ice-class in its fleet. These are ships designed with a reinforced bow that allows them to trade into ice-infested waters normally avoided by regular ships.

I left this two-hour meeting with a sense of disappointment. I was confident that I had displayed a deep understanding of the company's operations. No one else in the organization had this depth of knowledge, and I therefore fully expected him to discuss the president's position with me. It had ended without Ladi even mentioning it.

***

Ladi ended up nominating Carl Lee, who was a vice president of Fednav based in Montreal, to be a director of Navios International and Navios Handybulk, our two main operating subsidiaries. Carl was someone I had known for many years and liked; we got along well. After his appointment, he would come down to our office in Connecticut a few times a month to stay in touch with the business firsthand, while I continued to brief Ladi by telephone a few times each month.

In early October, Ladi called to say he would be back in New York the following week, and he wanted to invite Bruce Hoag and me to join him for dinner at the Metropolitan Club. We arrived promptly at 6:30 p.m. and were escorted into the dining room, where we found Ladi seated with John Weale—a surprise to us both. John had left Navios nearly a decade earlier to return to Fednav's head office in Montreal.

As we worked our way through the meal, Ladi and John asked Bruce and me several questions about the business. I had known Ladi for over twenty years, and not far into our dinner conversation, I could see he was uncomfortable. Following our main course, Ladi explained that he had been giving much thought as to who should head up Navios as president, and that he had decided it should be John Weale. I was floored. I was fully expecting Ladi to nominate me for the position.

As executive vice president, I had been effectively running the business since Sean's departure. As Ladi continued to expound on the reasons why he thought it made sense to have John move back down to Connecticut and rejoin Navios, my mind was spinning in a thousand directions.

As he carried on, I was thinking: *This is crazy. John is not a manager of a trading team, and he doesn't have experience managing the commercial side of Navios's business.* John was a detail-oriented man with extraordinary talent, but not, in my opinion, a good choice to lead the company.

I interrupted and calmly said: "Excuse me, Ladi. If you send John Weale down to run Navios, you will have my letter of resignation on your desk within the fortnight."

There was stunned silence at the table. Bruce had not spoken a word thus far, but he was taking it all in. John did not know what to say. It was obviously a very awkward moment.

Then Ladi looked at me and said, "Well, Tony, that's that, I suppose," and stood up, making clear that dinner was over. John followed suit.

Bruce and I had arranged a car to take us from the city back to Connecticut. The fifty-minute car ride seemed like a three-hour trip. Bruce was not one to rock the boat. His solid, Midwestern values would not have let him act the way I had at dinner, and he was very subdued. But I knew what he was thinking, because I was thinking the same thing: *Where the hell is all this going to lead?*

The following morning, I received a call from Ladi who said he thought my comment in front of John Weale was inappropriate. I explained to him politely that I was not happy with the apparent ambush and that I thought he should have discussed the proposed change with me before our dinner meeting. After a brief and somewhat uncomfortable exchange, we agreed to keep in touch over the next fortnight until I heard back from him with his decision.

But Ladi and I never had any further discussion about the matter. I continued to brief him on the activities of the company, and Carl continued to drop into the Navios offices for extended periods, but John never showed up to take the reins. So, I didn't resign and simply continued to execute the responsibilities as before. However, given that he had not made any formal announcement about my position, I quietly started to put out feelers through contacts around the globe to see what new opportunities might be available for a forty-five-year-old, seasoned, dry bulk shipping executive.

In November, Ladi asked me to fly up to Montreal for a meeting about the future of Navios. I thought this discussion would include his decision about the president's position. Instead, the meeting centered around his proposal to move the headquarters of Navios to Montreal.

I told him I thought this was a mistake for several reasons. I explained that perhaps no more than 30 percent of our staff would make the move. The brain drain would be devastating to the company. I also said that he could not just assume those in charge in Montreal could take over the running of Navios. It was a very different company from Fednav. Navios operated different-size ships in a freewheeling trading environment that Fednav was not accustomed to. My arguments must have hit home because nothing ever came of that idea.

***

It was obvious that Ladi was content to have me continue in my current role without giving me the official authority and the compensation that should come along with it. I'd spent sixteen years of my life at Navios. I had helped to grow it to be a profitable company with a solid, worldwide reputation. I felt confident it would continue to succeed under my management, if I were given the official authority. However, since that wasn't in the cards, I began to think about the nuclear option regarding my situation at Navios. Why not explore purchasing the company outright?

I knew I would have the support of all the staff at Navios. I had worked with many of them for close to two decades. But could I convince the senior managers to support the plan? Where would I get the capital to make a strong offer? I'd seen a brilliant dealmaker like Michael Bell fail. I'd also seen how Sean had succeeded in his reorganization of the company with an outside investor. Additionally, what would happen to me if the attempt to purchase the company failed? No doubt, my tenure at Navios would come to an end.

However, a key factor that made the proposition seem possible was that I knew Ladi was not comfortable with the direction Navios had taken. The company had evolved into a more decentralized organization, with traders and staff responsible for a wide variety of decisions, with senior management weighing in when needed. He did not understand the derivative market and was not comfortable with the complete reliance on chartering as opposed to owning ships to cover freight commitments.

In addition, Navios was a large company that was being managed by a group of executives well outside the visible purview of Montreal. Undeniably, the leveraged acquisition of the company in the early 1980s, just before the great dry bulk depression, had drained significant cash resources from Fednav in the mid-1980s. I knew all these factors weighed on him.

***

Invariably, most days Bruce Hoag and I were the last two individuals in the office. One evening in early January 1999, I sat down with Bruce to see if he thought my idea had any merit. Bruce was very conservative, and so I expected him to tell me we could never make it happen. But he surprised me when he said he'd like to look at the numbers before forming an opinion.

We had developed a comprehensive Excel data file that we called the Trading Fleet Balance. One was for our panamax operation and another for our supramax operation, both of which were updated at the end of each day, and which extended out twelve months with each column representing a week. The first column had the name of each ship in our fleet, and in subsequent columns the number "7" was inserted representing seven days of available ship supply that week. For instance, if we had a ship on charter for four months, the number "7" would be entered along the row for a total of sixteen columns representing sixteen weeks of available supply. The fleet list included all our long-term period charters, and our medium- and short-term charters. If we had forty ships at a given point in time, when the rows were tallied, they would show a vessel supply of 280 days per week. And this was done on a week-by-week basis, going forward twelve months.

Then, farther down the spreadsheet, we would have a section that represented freight commitments that the company had on its books. If we had a contract to move bauxite from Port Kamsar in Guinea, West Africa to Port Alfred, Quebec, we would enter the number of days required to carry the cargo. If the voyage, including load and discharge times, was estimated to take thirty-two days, in the row representing the cargo lift, we would enter four "7s" and one "4" under the five columns representing the dates during which the cargo was to be moved. And we would do this for all our freight commitments, going forward twelve months.

Following this, we would have a section for our derivative positions. For example, if we had booked four cargoes of grain at a fixed rate to be moved over six months, and following the lifting of the first cargo, we thought the market was moving up, we could "protect" the remaining cargoes by buying three thirty-day freight derivatives or a quarterly derivative covering ninety days. And we would enter this position on the spreadsheet.

The physical ship exposures, the freight exposures, and the derivative exposures were then tallied up to provide the profile of Navios's net long or short position every week, going forward a year. This was updated at the end of every trading day, and it was an important document, because one could look at it and very quickly get a sense of the company's exposure to the market. If our thinking was that the market was going to rally over the next six months, we would want to increase our exposure to the market, and we could do this in one of three ways: charter more ships to augment our existing fleet; try to fix (relet) some of our freight business to another owner; or buy some freight derivatives; or a combination of the three options.

The Trading Fleet Balance was a very effective tool to help us manage the exposure Navios had to the market on any given day. But for the uninitiated, it was difficult to understand and looked to be quite complex, even though its fundamental design simplified the strategic management of our business.

For about the next five hours, until just before midnight, Bruce and I reviewed our business lines, developed some very broad market numbers for the next few years, and played around with back-of-the-envelope calculations of valuation and projected profitability. We both came to the same conclusion: Subject to conservative market assumptions, Navios's future was strong and could possibly interest potential financial backers to invest alongside management in a buyout of the company.

Over the next week, I approached separately the nine or ten key managers in Navios (including the two Soler brothers, who ran our Uruguayan terminal business) to see if they would be receptive to the idea of our acquiring the company from Fednav. All but two of them were on board. One colleague said he thought we should stay in the Fednav fold, and another told me he had no interest in investing in a management buyout of the company. I was surprised by the reaction of these two integral executives. I had always assumed that everyone thought like me—get a piece of the rock. But that is not the case, of course, as different people have different tolerances for risk.

I decided that trying to develop a buyout of Navios quietly without Fednav first giving me the go-ahead to do so—in other words, going behind their back—might not be the best approach with Ladi. I also knew that he did not have anyone in Montreal whom he could parachute down to Connecticut to run Navios, should he decide to fire me. So, in February, I set up a meeting with him in Montreal.

Ladi struck me as being nervous, and I believe he was expecting me to tell him I had accepted a new position and would be leaving the company. He was therefore surprised when I told him that I would like to try and buy Navios from Fednav.

"Tony, where are you going to find the funds for this? Do you have backers already lined up for such an acquisition?" he asked.

I explained that I was not about to embark on such an effort without first getting his agreement to do so. I also told him that the key management team in Navios had agreed to support me in such an effort. Ladi said he would think it over and get back to me.

Although this was a gamble on my part, I thought my situation in Navios did not leave me much choice. Fednav was hesitating on a new management structure, and if something did not happen soon, I was likely to leave. Nevertheless, I knew I had significant bargaining power. Ladi had not sent John Weale down to run Navios, and following my earlier trip to Montreal, he had decided moving the company up to Quebec was not a realistic option. Perhaps most crucially, my instincts were signaling that Fednav wanted to get control of the Cominco contract, and I recognized that ultimately parting with this asset would be very useful in reducing the amount of cash required to buy Navios.

About a month later, Ladi called, catching me as I was about to depart on yet another trip to the Far East.

"Tony, raising capital is not an area in which you have any expertise, and I do not want to see us wasting our time as you try to acquire Navios, and you lose sight of running the business...my business."

"Ladi, I have a good team around me, and I believe that I can continue to effectively run Navios, while trying to put together a management buyout. In addition, over the past few years, I have learned much from Sean on the financial aspects of the business, and, in particular, dealing with sourcing outside capital." I also took the opportunity to remind him that I continued to have an invested interest in the business, as I owned 3 percent of the company.

He asked me how I would value the business. I explained that, given the company did not have a large base of assets, the simplest method would be to perform a discounted cash flow analysis of our various business lines. I said I could have the team develop a scenario based on estimated dry bulk market rates and plug these into a cash flow model that would punch out expected cash earnings, going forward for two years, and tie these back to retroactive earnings for three years.

He then asked how I would segment the business lines, and I said I would propose a breakdown by vessel and freight earnings against a given market scenario, and to that, I would add the earnings from our Uruguayan terminal business. I continued: "And the derivative side of the business, *which is growing rapidly*, is easy because we can mark-to-market our positions at any time." I threw out this last point in a somewhat cavalier fashion, which I knew he would not like and would make him nervous. But it was true—our derivative business was growing substantially. What had started as a few derivative contracts to help us understand this paper market, as it was developing in the 1980s, had morphed a decade later into a rather sophisticated, at least by maritime standards, business line for us.

Ladi again said that he would like to mull it over and that he would get back to me, which he did in early March, giving me the go-ahead. In the meantime, he had John Peacock, the executive vice president of Fednav responsible for financial management, call me. John asked, "Tony, do you really think you can pull this off?" And I replied, "John, I honestly don't know, but I promise you, I will give it my best effort."

∗∗

By the end of March, Bruce and I had put together a visual management presentation of Navios that covered the evolution of the company from a maritime transport company of ore for U.S. Steel to the complex, multifaceted, and leveraged trading business it had become. We laid out our primary lines of business: Navios International operating the panamax fleet, Navios Handybulk operating the supramax fleet, Navios Uruguay managing the terminal we had in that country, the company's overall derivative activity, and Navios Ship Agencies. In addition, the presentation reviewed the responsibilities and backgrounds of the key senior management team.

Once we had the presentation in place, I sat down with our integral executives to explain that Fednav had given me the green light to lead a management buyout of Navios. I told them that for the next few months I was going to focus my efforts on raising capital for such a buyout. The oversight of the day-to-day activity would be left to three key commercial executives: Mike McClure, Ted Petrone, and Shunji Sasada, all of whom were very supportive of the initiative and who would be management investors, alongside Bruce, me, and the Soler brothers. Mike oversaw the derivative trading activity; Ted was responsible for our panamax operation; Shunji for our supramax activity.

I liked that these three colleagues had different backgrounds, and when taken together, they provided Navios with a good deal of commercial firepower. Ted had graduated from a U.S. marine academy and spent some time at sea before joining Navios Ship Management in New York City in 1980. With the move out to Connecticut and the sale of the owned fleet, he progressed into vessel operations; and a few years later, he moved into the chartering area, where he quickly took on increasing responsibilities.

I hired Shunji in 1997 as Navios was becoming increasingly more active in the supramax arena. His background with MOSK in Tokyo, and later Trinity Bulk Carriers in Oslo, was unique for a Japanese national. Shunji complemented our other commercial executives.

Mike was one of the longest-serving members of Navios, having first arrived at the company in 1977, when it was still located in Nassau. He had an accounting background, but in the early 1980s, he moved into commercial contract negotiations. For a time, he also had responsibilities for our Uruguay terminal. Following Sean's return to Navios in 1989, we had set up a separate derivative trading desk; it was Sean who nominated Mike to manage and grow it.

In April, armed with what I thought was a strong presentation and a gung-ho attitude, I commenced the search for capital. I did not want to incur large advisory fees, so I contacted one of my close friends who operated a small investment advisory firm in New York. He provided me with a list of about thirty names that he thought might be possible candidates. I started knocking on the doors of banks, private equity groups, and some hedge funds, as well as some of the large North American pension funds and private family offices. When I discussed the plan with CVC they made clear they were not interested and preferred to be bought out of their equity position.

During April and May 1999, I must have made over fifteen presentations, most of them on my own, as I wanted Bruce in the office keeping an eye on things. But these meetings provided an interesting insight for me. Although my background was commercial, I was very comfortable with the financial aspects of the business, which reflected almost a decade working closely with Sean. Fortunately, most of the presentations took place in New York, Boston, and Chicago, so I was able to stay in touch if any serious operational issues arose. It was physically exhausting, and by the end of May, I still had not found any interested investors. I was beginning to doubt my ability to pull it off. But I knew I needed to stay focused on the long game and not let the daily grind get the best of me.

It was at the very end of May that I had a meeting with an investment banker at the Bank of Boston. After my pitch, he said the bank would not find such a deal attractive, but he thought there might be a group on the West Coast that might be interested in structuring an investment to purchase

Navios. Two days later, he called to tell me he had spoken with a company based in Seattle called Saltchuk Resources. They had indicated a preliminary interest in hearing what I had to say. To give him credit, he never charged me a finder's fee for the introduction.

***

I did a little digging into the company before the presentation. Saltchuk was created in the early 1980s by a group of Pacific Northwest investors as a vehicle to acquire Totem Ocean Trailer Express, a U.S. flag liner operation providing marine transport between the U.S. West Coast and Alaska. Later that decade, they acquired Foss Maritime, a large U.S. flag family-owned tug and barge company located in Seattle. The company has since expanded into ownership of other tug and barge services located in Hawaii, as well as domestic inland freight services.

Although I was unfamiliar with the Saltchuk name, I was very familiar with Foss Maritime because of the close working relationship Navios developed with this company in managing the maritime aspects of the Cominco Red Dog project. I suspected that Saltchuk must have received a positive report on Navios from them, which likely contributed to their interest in meeting with me.

Using the introduction from Bank of Boston, I called their office and arranged a meeting. A few days later, on Thursday, June 3, 1999, I flew out to meet them for the first time. I arrived very late that evening and stayed at a small, modest hotel located within walking distance of their office. I awoke the following morning thinking this could be our last opportunity. Their offices, located along the shore of Lake Union, were new and had a great vibe. I arrived there a bit early, and an assistant led me to a conference room overlooking the water. Within a few minutes four individuals arrived, dressed in jeans and casual shirts with down vests...the laid-back "West Coast" look. I immediately felt very overdressed in my "East Coast" business suit.

Brian Bogen and Chuck Kauffman were the two individuals I had arranged to meet with, and they had a few others from Saltchuk join the meeting. From what I could glean, Brian and Chuck were responsible for searching out new investment opportunities, and they were leading point on the meeting. I gave the Saltchuk team a two-hour presentation, and during a working lunch, I spent a few hours answering questions. About three-quarters of the way through the presentation, an older man dressed in workout sweats entered and quietly sat at the far end of the room listening to the

Q&A. He did not say anything and left shortly before the meeting broke up. I later found out that he was Mike Garvey, the CEO of Saltchuk.

I left the Saltchuk office without a strong sense that they were interested in the Navios proposition. On the way to SeaTac Airport, to catch my flight back to New York, I mulled over the meeting. I thought it went well, and their team had asked a lot of good, pointed questions. Nevertheless, I knew from my research that every maritime investment Saltchuk had was focused on the ownership of domestic U.S. flag physical assets. I wasn't sure Navios fit their investment criteria. I thought the trading nature of our business would probably seem alien to them.

The following Monday morning, my office landline rang. Brian Bogen was calling from Seattle.

"Tony," he said in his distinctive West Coast accent, "I am calling to say Saltchuk is interested in pursuing this investment. Chuck Kauffman and I would like to fly out tomorrow night to spend Wednesday through Friday in your offices to meet the rest of your team and start due diligence."

I was stunned. As I later learned, the quick turnaround was symptomatic of how this team operated.

Following three days of meetings with Brian and Chuck—which included me, Bruce, Ted, Mike, and Shunji—I came away thinking that we just might be able to move the process forward successfully. I reached out to Fednav to explain that we had found an interested investor, and I gave them some background on Saltchuk. They gave me the green light to pursue the opportunity.

We had some due diligence meetings throughout June with Saltchuk. These were focused and professional, largely because of the efforts of Bruce Hoag and his team. We managed to address all the questions posed to us about our corporate structure and finances. Saltchuk was not just focused on numbers. They took a close look at the Navios management team, and they came away impressed with what they saw. During my initial presentation to Saltchuk, I had expounded on the strength and experiences of our key managers. I had described how we all had witnessed and worked through the great dry bulk recession of the mid-1980s to make the company stronger and more agile. I explained that I believed the management team was a crucial asset of the company.

Bruce and I had a good "feel" for the Navios numbers. We knew how much we could afford to pay for the acquisition based on future cash flow projections derived from high, low, and base case market scenarios. But I made the decision early in the process that I did not want to negotiate a purchase price with Fednav until I had found an interested coinvestor for our business. I simply felt that it would make my life much easier if I could come to some broad understanding of how we jointly valued the enterprise and then present that number to Ladi and his team in Montreal.

CHAPTER 19

THE NAVIOS PURCHASE

*"'Price is what you pay; value is what you get.' Whether
we are talking about socks or stocks, I like buying
quality merchandise when it is marked down."*

WARREN BUFFETT

———————

B y the end of June, we had progressed sufficiently in our discussions
with Saltchuk that I felt it was time to do two things: set up a meeting with Fednav to explain that we had made considerable headway
with the buyout efforts and endeavor to get a price locked down with them,
and retain lawyers to represent management in our negotiations with both
Saltchuk and Fednav.

Having agreed to a ballpark value with Saltchuk for the acquisition of
Navios, I flew up to Montreal in early July 1999 to meet with Ladi and his
team to see if we might be able to reach an agreement on price. This was a
difficult negotiation for me because I was trying to buy the company from
the majority shareholder to whom I reported. If we were unsuccessful, I was
not at all certain I would have a future in Navios or within the Fednav group.
By that point, I had resigned myself to the fact that a failure would likely
mean a search for a new job.

Over a day, I managed to hammer out an agreement on price for Navios.
I was surprised at how quickly this came about. But again, it was an indication to me of how badly Fednav wanted to be rid of the business that had
drained significant financial resources from the company in the mid-1980s.

The agreed-upon purchase price was $28.8 million. The major valuation
metrics were as follows:

- Navios Pacific Inc. (NPI) owned the Cominco Red Dog contract, and NPI was itself owned 67 percent by Navios and 33 percent by Fednav. It was clear to me that this was the key asset that enabled us to get Fednav to the negotiating table. Ladi felt that the NPI contract should be controlled and managed by Fednav because it was a business that involved transporting commodities north of the Arctic Circle. The freight market was very weak in July 1999. We valued this contract by applying summer market time-charter rates against the adjustable fixed-rate contract that we had with Cominco. The baseline pricing of the contract was structured against the amortization of a hypothetical newbuilding panamax and supramax ship with a built-in return on equity, and there were annual allowances for cost-of-living increases applied to an assumed 1988 baseline vessel-operating cost. Essentially, the lower the freight market, the more profitable the contract. We agreed a valuation of $15.4 million for the remaining eleven years of the Red Dog contract, and Fednav "acquired" Navios's 67 percent ownership of the contract for $10.3 million, which meant we had to raise that much, less cash, to close the deal.

- Corporación Navios Sociedad Anónima (Navios Uruguay) was valued at $15.1 million based on financial metrics that incorporated balance sheet value, as well as three-year historical and two-year forward EBITDA numbers. (EBITDA stands for "earnings before interest, taxes, depreciation, and amortization.") What was very apparent to me, but understandably not on Fednav's radar screen, was that the throughput volumes of grain at our terminal could make a dramatic increase. I knew from some meetings over the previous twelve months with our large contract partners in South America that the export market for soybeans was expected to increase significantly because of new Chinese demand.

- Navios International Inc. (NI), our panamax operation, and Navios Handybulk Inc (NHI), our supramax division, were operating a time-chartered fleet of about forty ships that summer, most of which were on charter for periods of a year or less. We did have a half-dozen longer-term panamax charters with purchase options, which in the middle of the 1999 summer did not look too attractive. And all the freight business we had on our books was annually rated. We valued these business lines at $2 million.

- The Navios derivative trading operation was easily marked-to-market, and this part of our business was valued at just under $500,000.
- The balance of the acquisition was made up of $900,000 for our wholly owned subsidiary ship agency business, Navios Ship Agencies, and some working capital adjustments.

The goodwill associated with the Navios name had no value placed on it, and this, together with Navios Uruguay, to my mind, were the real gems of the company.

Because of the historical ownership of Navios dating back to U.S. Steel, our signature was considered sacrosanct in the marketplace. On any given day, NI or NHI could enter the market and charter a half-dozen ships without the owners questioning our motives or looking to see financials; and, perhaps more amazing, we were able to lock down multiyear charters with purchase options on the back of our name only. The same was true with contracts of affreightment. When we would chase after the transportation of a particular movement of commodity, there was never any question about who Navios was or what we did. I recall sitting in a meeting in Caracas in the early 1990s when someone looked at me and said, "The Navios name in this country is as well-known as Coca-Cola." We were always viewed as a company that "performed," through thick and thin. It was a well-earned reputation that was honed under the leadership of both Sean Day and me.

Navios had always been a subsidiary of other major corporate entities—U.S. Steel, Fednav, and Citigroup Venture Capital. The one concern I had about the acquisition was losing this ability to maneuver so easily in the dry bulk markets—chartering ships, fixing contracts of affreightment, trading derivatives—because the market might view the management ownership of Navios as being on a less sound financial footing. The reason for this is that in a management buyout, it is the managers of a business who are buying it. Because in most cases it is unlikely that management has the financial resources to offer up much equity, these transactions are generally viewed as being highly leveraged.

The tremendous flexibility of being active in the market would be essential to allow us not just to operate, but, more importantly, to grow the company in the years ahead. Before I departed Montreal, I reached an understanding with John Peacock and Carl Lee that if a sale eventually materialized, it could not be portrayed to the dry bulk market at large as a "management buyout," which is effectively what it was. We agreed that we would not use that term in any future negotiations, nor would it be used in any press releases, should the sale materialize.

***

Now that I had locked down with Fednav a price for the acquisition, I knew it was time to retain outside legal merger and acquisition advice. Immediately upon my return to Connecticut, a colleague suggested that there might be a lawyer at Healy & Baillie who would be perfect to represent management in our acquisition effort.

Healy & Baillie was a small firm based in Manhattan with about thirty lawyers, but it was perhaps the most prominent maritime legal firm in the United States. I reached out to John Kimball, who was the managing partner, and explained to him what we were up to. He told me his co-managing partner, a gentleman named Robert Shaw, would be the ideal candidate to represent us.

A few days later, Robert arrived in our office, and he was in our boardroom talking with two Navios executives when I walked in to greet him for the first time. There I found this tall, somewhat reserved, lanky Englishman, who spoke with an upper-crust British accent, the one associated with educational institutions such as English public schools (in the United States, these were private schools) and Oxford. He stood to greet me wearing a tweed jacket in the middle of summer, complemented by a ruffled pair of pants.

I knew this was not an easy legal project to consummate. Not only were we trying to buy Navios, but we still had to finalize detailed contractual terms with Saltchuk, as they would be new investors, alongside management in Navios. In a transaction such as the one we were contemplating, there were hundreds of documents to be negotiated and agreed upon between management and Saltchuk, and between the buyers and sellers of Navios. Besides the key documents we had various releases, resignations, indemnifications, noncompetes, board resolutions, etc.

To his credit, Robert seemed up for the challenge, and we retained his services.

From mid-July through the end of August, Robert, Bruce, and I spent much of our time in meetings with Saltchuk, primarily in Seattle. Two essential documents needed to be structured with Saltchuk: a shareholder's agreement that reflected management's ownership and control of the company, while always providing Saltchuk with sufficient protections as a minority investor; and the loan agreement between Saltchuk and Navios.

The Uruguay terminal was the one significant asset that we had against which we had no debt, but rather a steady stream of income, and it was this asset that we used to raise $15.5 million by way of a loan from Saltchuk. Navios was the borrower under the loan, which was secured by a stock pledge agreement of the shares of Navios Uruguay, which is relatively simple. However, the actual asset was based in Uruguay on land not owned, but leased, by Navios from the government. Saltchuk had no experience dealing with Uruguay (nor did their outside legal counsel), and so this part of the negotiation proved to be tedious. Fortunately, our long-term lease had recently been extended for twenty years to 2020, with an option for a further twenty years thereafter.

The loan document included some standard financial covenants such as current ratio, EBITDA/interest ratio, and tangible net worth provision, but Saltchuk recognized the trading nature of our business, and the covenants were not onerous. The loan specified an interest rate of 470 basis points above LIBOR, and a repayment period of seven years based on a fifteen-year profile, which we were able to service comfortably from the existing operations.

It was toward the middle of August when Robert pulled me aside to say we had a potential problem. Given that Saltchuk and the majority of the management investors were based in the United States, the new Navios would fall under the U.S. tax net as a controlled foreign corporation.

We agreed we should quickly take some tax advice on the matter. The tax advisor suggested the easiest way to address the situation would be to issue some preferred stock to a foreign entity, which, for the purposes of the U.S. tax code, would be viewed as equity on our balance sheet. He recommended that the level of preferred issuance should exceed the common by a comfortable margin. We had structured the management buyout so that $1.25 million bought 100 percent of the common shares of Navios.

I had very quickly come to realize that Robert was indeed a problem solver. Every time an issue crept up on us during the negotiations with Saltchuk, he found a work-around that satisfied both parties. Perhaps equally significant, he had a very deep Rolodex. Through a financial contact in Greece, whom he knew well and trusted, and whose company focused on the maritime sector, he was told that the Leventis-David family might well be interested in an investment in Navios.

This family is a large, prominent Greek-Cypriot family who has many investments in both public and privately owned companies throughout the world. Perhaps the thing I have come to admire most about them is their low-key approach to business and, for the most part, a propensity to stay outside of the limelight. After sharing some Navios data with them during the last two weeks of August, they requested a meeting. Because we were in the middle of detailed contractual negotiations, I decided to make a quick trip over to Greece to meet this family on my own, and left Bruce and Robert in place so as not to disrupt the negotiations, which were well advanced.

I arrived in Athens about midday on Tuesday, September 7, 1999, after an overnight flight from New York, and taxied straight to the Athens Hilton to check into my room on the eleventh floor. I quickly unpacked, had a good hot shower, and then decided to reach out to Bruce to make sure all was okay back at Navios. About three minutes into the phone call, the floor beneath me started to tremble. As it got progressively worse, the whole building started to sway, and I realized it was an earthquake. I hung up with Bruce, quickly dressed, and made my way out to the corridor and then the stairwell.

Many people were rushing down the stairs, and I bumped into a young woman who was carrying a small child, while holding the hands of a five-year-old, who was struggling to make her way down the crowded stairwell. I reached out and offered to help. She nodded gratefully, and the tiny child, who could not have been more than a year old, just jumped into my open arms. I proceeded to carry her down eleven flights, followed by the others. We then spent the next six hours walking around the outside of the hotel waiting for it to be examined to ensure there was no structural damage. This was a bad earthquake, with widespread damage throughout the city and about 150 deaths.

Needless to say, this did not seem like an auspicious way to begin a new business relationship.

I arrived at the Leventis-David family office the following morning to find cracked walls and some pieces of art on the floor. Anastassis David greeted me and we sat down in a large conference room. But due to a few small aftershocks, we eventually left to sit in the garden of a colleague's home to continue our discussions. I found Anastassis to be very focused, and for someone who was not directly involved in shipping, he seemed to know a good deal about it. We met again later for a dinner and we had a very collegial and relaxed time. We ended the evening with Anastassis telling me he would discuss the opportunity with some of his family members and get back to me quickly.

Two days after my return to the office, I received a call saying that Leventis would agree to invest $1.75 million for nonvoting preferred stock of Navios. Things were beginning to fall into place.

***

Most of the time spent in negotiation with Saltchuk revolved around the terms of the shareholders agreement, and this is one area in which Mike Garvey took an active role. He was a highly respected Seattle lawyer by background, but he was also a man with a considerable amount of common sense. Mike understood business, and he found his match in Robert. Many of the terms of the shareholders agreement were boilerplate: nomination and removal of directors, the definition of major decisions, dividend policy, etc. But it was the section on restrictions on the transfer of Navios shares postclosing where the negotiations got bogged down. Saltchuk was understandably very focused on the fact that their partners in the venture consisted of eight management investors who collectively ran the business they were investing in, and Mike was rightly concerned about two principal scenarios: death and disability or cessation of employment of one or more of the management investors.

We agreed to a formula whereby Navios would acquire a departing management investor share, with 50 percent of the purchase price of such shares reflecting shareholder equity, as of the date of departure; and the remaining 50 percent based on a five-year earn-out reflecting the preceding four years and the year of departure.

There was also a focus on the disposition of shares and who might have the right to buy them. Saltchuk agreed that in the event of a death or the involuntary departure of a management partner, Navios should have the right to buy the shares; in the second instance, the common shareholders should have the right to buy them in amounts proportionate to their respective shareholdings; and in the third instance, to a third party that Saltchuk and the management investors agreed to.

This type of sensible approach was characteristic of the Saltchuk philosophy.

Toward the middle of September, I received a call from Ladi saying he was sending John Peacock and Carl Lee down to New York to meet with me, and he asked if Bruce Hoag and I could drive out to LaGuardia Airport the following morning, where they would arrange a conference room for our meeting.

We walked into a dreary meeting room on the third floor of the airport and were greeted by John and Carl. After a few pleasantries, John announced Ladi had decided that as part of the sale of Navios, he now wanted Fednav to keep the Uruguay terminal. This created a huge problem, as the structure of our agreement with Saltchuk was very much dependent on this property. I could not believe they were changing a fundamental term of the purchase at this late date.

I stood up, looked at John, and said, "I have had enough. I am done! Go find yourself another CEO." And I walked out of the room, with Bruce scrambling to follow me. And I will never forget Bruce's words to me as we walked through LaGuardia terminal, out to the parking garage for the drive back to Stamford. He looked at me and, in his typical quiet demeanor, said, "Well, Tony, I think it is safe to say that meeting did not go well."

The following morning, I received a call from John Peacock telling me that he had convinced Ladi to reconsider, but that I needed to get the deal done quickly before Ladi again changed his mind.

The last surprise I had before closing the transaction was Fednav's insistence on Navios agreeing to a ten-year noncompete to "not directly or indirectly own, manage, control, trade, or operate international ocean tonnage trading into or out of the Great Lakes." This never came up until we first saw it in a late redline draft from Fednav of the stock redemption agreement. I balked at this: Trading oceangoing ships into and out of the Great Lakes was where I had first made my start in shipping, and I thought it was unsportsmanlike for Fednav to raise this at the eleventh hour. But Robert, who is always very levelheaded, quickly managed to talk me down and get me focused on the more pertinent issues. We did negotiate a carve-out that would permit Navios to "acquire a non-controlling interest in any publicly held entity" that was operating into or out of the Great Lakes.

We closed the management buyout of Navios Corporation on October 29, 1999, in New York City. The common stock of the company was bought for $1.25 million, with 55 percent owned by management, 40 percent by Saltchuk, and 5 percent by the Leventis-David family, with the latter group subscribing for $1.75 million of nonvoting preferred stock. This $3 million and the $15.5 million loan from Saltchuk, together with the sale of Navios's 67 percent interest in NPI, which was valued at $10.3 million, is how we funded the transaction.

CHAPTER 20

CHANGING COURSE

"Even if you are on the right track, you'll
get run over if you just sit there."

WILL ROGERS,
American humorist and social commentator

———————

For a period following the buyout, I worked with an outside management consultant to talk through issues the company faced. I retained him because it allowed me to speak freely and share thoughts I had with respect to the company and our employees. In return, he provided me with a completely impartial perspective on our business. One proposal he had was an inverted-triangle management structure, as opposed to the more common triangle where everyone reports "up" the triangle, eventually leading to a titular head.

I used this as an example with our employees to indicate that the Navios CEO was at the bottom of the inverted triangle, and it was the responsibility of that leader to provide financial, technical, and personnel support to everyone throughout the organization so that they could effectively execute their responsibilities. This floor-up, not top-down, flat organizational structure seemed ideally suited for the flexible, self-motivated, and adaptive culture of Navios. Everyone had an equal stake in making the company a success.

Now that we were free from Fednav's rigid corporate management paradigm, I realized we needed a strong new team to lead Navios. Bruce had the financials covered. Our talented senior executives and managers continued their excellent work handling the divisions they knew best. Given my new position as chief executive officer of Navios, I knew I had to spend more time focused across the broad spectrum of our business, with a new emphasis on strategic development. I wanted someone who would help me keep the big picture at the top of my mind and could help marshal my strengths to the best effect. Robert Shaw was the logical choice.

During the management buyout negotiations, for four extremely intense months, I worked very closely with Robert. Not only did he have an acute legal mind and tremendous experience in charter party disputes and maritime law, but he also had significant experience with corporate transactions, bond offerings, and some merger and acquisition work. However, he had built a successful career as a leading maritime attorney, and I was not sure he would be interested in making the change to corporate management.

About two months after we closed the deal, I reached out to ask if I might buy him lunch. We agreed to meet at his club in New York City. About halfway through a relaxed meal, during which we reminisced about some of the battles we had fought just a few months earlier, I told him that after giving it much thought, I wanted him to consider joining the Navios executive team.

Robert was quite surprised and flattered by my offer. But his initial reaction was negative. He explained that he had never worked on the operating side of the maritime business, but rather always on the legal/service side. There was also the issue of compensation. He shared what he was earning as a senior partner at Healy & Baillie. Because Robert had been involved in all the details of the management buyout, he knew the salary structure of the Navios executives. He recognized his current compensation package was much more than Navios could afford to pay.

But I knew I could offer him something the law firm could not: an equity stake in a successful and growing maritime company.

He seemed intrigued but voiced his concerns about how the other management investors might react to his arrival in the company, his operational inexperience in the nuts and bolts of the maritime industry, and the change in his perceived role as an outside attorney to an executive manager.

"And what about Saltchuk? I am not sure they and the other management investors would be open to having their stake in the company diluted with the issuance of additional stock so soon after closing the purchase," he explained.

My response was that all the parties had come to know him during the buyout negotiations and had been very impressed with his knowledge and capabilities. I was confident that they would welcome him as an asset to the team to assist moving the company into the future.

By the end of our lunch, Robert agreed to think about the proposition and get back to me.

Up until the time of my lunch meeting, I had not divulged my thoughts concerning Robert to any of the other senior executives. The dust had only recently settled from the management buyout, and I felt it was important to get everyone focused on the business of managing and growing the company. But having finally broached the matter with Robert, and sensing that there was indeed an interest on his part to consider the matter further, I decided to discuss the idea with Bruce. It would be crucial for me to get a "buy-in" from him on what I was proposing. Bruce responded in his usual reserved manner: "I think this is a brilliant idea, Tony." The conversation quickly turned to another pressing personnel concern: the employment termination of the senior executive in charge of fleet operations.

When I announced the plan to acquire the company from Fednav, he had voiced concerns about the buyout. He had worked at Navios for about twenty years and was comfortable working within the larger corporate structure of Fednav. Perhaps more significantly, he doubted management could assume ownership of Navios and successfully grow the business. But despite his concerns, he signed on.

While he had executed his responsibilities well, I believed he did not have the same "fire in his belly" approach to the business that I knew the new Navios team would need. I required an enthusiastic commitment from every management partner in order to make the buyout succeed. I had shared my concerns with Bruce, but we hadn't arrived at a decision about the future of this senior executive.

Under the terms of the new shareholders agreement, we had the option of terminating the employment of a management shareholder and buying out his equity based on a pre-agreed formula.

As Robert noted, I thought it was very important to get a buy-in from Saltchuk on what I was considering, both in having Robert join the team and the possible termination of a senior management investor. So, I flew out to Seattle for a face-to-face meeting to walk through with them the ramifications of what it was I was proposing.

As I thought, they respected Robert and felt he would be an asset. However, their main area of concern was the fallout it might create with the other management investors. In other words, "If this can happen to him, I suppose it could happen to me." Nevertheless, because they could see I felt so strongly that this was the right strategic move for Navios, they went along with my proposal, although I sensed somewhat reluctantly.

It caused me some sleepless nights as I stewed and thought through the ramifications of what I was proposing. But I kept thinking back to one of the lessons I had learned from Michael Bell years before: Sometimes, if you think you have a great idea, you just have to barrel ahead with it and deal with the consequences. And so that is what I did.

It took another three months of cajoling and off-site meetings before I eventually managed to convince Robert to come on board as executive vice president and general counsel for the corporation. He would work closely with me in formulating a growth strategy for the company. Once Robert accepted the offer, I terminated the employment of the other executive, had the company buy back his stock, and then sold this equity share to Robert as part of his employment agreement.

It was not an easy decision to hire a second-in-command from outside the organization, particularly in a tight-knit community such as Navios, while at the same time letting one of the other integral executives go. It was probably the most difficult decision I had made during my tenure at the company. But with the benefit of hindsight, I can say that it was the right decision.

***

A year after Sean Day rejoined Navios in 1989, we had moved the head office from Greenwich to Stamford, Connecticut. Now our lease on the Stamford office was about to expire, and the building management wanted us to extend at a higher rent. But I was very focused on keeping a tight rein on our corporate overhead, particularly as we had just concluded the management buyout. Further, as the area of lower Fairfield County developed, the traffic along the I-95 corridor had become much more intolerable. So, early in 2000, Bruce Hoag and I spent several weeks visiting second-tier office buildings located primarily in the immediate area to get a sense of what else might be available for less money.

One day, the broker we had retained to help us look for new offices showed us a listing in an old three-story, long-abandoned lock-manufacturing building, located down near the waterfront in the center of Norwalk, Connecticut. It had been shuttered for years, required a great deal of work, and was in the process of being renovated. The day we visited the space, we were told to watch out for holes in the floor and beware of exposed steel beams and nails that were being uncovered from layers of cement. I walked out thinking this space would never be appropriate as the head office for a company like Navios.

But, as Bruce pointed out, it had some pluses. There would be a 25 percent reduction in our annual lease expense. The landlord would pay for the up-front build-out of our space. It was within walking distance of numerous restaurants, shops, and pubs, something that was sorely lacking with our old Stamford office. Perhaps the biggest advantage was that relocating to Norwalk would significantly cut the commute time for 90 percent of our staff.

Two weeks later, we returned with a design consultant and walked around the space for a second time. She was able to help Bruce and I visualize what could be achieved with the space. Leaving the exposed steel beams, original red brick walls, and uncovered commercial venting systems running throughout the ceilings would give the space a "hip" deconstructed look and allow for an airy feeling associated with an open-plan concept, with very few offices. We decided to take the plunge, and six months later, we moved into more suitable, fresh new offices at considerably less cost than our previous building.

Concurrent with the move, we decided to establish new office hours: Monday through Thursday, 7 a.m. to 5 p.m., and Friday, 7 a.m. to 11 a.m. There were two benefits to the early-morning start: A significant amount of our business was centered on European time, so we were able to work this geographic area more efficiently, and the early commute meant there was much less traffic on the roads, making it an even easier drive. And everyone, of course, loved the early getaway on Friday.

***

One of the benefits of having been Sean Day's right-hand man for close to a decade was that I was able to watch how he allocated his time amongst the commercial, financial, and operations areas of Navios. I was fortunate that Sean had a background in operations and finance, so, to a great extent, he gave me free rein to run the commercial side of the business. But I learned a great deal from him concerning overall management, and some of this I was able to apply to the "new" Navios. Initially I spent most of my time working with Bruce focusing on the financial areas of our business. This was very important, given that we had just structured a highly leveraged transaction and no longer had CVC or Fednav behind us to prop us up if we got into trouble.

Robert arrived at Navios in early 2000. Because many of the legal disputes that arise in the maritime business revolve around operational issues, I had him take over responsibility for the operations of our chartered fleet, in place of the senior executive who had left. In the early months following his arrival, I spent a considerable amount of time with him, knowing that he would have an adjustment period. While he knew about our operations theoretically, most of his onboarding dealt with the everyday practicality of running a large fleet of ships, finding his way with the other operational managers reporting to him, and, of course, the many and sundry legal issues that crop up in fleet operations, in which he was able to quickly immerse himself, much to the benefit of the company.

Following the new, more inclusive corporate structure, we initiated a daily morning trading meeting that was attended by all the commercial physical and derivative traders in Norwalk, and later, our Piraeus office via videoconference. Robert and Bruce would join most mornings as would I when I was not traveling. It was a great way for me to maintain a perspective on the pulse of the commercial activity of Navios.

I made it clear from the outset that everyone who sat in on these morning meetings was encouraged to voice their opinions openly and without judgment. It made for some interesting debates. I recall shortly after we had instituted these meetings making a comment about the derivative market and getting blindsided by a young trader who explained why my thought process was all wrong. Although I disagreed with his thinking, I loved the fact that he felt comfortable enough to push back on the CEO.

These morning trading meetings quickly became no-holds-barred gatherings, and I, as well as all the commercial staff, thoroughly enjoyed them. Everyone felt free to comment and debate various commercial initiatives the company was undertaking every day, and I believe it helped to strengthen our trading capabilities.

***

As part of the restructuring of the company, we decided to sell Navios Ship Agencies. I met with George Duffy, its longtime president, and explained our position. Before opening it up to a competitive bidding process, we wanted to allow him the opportunity to conclude a management buyout of the agency business. Grateful for the opportunity, he and a few of his leading managers bought NSA for $1.5 million, with very little fanfare in the marketplace.

We agreed to allow them to continue operating under the name of Navios Ship Agencies, which was crucial for them to help retain existing business and find new clients under the established brand. It had the added benefit of shielding us from questions concerning our financial stability so soon after the acquisition.

It was also a small but welcome cash infusion into Navios at a time when I was very focused on deleveraging the business.

***

I continued traveling to Asia, regularly visiting Japan, mainland China, and Hong Kong, but Indonesia and Singapore less frequently, to maintain relations with important maritime chartering clients there. Many of these trips were to meet with other shipowners or ship financiers to our industry as well as to meet with existing customers. I had witnessed the tremendous growth in and around Tokyo in the 1980s, and by the end of the 1990s, it was apparent to me that several cities in China were starting their period of tremendous development. The expansion that one could see in and around the cities of Beijing, Shanghai, Dalian, and Qinhuangdao was staggering; and every time I returned to these growing cities, entire sections were unrecognizable because of new construction.

I became increasingly convinced that the dry bulk markets eventually had to be impacted by this new wave of urbanization. Then in late 2001, China was admitted to the World Trade Organization (WTO), which accelerated this growth exponentially.

During the Clinton administration's second term, the U.S. government became a strong proponent of China's inclusion into the WTO for two overriding reasons: one economic and the other political. China was then the world's sixth-largest economy, and the thinking was that its acceptance into the WTO would promote increasing levels of global trade, which would benefit the United States. And this is precisely what happened, although to a much greater extent than anyone ever imagined.

Following China's admission into the WTO, its economy experienced one of the most remarkable surges in history, causing demand for, and the price of, dry bulk commodities to increase enormously as the country expanded its industrial and manufacturing bases and grew its modern cities. The impact this had on our freight markets was dramatic. China's economy surged, as did the dry bulk markets. The daily spot market earnings for supramax and panamax ships went from an average of about $10,000 or $11,000 per day to about $35,000 per day.

However, the U.S. government also believed accession into the WTO would act as a check on the Communist Party's centrally planned economy and help transition the country to a more liberal-democratic system of government. The opposite has happened, as we've seen throughout the decades since. China's current leader President Xi Jinping tightly controls its centralized economy and financial markets, and has been a forceful impediment to any democratic developments.

CHAPTER 21

TIME TO GET BACK INTO SHIPOWNING

"If you always do what you've always done,
you'll always get what you've always got."

HENRY FORD

N avios had not owned a fleet of ships since the early 1980s, when, because of market pressure, the company had been forced to sell off its vessels. Fortunately, our market presence and brand name allowed us to operate a large fleet of chartered ships.

Following the management buyout, we gradually initiated a macro strategy to reduce our exposure to fixed-rate contracts of affreightment. When we did provide end users with freight commitments, we increasingly hedged out these positions by taking on additional short- or medium-term vessel capacity or going long (buying) ocean freight derivatives. But as our expectations of a bullish dry bulk market started to emerge, I began to search out opportunities to expand our long-term chartered-in fleet and possibly augment it with the acquisition of ships.

A few months after closing our deal, I flew to Europe to visit various customers and some of our bankers to reconfirm and recommit Navios's engagement with each of them. I decided to finish the trip in Athens to meet with Anastassis David, to let him know that although his family's investment in the newly restructured Navios was small, I nevertheless felt they were valued constituents in our new venture.

Since we had acquired Navios, I had developed a good relationship with Anastassis. As he learned more about our business, it was apparent to me that he was very intrigued by our asset-light model. He was not a traditional Greek shipowner—far from it. He was a hard-nosed businessman who supervised many of the family's investments across a broad spectrum of industries. I could sense that the returns we generated with the limited capital we had invested in the business impressed him.

It was during this trip that Anastassis first told me the family had a separate company called Levant Maritime, which was operated by two managers out of offices in London. The family had decided to order nine newbuilding supramax ships at Sanoyas Shipbuilding in Japan. At the time of our meeting, Levant had taken delivery of the first three units, with the other ships scheduled to deliver from the shipyard in 2001 and 2002. Anastassis told me that the company undertook its own technical ship management out of a separate office they had in Piraeus, the port area adjacent to the city of Athens, which employed about twenty people.

This company was a surprise to me, as it supported the family's commitment to traditional shipowning, which was something altogether quite different to Navios's business strategy. It also indicated that, like me, Anastassis believed in the growing strength of the dry bulk market.

I kept my eyes on the Levant Maritime operation from a distance. In the early fall of that year, on yet another trip to Athens, I was introduced to Michael Moschos, the president of Levant and his number two, Gregory Parissis. Both Michael and Gregory were what I would describe as traditional Greek shipowners; both their families had originated from the Greek island of Chios, located just off the coast of Turkey in the Aegean Sea. Many of the prominent names in Greek maritime transport today, such as Angelicoussis and Chandris, are families that hailed from this island.

We had a relaxed lunch in a wonderful fish restaurant along the Piraeus waterfront, where the waiters and busboys run back and forth from the kitchen across the street to the tables set up alongside the pier. I learned that the three supramax ships Levant Maritime had on the water were traded in the spot market on short period time charters. I asked them what their goals were as managers of the company, and they explained that providing cost-effective technical ship management was their main area of focus. In other words, concentrating on the nuts and bolts of running their ships, not the chartering business. They stressed that technical management was the area of shipping in which Greek shipowners could outperform their competitors.

They accepted the prevailing level of the time charter market whenever they fixed their ships. When I asked about the company's exposure to the freight market, they seemed to be rather nonplussed.

Our perspectives of the dry bulk market could not have been more different. We lived and died by the market every day at Navios. We owned none of the ships we operated, and so the problems associated with technical ship management fell to the owners from whom we chartered our ships. If there was a problem with the operation of one of our ships, we simply put it **off hire**, until the problem was remedied by the owner. I viewed technical ship management as a function that could be farmed out to any number of very professional firms located in various parts of the world that specialized in providing technical ship management services for shipowners.

***

If you have visited or looked at a map of Greece, you realize why the country and its people became such an independent maritime nation: geography. The location of Greece in the eastern Mediterranean places it next to Asia Minor and close to many of the historic sea-lanes and trade routes that run along the southern Mediterranean into the Black Sea, many of which were developed by Greek traders and seafarers. In addition, there are more than one thousand islands in Greece, so life in this country has always been intertwined with the sea. The country's terrain is surprisingly mountainous, and although one does find some large fertile valleys, there is limited farmland. Imports of grain have been a fact of life for millennia. The mainland also has an extensive coastline, so trading by sea has been part of the Greek national character for eons.

In 1948, the United States created the Marshall Plan to aid in the recovery of various European countries from the economic devastation caused by the Second World War. It was not just cities that had incurred widespread damage during wartime, but also a large portion of Europe's transportation infrastructure, such as railroads and their terminals, roadways, tunnels, bridges, and ports. During World War II, Greek shipowners aided the war effort by offering their ships to the Allied convoys to help move war materials, food, and clothing from the United States to Great Britain. It is estimated that about 75 percent of the Greek merchant fleet was destroyed by Nazi U-boats from 1941 through 1944. As part of the Marshall Plan, in the late 1940s, the United States sold one hundred Liberty ships to various Greek shipowners for less than scrap value, and this is the genesis of this country's modern, vast, controlled fleet.

Today, the Greek-owned (but not necessarily domiciled) fleet of tankers, bulk carriers, container ships, and specialized and general cargo ships totals about 250 million gross registered tonnes, or about 17 percent of the global fleet of ships. The second largest is China, with about 235 million **gross registered tonnes**, representing about 16 percent of the world's fleet of ships. Greece has a population of 11 million people. China's population is 1.4 billion. What is perhaps even more remarkable is that most of the Greek-owned fleet is controlled by private shipowners—quite often family businesses. The Chinese-owned fleet, in contrast, is controlled by massive state-owned enterprises, such as COSCO, or the China Ocean Shipping Company.

There is absolutely no doubt that the Greeks do have a nose for ships. So, how, you may ask, do the Greeks do it? Well, they are smart, tough, agile, aggressive, and entrepreneurial. Culturally, they are traders, and their commodity of choice is ships—specifically, the buying and selling of ships. Some outsiders describe the international business of owning ships as the biggest casino in the world, and given that most of the world's fleet is privately owned, it is a big-dollar game with attendant big risk. This is not a market for the uninitiated or the easily intimidated.

Greek shipowners are known for the proficient buying and selling of secondhand vessels, as opposed to ordering newbuilding ships. They are also very adept at searching out turning points in both the short-term and long-term market cycles and stepping in to acquire vessels when things look particularly bleak. The definition of a market bottom is when most others have given up all hope for a rebound, so it takes stamina and guts to enter a position at this point in the process.

The focus on acquiring secondhand ships, as opposed to newbuildings, is driven largely by the requirement for less equity capital. But even Greeks who have been successful, and have built up large fleets of ships, generally continue with this strategy. They are comfortable with the formula, and a secondhand asset has the added advantage of being acquired within a few months. Ordering a newbuilding vessel means delivery on the water two years, or perhaps longer, into the future, when no one knows what the market might look like.

Much like the international ocean freight markets that I have described earlier, the market pricing for ships is highly volatile, and values for these assets can move dramatically from month to month. When one buys a ship, one arranges to have it inspected by a technical engineer, much like the inspection undertaken when buying a new house. The ship may require some upgrading work, or it may not; it depends on the quality of technical ship management of the owner from whom the unit is being acquired.

In the spring of 2016, during a particularly difficult time in the dry bulk markets, one was able to acquire a five-year-old supramax bulk carrier for about $13 million.

Let's assume that a fictional, aspiring Greek entrepreneur stepped into the market in 2016 and bought a supramax ship. He would have conservatively financed 55 percent of the purchase price and therefore had $5.85 million of equity invested into the asset and taken on $7.15 million of debt. Let's further assume he arranged for first-mortgage debt financing with principal repayments of $900,000 per year. The cost to service the debt would have worked out to about $3,000 per day (principal and interest), and his running costs at that time on a five-year-old supramax might have been about $4,500 per day, excluding an accrual for dry-docking. So, the entrepreneur's cash breakeven would have been about $7,500, and during 2016 through 2017, he should have been able to operate his ship in the ocean freight markets at a breakeven.

Two years later, that same ship would be worth $18 million, and let's assume in the spring of 2018 he decided to sell the ship. Following transaction costs, he would have received about $17.75 million and paid off his remaining $5.4 million of debt, netting him about $12.4 million on a $5.85 million investment two years earlier. Not bad.

And if the Panama Canal closed for two years in 2017 because of a terrorist attack on the canal locks, the value of his ship might have quite possibly doubled to $26 million, netting him about $21 million on his $5.85 million investment. Sounds simple in practice, but it's not. It requires a very sound grasp of the international commodity and maritime finance markets; the contacts in the sale and purchase market to bring the ship to one's attention; you have to have a technical team that knows how to inspect the ship; and the knowledge and contacts required to operate the ship in the international ocean freight markets.

And to make such an investment even more attractive, since 1953, the Greek government has enshrined into law a tax exemption on revenue related to maritime income. In the shipowning business I am involved in today (more about this in Chapters 23 and 24), we do not pay tax at a corporate level, but any dividends earned or any return of capital that I receive requires me to pay tax here in the United States. The Greek shipowner does not have to pay any tax on repatriated funds into Greece. So, essentially, the Greek shipowners can invest their earnings on a tax-free basis—not tax-deferred, but tax-free—which is why ocean-shipping fortunes in this country can grow, and often do, dramatically and rapidly.

***

In April 2001, Robert and I flew to Athens to meet with various Greek shipowners to see if we might conclude some attractive long-term time charters. As I found out much earlier, Robert was of Greek descent on his mother's side and spoke Greek fluently—a great asset in dealing with Greek clients. While there, Anastassis David suggested a meeting with him and Michael Moschos, at which he floated the concept of merging Levant Maritime and Navios. Given the very different yet complementary business models of each company, I thought it could make a great deal of sense. However, Michael did not seem open to this possibility and did not engage in the discussion.

There were several benefits associated with merging Levant Maritime into Navios. It would fit nicely with our strategy of "going long in the market" by increasing, by about 50 percent, the amount of controlled tonnage that we had in our core long-term chartered fleet. Navios was developing its supramax trading activities, and so the six supramax newbuildings Levant had on the water, with three more to deliver in 2002, would help to support and expand Navios Handybulk. It would also enable us to build up the asset side of our balance sheet, which continued to look weak. A stronger balance sheet would provide us with more opportunity in deal flow.

In the two years that we had been working with Anastassis David and his family, I had become very comfortable with their approach to business and the family's high level of integrity. I felt they would make excellent partners.

Nevertheless, three main obstacles concerned me with such a transaction:

Saltchuk had made clear to us from the time of our first meeting that what they found attractive about Navios was the lack of "steel" on our balance sheet. All their other businesses were heavily invested in maritime assets, primarily U.S. flag roro ships, and tugs and barges, whereas Navios was an asset-light company that still managed to generate attractive returns. Merging the Levant fleet into Navios would shift this paradigm, and it concerned me that this might not be what Mike Garvey wanted for his company.

The second had to do with valuation. The Leventis-David family knew that, between the common and preferred stock, the shareholders of Navios had $3 million invested in Navios and one asset in the Uruguay terminal against which we had, by then, about $14 million of remaining debt. In discussions I had with Anastassis, I knew that Levant Maritime had managed to achieve an advance rate of debt financing (a fraction of the value of the ships) of about 78 percent on the cost of the newbuilding program, and that the average cost for each of the nine ships was about $21 million. This meant they had about $42 million of equity capital invested in their fleet, plus perhaps another $12 million covering minimum pledged liquidity provisions in each of the owning vessels' bank accounts, and some additional amount for working capital purposes. So, Levant had about $54 million of equity capital invested in their business versus the $3 million we had invested in ours. If one were to value the two businesses on this metric alone, it would be a 95 percent to 5 percent ownership allocation.

However, even though Levant Maritime owned nine supramax ships, its business was dwarfed in size by the scope of Navios's operations, which were made up of a large, chartered fleet of forty to fifty ships, contracts of affreightment, ocean freight derivatives, and the Uruguay terminal.

The third concern I had was how the two managers of Levant Maritime would fit into the Navios organization structure. Through family contacts they had managed to form Levant Maritime with the financial support of the Leventis-David family five or six years before, which had enabled them to access capital to acquire tonnage. The family's primary relationship was with this group, not Navios. The managers had been given the mandate to operate the business by the Leventis-David family, and any merger could affect their leadership positions within the larger organization.

Robert and I discussed the situation. He liked the idea, although he shared all my concerns. Nevertheless, we decided I should revisit the matter with Anastassis, which I did in a very low-key manner during a call with him just before the 2001 Christmas holiday. His reaction was subdued compared to our initial discussion in Athens. I suspected he had run into resistance from Michael and Gregory. He said he would think more about it and get back to me.

He reached out to me in late January to say he had given the idea some thought. Like me, he could see the benefits of merging the two companies, but he wanted to better understand how the numbers might work.

I explained it would not work based on equity capital invested in each of the businesses, because of Navios's unique structure. Unlike Levant Maritime's emphasis on steel assets, we had significant off-balance-sheet assets. These included Navios's reputation going back close to fifty years of trading in the global maritime freight markets; a depth of management that equaled or surpassed many of the prominent global maritime operations; a large amount of positive working capital required to operate our business; and a long-term chartered fleet, with purchase options, that could look very attractive in the coming years. We finally agreed that Levant would be valued on the basis of net asset value (NAV) of their fleet, and Navios on a multiple of its earnings. This turned out to be advantageous for us because the NAV values in the fall of 2002 were still low.

Anastassis then raised the issue of management structure. I explained the reasons why I thought any deal had to be structured as a merger of Levant Maritime into Navios, which meant that Navios would assume management responsibility for the merged entity. He told me this would be a nonstarter with Michael and Gregory, both of whom had a small equity stake in the Levant Maritime business. I told him that if we could find a way to work out a solution that would be acceptable to both management teams, then we might be able to move forward.

Anastassis and I could see the benefits of merging the two companies—the intellectual capital associated with a trading business, together with the control of steel hardware associated with the owning of ships. We initiated more formal discussions a few months later, some of which included Michael and Gregory. Over the next several months, we had numerous meetings. By August, we had agreed to the broad outlines of a deal. But there remained the two vexing problems: the management structure of the new entity and the respective valuations.

We came up with an innovative solution to the first issue. We would create a new holding company called Nautilus Maritime, which, in turn, would have two divisions: shipowning and technical management under Levant Maritime, and all the other business lines under Navios Corporation. But ultimately someone had to oversee the holding company. I had made clear to the Leventis-David family throughout the negotiations that I was not about to relinquish my role as CEO of the newly formed holding company. They proposed Michael Moschos and I share a co-CEO arrangement. I simply did not think it made any sense to have two individuals responsible for managing one business, particularly as our approaches to the industry were so different.

Then there was the issue of relative valuation and percentage ownership. The Navios shareholders wanted 40 percent ownership of the combined entity; the Leventis-David family, with input from their financial advisors, was offering 35 percent. After many conversations we couldn't come to an agreement on these two important issues by phone or fax.

Anastassis suggested we meet in Athens to work out these outstanding points and move forward. Forty-eight hours later, I was sitting with him and his father, George, in the latter's study at his home in Athens. Out came the single malt Scottish whiskey, and over the next few hours, we had more of what I would describe as a fireside chat than a negotiation. They tried hard to get me to accept the 35 percent and the co-CEO arrangement, but I held firm on both issues. We shook hands and agreed to continue talking. The following morning, I headed back to the airport.

It was on this flight home that I started to question the merits of the merger. Just three years earlier, Navios management had successfully structured a deal that allowed us to control our destiny, as management owned 55 percent of Navios. Given the relative valuations, the merger with Levant would require us to give up that control, notwithstanding that we would still be managing the merged businesses. Taking on debt of about $147 million linked to nine new buildings also gave me pause. Although I was becoming increasingly bullish on the prospects of the dry bulk market, what might happen to the new company if the market took a surprise nosedive? The advance rate against these units was about 78 percent, so they were significantly leveraged. In addition, the continued haggling over the management structure and the headache of "managing" the two executives of Levant Maritime—who were certainly not in favor of the transaction—made the deal seem less desirable.

Before I landed in New York, I had drafted an email to Anastassis explaining I had decided to back away from the proposed merger and setting out my reasoning for such an about-face. I also wrote that I was uncomfortable with the overall leverage of the transaction. He dubbed it "the email from thirty-six thousand feet," and we still sometimes laugh about it today. A week after he received it, the family agreed to my role as sole CEO of the merged entity and agreed to provide an additional financial facility for Navios to borrow from the family, up to $12 million for working capital purposes.

We now had one outstanding issue—relative valuations—and given their movement on the two items above, the family was not inclined to offer more than 35 percent. Anastassis flew to New York in early October with some of his advisors. Robert, Bruce, and I met with them in a conference room he had arranged at the Peninsula Hotel. We had debated the 40 percent versus the 35 percent for an hour, when Anastassis suddenly asked everyone but me to leave the room. The two of us chatted around the issue for about twenty minutes and finally shook hands at a 38 percent valuation.

The next six weeks were a blur of meetings with lawyers and bankers to codify the deal before the end of the year. As part of the transaction, we arranged a $50 million debt facility with Norway's DnB NORD bank, and the German lender DVB Bank—$14 million of which was used to pay off the Saltchuk loan, and $30 million to refinance two of the Levant ships. We retained a $6 million revolving-credit facility for working capital purposes.

As I had expected, Saltchuk was not enamored with the merger. But to give them their due, they agreed to allow us to move forward against paying down the outstanding debt Navios had with them on the Uruguay terminal, and buying back most of their common equity so that post-merger they only owned 4 percent of the newly formed merged entity.

Robert and his team did all the heavy lifting on contractual details, and we closed the merger on December 11, 2002, but it was not without some last-minute concerns for my position in the deal. Robert had advised me that I should retain a personal lawyer to represent me in the transaction. To protect my interests, she proposed that the Leventis-David family agree to the following terms in writing: If I were removed from my position, or the company was merged or sold and my position as CEO was terminated, or if the head office of Navios was moved more than 40 kilometers from Norwalk, Connecticut, they would have to pay me a seven-figure sum.

The day of the closing, which was held in London, we had the usual battery of lawyers, advisors, bankers, and executives from the other side in attendance. At some point, there was a small commotion in one of the offices with Robert, Anastassis, and the Leventis-David family lawyer. As Robert walked out, rolling his eyes at me, Anastassis asked me to join him and his family attorney in the private office.

His lawyer explained to me that the family had never had to provide such personal assurances to the CEO of any of their businesses, and he went on to say he was advising the family against doing so. The lawyer did all the talking for about three minutes and Anastassis said nothing.

Although this coda to the agreement had been drafted to protect my interests, I looked at it from a different perspective. Navios management was giving up control of the business, and I thought this agreement in a small way helped to protect the overall management team.

I listened, then turned to look at Anastassis, completely ignoring the lawyer, and quietly said: "No assurances, no deal," and walked out of the office. Five minutes later, Anastassis ambled out, with a resigned grin on his face, handed me the signed agreement, and said, "Well, Tony, I had to try!"

Celebrating the Navios–Levant merger in London, 2002. Left to right: Anastassis David, Brian Bogen, and the author. Credit: Author's Collection

About a year following the merger, we changed the Nautilus name to Navios Maritime Holdings (NMH), and did the same with all the various operating subsidiaries, including Levant Maritime, reporting into it. This included all the Levant ships, which we renamed with a Navios prefix. We did this with a view to streamlining the company and branding everything with the Navios name.

It was about this time, and came as no great surprise, that Michael Moschos and Gregory Parissis decided to resign their positions overseeing the technical management of the owned fleet and departed the company. NMH acquired their very small equity ownership in the merged entity and we had other executives assume their responsibilities.

CHAPTER 22

JUST GOOD BUSINESS SENSE

"Missing the bottom on the way up won't
cost you anything. It's missing the top on the
way down that's always expensive."

PETER LYNCH,
American investor

W e were very fortunate that in the period immediately following
the merger, the dry bulk markets commenced what turned out
to be a five-year rally. It was not three months following the closing in London that market earnings and hull values started to increase significantly. Our general strategy of reducing exposure to freight and increasing our exposure to ships proved correct, and we quickly built-up significant
cash reserves.

By the fall of 2003, I thought it was time for the board of directors of
NMH to see for themselves our terminal in Uruguay. I decided to schedule the second of our 2004 NMH board meetings down in South America.
I thought this was important because it was the loan we obtained using the
terminal as collateral that allowed us to conclude the management buyout. I
also felt it was time for everyone to see the significant upgrades we had been
making to our port operation in Nueva Palmira.

Through the 1980s and 1990s, we had transformed the terminal facility into one of the premier grain-loading operations in the region. It was
becoming an ever-more-important asset for the organization. A new Four
Seasons resort hotel had opened just outside Carmelo, a small town located

about a twenty-minute drive from Nueva Palmira. I thought this would be an ideal venue for our meeting, so I scheduled it for May 2004, early fall in Uruguay.

The first day, I had the entire board take a detailed five-hour tour of the terminal complex. It had grown to include four large cement silos, with a total storage capacity of about 150,000 metric tonnes, as well as the second new dock dedicated to the discharge of river barges and new ship loaders.

The second day, our board meeting lasted the better part of eight hours. The last item on the agenda, as was normal with all our board agendas, was "Any Other Business." It was at this point in the meeting that Brian Bogen, who continued to represent Saltchuk on our board, and whose background was that of an investment banker, asked: "Tony, what is Navios worth today?"

The question came out of left field, and I was not prepared to answer it. I fumbled a little, spoke about our various business divisions and the jump in revenue caused by the bullish dry bulk market. I said I thought it was probably valued between $250 million to $275 million, net of debt.

Following a general discussion about valuation, it was again Brian who managed to get everyone focused on what was important. "Given that about fifty million dollars of equity is what we have collectively invested in this business," he responded, "would it not make sense to retain some professional advisors to undertake an analysis of our business and provide us with a valuation?"

I sat there dumbfounded. His suggestion implied that we obtain a precise valuation to explore a possible sale. It was only five years earlier that we had acquired Navios from Fednav, and two years earlier we had merged Levant Maritime into Navios to create a formidable maritime transportation company. We had gone from having an asset-light balance sheet with reasonable but small earnings to having a meaningful balance sheet with significant earnings. Why would we want to sell? We were just getting started.

That is one of the benefits of having outside members on a board of directors. It can get management to focus on areas that would not normally be part of its purview.

Shortly after my return to the United States, I had several telephone conversations with Anastassis David, who was the nonexecutive chairman of Navios. Although market pundits were forecasting very bullish scenarios for our markets for the next few years, we were still operating in a highly cyclical industry. I felt it was important not to lose sight of the fact that 80 percent of the time shipowners were "price takers" in what was a highly commoditized market. We agreed that we had a responsibility to all our shareholders to ascertain what the company might indeed be worth, should we decide to sell.

In the fall of 2004, Navios celebrated its fiftieth anniversary, and in the year leading up to this, we created a new marketing campaign that included an updated website, new marketing brochures, tabletop ornaments with the Navios flag, and a beautiful leather-bound book of marine distance tables. We felt this was an achievement that we should celebrate with many of our customers and friends around the world. We arranged to have four large celebratory cocktail receptions in Montevideo, Norwalk, Athens, and Tokyo. The largest was the reception in Norwalk, which was held at the Norwalk Maritime Aquarium with more than three hundred guests in attendance.

I was very proud that Pino Colombari, Bob Goldbach, and Sean Day, all previous presidents of Navios, attended the Norwalk reception. In addition, we had several individuals in attendance from Fednav, including Ladi Pathy and John Peacock.

At the fiftieth anniversary party of Navios in Norwalk, Connecticut. Left to right: the author, Pino Collambari, Ladi Pathy, and past Navios presidents Bob Goldbach, Don Szostak, and Sean Day. Credit: Author's Collection

The dry bulk markets, by this time, were in the second year of a five-year run, and we were feeling flush with cash. It was a relatively easy decision for me, then, to arrange to fly all the head office staff, with their significant others, to Bermuda for a three-day getaway in the middle of September 2004. It was a marvelous opportunity to say thank you to everyone who had been with the company through thick and thin for so many years.

***

The summer of 2004, we reached out to a few investment banks with strong financial advisory divisions and several law firms. On September 8, Navios executed an engagement letter retaining Lazard Frères & Co. (Lazard) as our investment advisor in connection with the possible private placement of equity, equity-related, or debt securities of the company, or a possible sale.

We provided Lazard with Navios historical financials and simple forecasts for 2004 through 2005 and requested them to advise what they thought our business was worth. They came back and told us they believed a realistic price range for the equity of Navios, net of debt, was $375 million to $450 million. Robert, Bruce, and I were the first people to see these numbers, and we were very surprised by the high valuation.

During this period, we also considered an initial public offering (IPO) for NMH. Not only were the commodity markets very strong, but the capital markets were as well. The dry bulk markets were now viewed by the investment banks as an extension of the commodity markets, and everyone was quoting the BDI, so there was, for the first time in my career, a serious focus from the financial community on our space.

When we met with investment bankers, many of whom were not familiar with maritime transport, and talked through our model with them, you could sense that they thought it might be difficult to market our business through an IPO. The model of most publicly listed dry bulk maritime companies was simply to charter out their fleet of ships to provide the financial analysts with visible forward earnings. The Navios model was quite different.

We had seven owned ships (as the market price for ships had increased, we had sold off a few); a long-term chartered fleet of twenty-two ships, all with purchase options, fifteen of which were on the water, and the remaining seven scheduled to deliver into our fleet in 2005 through 2007; a medium- and short-term chartered fleet of an additional twenty to twenty-five ships; and various contracts of affreightment, primarily in the Atlantic basin, but some in the Pacific as well. By the standards of the shipping industry, we also operated a very large and successful derivative trading desk, which was active in both hedging and speculative strategies. And we had the bulk terminal facility in Uruguay.

Two other factors affected our thinking concerning initiating a public offering. I felt strongly that the trading nature of our business was not conducive to operating as a public company. First, we were too small. Even today, the largest dry bulk listed companies are considered microcap stocks, and so the float is small and therefore the stock price can be easily impacted by day traders. The other concern had to do with the street's short-term focus on quarterly earnings and EBITDA, which over the long term simply does not work when you operate in a volatile trading environment. The pressure for EBITDA has forced the management of some publicly listed maritime companies to focus on their financial "engineering," to the detriment of their underlying business.

As a result, we abandoned the IPO option.

As we moved forward with the sale of NMH, I discovered that the process of selling the company in 2005 was easier than the process of buying Navios six years earlier. Because of the sums that were involved, we retained more outside advisors. Unlike the purchase in 1999, when we were the acquirers of the company—but simultaneously also having to work out new loan documentation and a complicated new shareholders agreement—this was a straightforward process. The Lazard team was led by Jamie Kempner, a Manhattan native who happened to own a home in Greenwich, and was therefore close to the Navios head office in Norwalk. He had a team of three Lazard investment bankers working with him.

Through a very intensive five-week period, beginning in the middle of September, Lazard worked with Bruce, Robert, and our key executives to put together a detailed confidential information memorandum regarding Navios's business and operations. Bruce and the financial team did the heavy lifting, spending hours on the historical financials and developing forecast earnings. Robert led the charge of creating a proper data room so that when we found prospective buyers, we could work with their financial and legal advisors to comb through all the ownership details, the commercial and technical contracts, legal items, and financial information pertaining to the sale.

Once the overall plan was established, Lazard approached about seventeen strategic maritime and commodity companies, and about thirty financial institutions and private equity groups, to see if they had any interest in acquiring NMH. By early December, about twenty maritime and financial companies had signed the nondisclosure agreement and expressed intentions to consider an acquisition.

Because of the strength of the dry bulk market and, equally importantly, the global commodity markets, many major investment banks and some financial firms, which now viewed dry bulk freight as an extension of the commodity markets, wanted in on the action. Dry bulk was emerging into the mainstream marketplace, and some financial market prognosticators were referring regularly to the BDI, calling it a leading economic indicator. We received letters of interest from Morgan Stanley and Goldman Sachs, among others. It soon became apparent that the overall auction process was going to be very competitive.

In early January 2005, after poring over the initial indications and the pros and cons of potential buyers with Lazard, we notified six companies that they were short-listed for the second round of the auction process. The criteria used to make this determination were the price level indication and the potential acquirer's perceived ability to close a transaction. We invited them to conduct preliminary due diligence and meet with the senior leadership team, which consisted of Robert, Bruce, and me. We delivered long, detailed presentations to them that month and spent many grueling hours answering numerous questions, not just about NMH, but about the maritime industry and our markets.

***

All six prospective buyers came back with proposals higher than their original bids. We narrowed the potential pool to two buyers: DryShips Inc., run by George Economou based in Athens, and a special-purpose acquisition company (SPAC) called International Shipping Enterprises (ISE), led by Angeliki Frangou. Both companies had indicated an initial willing purchase price of about $550 million, but following due diligence, they increased their offers to $580 million, levels that were significantly more than other indicative amounts.

George Economou is a self-made, successful shipowner who came up through the ranks of Greek shipping on the technical side of the business. He formed Cardiff Marine and used this company to acquire, slowly but surely, a fleet of ships. Although he had shown a remarkably successful commercial flair, we were nervous whether he could close a deal. In 2004, he had formed DryShips Inc., which he took public just at the time of his negotiations with us. In our discussions, George was reluctant to disclose which entity he was planning to use to acquire Navios and where his finance for the acquisition would originate.

Angeliki Frangou grew up in a multigenerational Greek shipping family, which included her father, Nikolas Frangos, a well-known Greek shipowner. She graduated university with a degree in mechanical engineering and has a background in finance, which gave her an understanding of both the financial and shipping markets. She acquired her first ship in the early 1990s and formed the ISE SPAC in 2004.

A SPAC is a "blank check" company that allows retail investors to invest in private-equity-type transactions that are generally highly leveraged. Normally, the management of the SPAC has a fixed period—then generally about eighteen months—in which to complete an acquisition. If they don't, the equity capital is returned to the investors. At the time of its formation, a SPAC has no existing business, but rather states its intention to acquire a business in a particular space. ISE had raised about $200 million for acquiring ships or maritime-related businesses. By January 2005, ISE had about ten months left on the use of this resource; Angeliki was incentivized to get a deal closed quickly.

During January 2005, we had multiple meetings with both, and their teams were allowed access to the data room. By the end of January, they had signed off on the details of the planned sale and provided comments to the proposed stock purchase agreement.

It was obvious to both Robert and me that George and Angeliki were very keen to move forward with the acquisition, and in early February, we invited both parties to the Navios head office to see if we might be able to finalize the sale. We scheduled them to arrive on the same day, George in the morning and Angeliki in the afternoon. But George's arrival was delayed by some hours, so they arrived at about the same time. We had Angeliki and her team stationed in our boardroom, located on the second floor of our three-story building, and we placed George and his financial manager in a first-floor conference room. Neither group knew the other was in the building. We explained to both parties that they were one of two short-listed candidates. Over three hours, Robert and I ran back and forth between the two conference rooms, trying to firm up the final price and broad terms.

The final sticking points with George remained his financing and which company he would use to conclude the transaction. We just could not pin him down on the ratio of equity versus debt financing that he was proposing. He seemed unwilling to give us evidence of his resources, so we respectfully declined to move forward with his bid.

On the other hand, we knew that after deducting the promote fees Angeliki was earning from the SPAC, and the fees of her investment advisors, she had about $180 million of equity capital available. More significantly, she had a commitment letter from HSH Nordbank AG, a commercial bank headquartered in Hamburg. It was one of the largest lenders to the maritime industry. The letter indicated the bank's willingness to finance up to $520 million of the acquisition.

We agreed on the broad terms of the deal with ISE on February 9, at an agreed purchase price of $608 million. On the following day, ISE insisted on issuing a press release announcing that it had entered into an exclusive negotiating agreement for the acquisition of NMH and all its related subsidiaries. The dry bulk market was very strong, and it dawned on us that the press release was effectively Angeliki's attempt to stave off the threat of any other potential buyers coming forward to try and insert themselves in the sale process. This reconfirmed our resolve to be very aggressive with the contractual terms related to the sale.

Throughout the balance of the month, there were numerous meetings between ISE and our management related to due diligence issues and the precise terms of the stock purchase agreement. On March 1, ISE and Navios issued a joint press release announcing that the parties had entered into a definitive stock purchase agreement pursuant to which Navios and its subsidiaries would be acquired by ISE.

However, the dry bulk market was entering a period of high volatility. The first significant dry bulk market peak of the current century occurred in Q1 2004, followed by a second peak at the very end of that year. By mid-December 2004, the BDI was marked at about 6,000; six months later, it was down to about 2,500. All the market exuberance that had built up in the prior year seemed to dissipate, just like air slowly leaking from a balloon. It reached a bottom a few weeks before we were scheduled to close the sale. On August 1, the BDI was marked at 1,769—a 70 percent drop off its high, just seven months earlier.

In fact, given the dramatic falloff in rates, Robert, Bruce, and I had several sleepless nights during the early summer of 2005, as we were very worried that ISE might try to wriggle out of the sale. The market was 56 percent off its highs by the time the proceeds of the sale hit our various bank accounts. It took about eighteen months for the BDI to retrace its steps back to 6,000, and about thirty months for it to reach about 11,500, a 550 percent improvement from the August 2005 low.

But it was not just the dry bulk markets that we were focusing on back in 2005. The capital markets were very liquid then, perhaps "frothier" than they had ever been. This was fueled by several independent events that together conspired to ensure the world was flush with capital as we entered the twenty-first century.

What first set these markets on this path was the arrival in the 1990s of new technology in the form of enhanced computer logarithms and communications creating an instantaneous flow of information across the globe. Innovations such as electronic exchanges and high-frequency trading, not just of stocks and bonds but of currencies and commodities as well, added to information liquidity—all of which led to more integrated capital markets.

In addition, there were some structural changes taking place. The most notable was the repeal of the Glass-Steagall Act of 1933, which separated commercial from investment banking. The idea behind this act was to ensure that the trading results of investment assets did not have an impact on the commercial activities of the banks. It was replaced, much to the consternation of Paul Volker, by the Financial Services Modernization Act of 1999, which allowed banks to use their deposits to invest in derivatives; and regulated the derivative market to remain largely a market between "sophisticated counterparties."

The dot-com bubble burst in the first half of 2000, and in September 2001, we experienced 9/11. To help counteract these two events, the Federal Reserve started to lower the federal funds rate aggressively, from 6.25 percent in the spring of 2000 to 1 percent by the summer of 2003. The reduced rates caused banks and private equity groups, as well as hedge funds and some other investors, to search out riskier assets that offered higher returns. With interest rates so low, deals were structured with increasing amounts of leverage. The European banks were very active in the **Eurodollar** market, and they borrowed heavily during this period.

I recall sitting with Bruce Hoag in his office shortly after we had announced that ISE and NMH had entered into a stock purchase agreement. He looked at me and said: "Tony, it is amazing that a buyer has arranged $520 million of financing against the agreed purchase price of $607 million. That is eighty-five percent leverage. It's nuts!" Had we waited to sell NMH in 2007 or 2008, it would have been doubtful that the capital required for such a transaction would have been so readily available, especially as fear of the subprime market was just starting to filter through the capital markets generally.

One additional factor driving the sale from the perspective of the U.S.-based management investors was that the long-term capital gains rate at the time of sale was 15 percent, implemented by the administration of President

George W. Bush. We were apprehensive about whether a future administration would increase these rates.

One of my real concerns from March through to the closing at the end of August was the impact the proposed sale was going to have on our employees, primarily those located in our Norwalk head office and our technical ship management office in Piraeus. There was no doubt going to be a period of some confusion and uncertainty. I was worried about the effect this would have on employee morale.

We still had a business to run in a market that was roaring, so it was crucial that we keep everyone motivated and focused. In this way, the performance of the organization did not suffer. I was particularly concerned about the accounting and financial teams, as they would, by necessity, have to get involved in the detailed due diligence process.

Shortly before the first press release, I reached out to a friend who had been involved in a similar situation. The advice he gave me was to try and keep the employees apprised of the situation as it unfolded. He explained that a lack of communication from senior management would simply lead to the rumor mill working overtime, so we tried to do what he suggested. I communicated a few times to all the employees, outlining where we stood in the sale process, and I had the other seven management shareholders speak on a more regular basis with their respective teams.

No one departed Navios during the entire process, which I believe reflects that senior management did handle the process well with our employees.

Although Angeliki had indicated to me personally that she would initiate few changes in staffing, and that she would likely leave the management office in Norwalk, I was not sufficiently naïve to think that there would not be few changes. I was very concerned about what this might mean for our employees, many of whom had been with the company for fifteen, twenty, or twenty-five years.

Well into the process, I approached Anastassis David and explained that, assuming we concluded a successful sale, I wanted to set aside a sum of money from the sale proceeds to distribute to all the head office employees to provide some level of financial comfort. Quite honestly, none of us knew at that point what the buyers would do. We agreed on a sum of $2.5 million to be paid out from the proceeds of the sale.

During the period from April through July, as our respective legal teams worked through the details of the sale, we had some board meetings. It was at one of these, attended by the other board directors, that I first raised the prospect of an employee fund. All of these directors, but one, would benefit directly from the sale proceeds. Anastassis indicated to everyone that he was on board with what I was proposing, and he explained that the eight management investors would not be included in this distribution. The next issue we had to grapple with was how to distribute the proceeds of the fund.

We had discussed various alternatives: One was to have specific amounts set aside for different levels of management and staff. Another was to base the distribution on how we had disbursed bonuses over the previous few years. Yet another was to base the distribution on seniority, the idea being that older employees with more tenure should receive a larger payout because a job search for them might be more difficult than for a younger employee.

We eventually settled on the third option, which was to base the payout on an employee's length of tenure with the company. Very simply, the longer the individual had worked at Navios, the larger the distribution. It was clean and simple, and notwithstanding his or her position in the company, it served to reward the people who had been with the company the longest and who had worked through all the ups and downs that we had experienced over the years. However, we agreed that this **sinking fund** would remain strictly confidential until after the sale was complete.

We closed the sale of Navios Corporation on August 25, 2005, for a price, net of debt, of $607 million, less an EBITDA adjustment of $13 million, a $7 million success fee to Lazard, and the $2.5 million payout to Navios employees.

Approximately $200 million of the sale proceeds was attributed to twenty-two long-term time charters from Japanese Shikoku owners, fifteen of which had purchases options that were significantly "in the money." About $190 million of the net proceeds was paid out to the eight key management shareholders of the company who had a collective tenure with Navios of 19.6 years.

***

Following the sale, Angeliki asked me to remain on the Navios board, but I declined. I thought the new owners should have a clean break from the previous CEO. So, I agreed to step down the following day.

On the morning of Friday, August 26, I arrived at our headquarters in Norwalk. I had everyone gather in the bullpen area of our office at nine o'clock and I stood up on a desk to address all the employees. I confirmed that the previous afternoon we had closed on the sale of the company; then I announced that as part of the process, the Navios board of directors had decided to set aside a fund of $2.5 million that would be distributed to all the employees, whether they remained with the company or left, on a scale based on their length of service with Navios. The news of the sale was expected, the news about the fund was not, and a few employees became emotional.

Someone asked if there were any plans for personnel changes. I said the new management had assured me that there were no plans for staff changes, but that ultimately it would be up to them. I paused, then said that the only immediate personnel change I knew of was that I would be departing the company, effective at the close of business that day. As I said those words, I broke down and could not continue.

Navios had been a major part of my business life for twenty-three years, and having succeeded in creating a corporate structure with a strong balance sheet, a great core fleet of owned and chartered dry bulk ships, a true collegial atmosphere throughout the organization, and a company where management owned significant equity, it was a profoundly sad day for me.

But it was probably the best "fixture" of my career.

CHAPTER 23

NEW HORIZONS

"You can't go back and change the beginning, but you
can start where you are and change the ending."

C.S. LEWIS,
British author

———

I awoke on Monday, August 29, 2005, and lay in bed with a very strange
sensation in my stomach. I did not have to jump out of bed and head off
to the office for a day filled with work and meetings. As I lay there, gaz-
ing up at the ceiling, I was unsettled. I felt a real sense of unease, because
for the first time in decades, I was not quite sure what to do. It might have
been panic.

I was fifty-two years old, and retirement still seemed to be a long way
off. I had, up until that point, never really given it much thought. I always
had a sense that I would somehow be employed well into my elderly years. I
had my first summer job at the age of fourteen as a "runner" in a stock brokerage firm in Montreal and had worked every year since. Most people have
a few years before their retirement to think about the future and plan for that
eventuality. I, however, had spent the past ten months with a singular focus
on getting to the finish line with the sale of NMH.

I had always enjoyed the mental challenge and stimulation that came
from being part of the fast-moving, volatile maritime industry. What would
be the next phase of my life? I loved to cook, and I had been collecting and
enjoying wine for decades.

I also enjoyed traveling about the world, and now I had all the time to do so. It would also afford me more family time. Later in the day, I looked at my wife and said: "Jen, let's hop on a plane and head off somewhere for a month. I don't care where, anywhere, but you choose."

I was surprised when after some thought she looked at me and replied, "Well, I have never been to Greece, so why not plan an extended holiday there?"

Having spent considerable time there on business trips, it was not at the top of my holiday list, but I had never explored the country beyond Athens and Piraeus, so Greece it was.

Greece has so many incredible attributes: breathtaking scenery, an incomparable depth of history and culture, a glorious climate, superb cuisine, some of the best beaches to be found in Europe, and, of course, a society based on democratic norms that date back to the days of classical Athens.

We departed in the middle of September, and following five days in Athens, we flew off to Mykonos and Santorini for a week, which was nice because the "high" season was behind us, and these high-tourist islands were more welcoming without the usual crowds. But the highlight of our trip was the two weeks we spent traveling throughout parts of the southern Peloponnese, which is an area I had never visited and which most tourists to Greece never see.

The geography of the Peloponnese is what surprised and delighted us: the lofty Taygetos Mountains, great river gorges, beautiful sand and rock beaches, and azure water made for stunning scenic drives, many of them along tiny coastal roads. We spent a good part of our time in the Mani, which is a peninsula located at the southern end of the mountain range.

The land there is rugged, with few trees. There are stone towers scattered about that were erected centuries ago as families feuded. Animals walk aimlessly across deserted roads, and the local cuisine rivals that of any I have had elsewhere in Greece. What you won't find are picturesque village squares with cobbled streets and a *kafenio* surrounded with whitewashed buildings leading to a pretty beach, as you find in the Cyclades Islands. Instead, there are little harbors with structures built of stone, many of them jutting straight out from the sea. And there were no tourists. And there were no signs in English anywhere. It was marvelous.

But as much as I enjoyed our vacation in Greece, when I returned home, I knew that traveling from place to place would not satisfy my need to be engaged in a challenging activity. I reconnected with Queen's University and gave some lectures. Jen and I became involved in a local school program for disadvantaged kids. We had some wonderful family holidays and enjoyed spending time on our property in Quebec. I spent considerably more time on my golf game and enjoyed skiing during the winter months. But it soon became apparent to me that I missed the rough and tumble of the maritime industry.

Following the sale, Anastassis David had said to me that if Robert and I ever became involved in another maritime adventure, his family would very much like to support us. A few years later, following the expiration of our noncompete clauses in the NMH deal, we started to contemplate our next move. I felt it was premature to be investing back into the dry bulk space, because the market was still quite firm and ship values were elevated. I considered other options, some of which I discussed with Robert and Anastassis.

Three years after the sale of NMH, Robert and I, together with the Leventis-David family, formed a small maritime hedge fund, which we collectively capitalized privately with about $20 million. We hired a few young quants, rented a small office in Stamford, and we were off to the races. The hedge fund was focused on trading ocean freight derivatives, known as **forward freight agreements** (FFAs). But I did not find this activity as intellectually stimulating as operating in the physical side of the business; and so after a few years of breakeven returns, collectively we decided the risk was not worth the return and we folded the operation.

About eighteen months later, Robert and I started to think about forming a new shipping venture, and we traveled to Athens to meet with Anastassis to discuss our plans. By 2011, the dry bulk markets had fallen from their historic highs of the previous decade, and since the value of ships had fallen, we thought it might be a good opportunity to invest in some secondhand vessels.

We agreed to focus our efforts on buying secondhand supramax ships for two reasons: First, their smaller size and deck cranes made them more flexible assets than the larger, **gearless** bulk carriers. Second, because they were more dependent on the minor bulks (fertilizers, cement, sugar, bauxite, scrap, petcoke, forest and steel products, among others), we could trade with a wide variety of clients and be less reliant on the high-volume China trades.

It was a few months following that meeting that we formed Sea Trade Holdings (STH).

Anastassis thought we should bring another partner into the STH venture, not only to raise more equity capital, but to bolster our expertise on the technical side of the operation. He introduced us to George and Zenon Mouskas, the second generation of a Greek-Cypriot shipowning family who manage a company called Olympia Ocean Carriers, out of Cyprus. They owned capesize and kamsarmax ships (the latter is a larger-size panamax whose deadweight is maximized for entry into Port Kamsar, in the republic of Guinea).

However, Robert and I were initially concerned about bringing a partner into STH who was already established in the dry bulk sector. Nevertheless, we agreed to have a few preliminary meetings with them and quickly became convinced that they would make excellent partners. We were impressed with the Mouskas family's experience in shipowning and their justly earned reputation for integrity and loyalty, practicality, and common sense. Early in 2012, we struck a deal with them to subscribe for common equity in STH, alongside Robert, myself, and the Leventis-David family.

***

While we originally thought the best way to begin was to acquire supramax ships from the secondhand market, the introduction of a new size category of bulk carrier, the ultramax, changed our plans. Similar in design to the supramax, but with an increased deadweight of between sixty thousand and sixty-five thousand tonnes, the ultramax offered economies of scale when compared to the supramax.

Toward the end of 2011, Robert and I also started to research the new "eco" electronic engine being introduced to the maritime industry. In addition to the significant environmental benefits, depending on the price of fuel, the savings can be as much as $3,000 per day for an ultramax-size ship over a similar-size vessel with a regular mechanical engine. The more we learned about it, the more convinced we became that STH should be ordering new-building vessels with eco engines.

STH decided to order nine 60,000-deadweight-tonne eco ships designed with electronic, as opposed to mechanical, engines. At fourteen knots laden with cargo, our units burn about twenty-five tonnes of fuel a day. A supramax vessel built just two years earlier, with a deadweight of about fifty-eight thousand tonnes and a mechanical engine, will consume about thirty-one tonnes of fuel a day—six tonnes per day more than the STH ships in a similar condition.

We canvassed yards in Vietnam, the Philippines, Japan, and China. The ultramax designs in each of these countries were almost the same. Ultimately it came down to the shipyards in China and Japan. While there was a tendency to favor Chinese yards because of their relatively lower pricing, there were additional costs involved in building there.

Even though the Chinese ultramax ships were priced about $2 million less than those built in Japan, there was an additional cost we would have had to incur for yard supervision in China, which we estimated reduced the cost differential to about $1.5 million. We would not need this level of oversight in the Japanese yards because of their reputation for high quality and efficiency.

But perhaps more importantly, when Robert and I reached out to some independent technical ship managers to review the running cost differential between Chinese- and Japanese-built vessels, we found some sobering information. The data indicated that for the first three to four years, the running costs were similar, but as the five-year **Special Survey dry dock** approached and beyond, the running costs on the Chinese-built ships started to increase more rapidly than the Japanese-built units. Taking the long view, we decided to order in Japan.

I had been out of the actual dry bulk markets for about seven years at that point, and the industry had experienced some significant changes. Financing was more difficult to arrange, and much of the commercial activity of the dry bulk markets had shifted to Asia. STH was barely a year old and had no performance profile. We were viewed as a start-up.

While the Mouskas family business was shipowning, they had less newbuilding experience, having acquired most of their ships over the years in the secondhand market. And they were less familiar with the Japanese market.

The Japanese have a tradition of engaging in long-term relationships and are very cautious dealing with new companies approaching them. But I had about thirty years of maritime experience in Japan: I knew the major trading houses, as well as many of the local Japanese owners. I had been involved in newbuilding orders, as well as long-term time charters from Japanese shipowners. I had experience with contracts of affreightment with Japanese steel mills.

In the years since my departure from Navios, some of my Marubeni contacts had retired, while others had been promoted into senior management positions beyond the traditional maritime divisions of the trading house. I decided to reach out to Shigeki Nakagawa, who was still active in his role as president of Fednav Asia. Nevertheless, he suggested I approach Marubeni, the Japanese trading house with whom I was closest, and get their support for our new venture.

On my first trip to Japan as managing director of STH, in February 2012, I met Satoru Nakagawa (no relation to Shigeki), and we spent a week together in Tokyo doing the rounds of the major shipbuilders. I also took the time to visit and reconnect with some of my Japanese business contacts.

With the assistance of Marubeni, and in particular Satoru-san, as well as the technical oversight of Olympia Ocean Carriers, and access to attractive financing through the Leventis-David family connections, STH was able to order nine new ultramax ships.

The erection of the immense, permanent hold ladders in the forward cargo hold of the MV *STH Montreal*. Credit: Author's Collection

***

The shipyards in Japan, and indeed around the world, offer to prospective buyers predetermined technical designs for the ships they build. Items such as length, beam, depth, propeller size, engine specifications, and machinery lists are all standard features that are incorporated into the newbuilding contract. It is known in our trade as a "cookie-cutter" design. The details of the yard's vessel specification sheets are reviewed and compared by prospective buyers, and a decision is made on which yard to choose for the project.

The next step is to negotiate the broad contractual terms with the shipyard. These terms include such items as place of construction, when the ships are to be delivered from the yard, the price of the newbuilding contract, terms of payment, and the buyer's right for technical supervision during the construction period. Many Japanese shipbuilders do not like to have an owner's technical representative on-site during construction, and because the quality of the build is so good, many owners do not insist on this. In contrast, for orders in China, it is very much the norm to have on-site yard supervision.

The construction of the MV *STH Tokyo* in Japan. The two workmen in the lower center of the picture provide scale as to the size of a ship's hold.
Credit: Author's Collection

Of course, once detailed contract negotiations are commenced, certain changes or additions can be made to the yard's cookie-cutter design. For example, one can choose the type and grade of self-polishing copolymer paint for the ship's hull. Some paints are better than others, with anti-fouling characteristics that last longer. Ships are designed with CO_2 (carbon dioxide) systems in the engine rooms that come on automatically in case of fire; we opted to have our ships designed with CO_2 systems in the cargo holds as well, which provide us, and more importantly our charterers, greater flexibility in the types of cargoes that can be loaded. We opted to have air conditioning throughout all the officers' and crew quarters, and we also chose to have individual bedrooms for each crew member.

In addition to the new electronic engines, we also chose to have certain energy-saving devices (ESDs) built into the design of our ships. Vessels in the

STH fleet are equipped with a bulb and fin system on the rudder, as well as a Super Stream Duct® built onto the stern of the vessel in front of the propeller. ESDs such as those I've mentioned help to improve the flow of water into the propeller and following on from the propeller as water exits and moves past the rudder. These ESDs have improved the fuel efficiency on our vessels by about 4 percent.

The construction of MV *STH Athens* in Japan. Note the prefabricated steel in the foreground. Today, ships are built much like a Lego set. Credit: Author's Collection

In the fall of 2013, we signed the first contracts with Mitsui Engineering & Shipbuilding and Japan Marine United (JMU) for two ships to be built by each of them. During the period from 2014 to 2016, we followed up with an additional five orders for new ships, three with MES and two from JMU. The JMU ships were built at the same yard at Kure that was controlled by D.K. Ludwig sixty years earlier and which built the Navios ore-class ships in the late 1950s.

CHAPTER 24

SEA TRADE HOLDINGS

"The pessimist complains about the wind;
the optimist expects it to change;
the realist adjusts the sails."

WILLIAM ARTHUR WARD,
American writer

———————

W e set up the corporate organization structure for STH in a simple
format that is used widely throughout our industry. Each ship is
owned by a single-purpose owning company, and all nine companies are owned by STH.

From the outset, we decided that we would finance the ships conservatively. Robert and I reached out to several potential lenders and concluded
first mortgage loan financings with four different banks across our fleet of
nine ships. The gearing was conservative, at least by maritime standards. We
financed about 55 percent of the cost of each ship with our lenders, and the
balance was equity capital paid into STH by the partners.

We took delivery of the first three ships in 2015, three more in 2016,
one in 2017, and two more in 2018. So, as I write, the average age of our
fleet is about five and a half years, which is considered young by global
standards. We hired a small group of experienced commercial and operational personnel and set ourselves up in a small but comfortable office in
Stamford, Connecticut.

The STH commercial strategy is to act as a provider of tonnage to
charterers around the world. When I was at Navios, we employed our ships

in contracts of affreightment, which we largely controlled, and supported our commercial activity with FFA trading. The STH business model, on the other hand, is much simpler. We own the assets and arrange financing for the ships. We employ a third-party technical manager to oversee the technical ship management of our fleet. We charter them at daily rates of hire to end users, who employ the ships in their own trades. It is rare that we ever have shipbrokers quote any of our ships as being "open charter free" in the market. We have found the charterers of our vessels generally approach us privately to extend the charters with them or to ask when the next ship in our fleet will become available for charter. I believe this is largely a result of the Japanese pedigree of our assets and the quality of our small but very experienced staff.

However, challenges remained. When we ordered our ships, we believed we were entering the market at an opportune time, given the historical pricing of newbuildings. But, by the time they delivered to STH, the dry bulk markets had not rebounded to the extent we had hoped. We were nevertheless able to charter the ships out to industrial end users, commodity traders, and grain merchants. The level of charter hire we were able to achieve from 2015 through to late 2020 covered all our costs: servicing our debt, employing crews, and covering all our shoreside general and administrative expenses.

***

Over the years, I have had many opportunities to visit ships in different locations around the world, including opportunities to attend ship launchings in Japan. But even during my voyages on board Fednav's *Federal Saguenay*, I had never crawled throughout the insides of an entire ship, bow to stern. It was something I had always wanted to do, but I was always too busy to set aside the time. The opportunity presented itself in November 2016, which was just two months before the completion of construction of the MV *STH Chiba*, a sixty-thousand-deadweight ultramax bulk carrier, and the seventh unit to deliver into the STH fleet.

I was in Tokyo on a seven-day business trip and was able to free up one day for this adventure. Early one morning, I arranged for a car to take me out to the MES Chiba shipyard, which was ideal because it was located a relatively quick one-hour car ride from the center of Tokyo. The managing director of the shipyard and a few of his management colleagues met me there. Of course, they all thought it was rather strange that the managing director of STH was coming to their yard to take a detailed tour of the ship so late in the building process. When I arranged this outing, it never occurred to me that the yard personnel might be concerned that I was going to inspect their work; so, I immediately tried to set them at ease by explaining I was not an engineer, and the visit was purely for personal reasons. They seemed incredulous, but in typical Japanese fashion, they were too polite to question it.

Because we lacked any technical management expertise in our small STH office, and unlike most other shipowners who order ships in Japan, we felt it would be beneficial to have "our" representative on-site during construction. We retained an experienced technical superintendent, a Romanian named Petrut Palade, and stationed him at the yard to keep an eye on things during the thirteen-month building process. He is the one who met me and gave me the grand tour. I donned coveralls and a hard hat, and at sixty-three years of age, I spent six hours exploring every nook and cranny of that ship.

The ultramax ships in the STH fleet are midsize dry bulk vessels of sixty thousand deadweight tonnes, with an overall length of two hundred meters, a beam of thirty-two meters, and a draft when fully loaded of about thirteen meters. Their lightweight is about 10,500 tonnes. Our ships are designed as single-hull bulk carriers, with five holds and five accordion-style hatch covers that open in the fore and aft directions. Thirty-tonne-capacity **pedestal cranes** are spaced between the number-one and number-five hatch covers. These four cranes can rotate 360 degrees, and each of them can access the holds fore and aft.

We started at the lowermost extremity of the engine room and worked our way up. From the main weather deck, through a watertight door at the stern of the ship, we climbed down three stories of very steep metal stairs to the very bottom of the ship. The immense six-cylinder engine loomed two stories above us. I was able to touch the intermediate tail shaft that protrudes out from the engine and connects through the after-peak collision bulkhead (the first main transverse watertight bulkhead forward of the stern of a ship) to the propeller of the ship. The propellers on our ships consist of five large brass blades that have a diameter of about twenty-one feet.

The massive brass propellers of the MV *STH Kure*. Note the zinc anodes attached to the hull and rudder. These are used to help reduce steel degradation. The saltwater acts as an electrolyte and transfers electrons from the anodes to the steel plate around it helping to act as a protective layer. Credit: Dave Van der Linden

I was particularly interested to see the **ballast water treatment system** (BWTS), which is a new technology that has been mandated to be retrofitted on all ships by 2023. Ships take on ballast water in one part of the world and quite often discharge it in another, and as a result, invasive marine species are moved around the world in this ballast water. The BWTS essentially "cleans" ballast water before it is discharged so that this egress does not occur. Each of the STH ships was designed and built with BWTS in its engine room. While I had seen the design plans, I had never before seen the actual mechanism.

I visited the main engine control room, which was about the size of a forty-foot transport container filled with all types of electronic controls, most of which I could not make head or tail of. Our superintendent also showed me the freshwater generator (a unit used for conversion of salt water to fresh water for daily use on board a ship), various pumps, the **auxiliary boiler**, and the sewage treatment plant. There is a plethora of systems required to run a large bulk carrier, in addition to an officer and crew complement of twenty people.

**The engine room of the MV *STH Chiba*. Note the stairs
to the right that provide the reader a sense of the size and
depth of the space. Credit: Author's Collection**

Upon exiting the engine room, we made our way through the super-structure of the ship, located directly above the engine room area. The first deck, or A-deck, is located at the same level as the main deck of the ship and houses separate officer and crew dining areas, as well as a large galley, a walk-in freezer area for provisions, laundry facilities, and a meeting/recre-ational room for the crew. The B-deck houses the petty officer and crew bed-rooms, with a shared bathroom for every two cabins. The C-deck is where you find the captain's and the chief engineer's bedrooms, with adjoining day rooms and private bathroom facilities. The second engineer and chief mate are also housed on this deck.

Just above the C-deck is the bridge, or D-deck—the command room of the ship—from which vantage point the officers have a clear view of all aspects of the ship. Equipment on the bridge includes: a gyrocompass; auto-pilot; an echo sounder; a Doppler speed log; radars with automatic radar plotting capability; an electronic chart display information system, which is a computerized navigation system; GPS; an automatic identification system, which continuously transmits a ship's identification and navigational posi-tional data so that maritime authorities and other ships are aware of its posi-tion; a voyage data recorder, which collects data from various sensors located throughout the ship; global maritime distress and safety systems; and bridge navigational watch alarm systems.

From there, we made our way down to the main deck and through a small watertight door built into the number-four **hatch coaming**. We climbed down a ladder, about eighteen meters in length, to the bottom of one of the ship's holds. It is only when you stand in the middle of an empty hold on one of these ships that you come to realize just how large they are. The average length of our holds is 31.2 meters, the width is 32.2 meters, and the height is about 18.5 meters.

All large ships today are built with double bottom tanks located just beneath the steel plate floor of the cargo hold. In other words, ships are double hulled, which provides two essential features. The most important is that double bottom tanks, which generally run the length of the ship from aft of the fore-peak collision bulkhead to the after-peak collision bulkhead located at the stern of the ship, offer a measure of safety to avoid the ingress of water into a cargo hold in case of a grounding or collision. In addition, double hull bulk carriers offer more efficient cargo handling because there are no hull frames or brackets protruding into the cargo holds, just the smooth side of the inner hull. Double bottom tanks are often used to store fuel oil and water ballast. We spent the better part of an hour walking through various parts of the double bottom tanks with flashlights, most of the time bent over as the height was probably not much more than one and a half meters.

Petrut arranged to have one of the ship's cranes with a basket attached to its hook lowered down into the hold to retrieve us from the **tank top** back up to the weather deck. Each of the four cranes on the ship is located atop a raised pedestal of about nine meters, which allows the driver of the crane better visibility when loading and/or discharging cargo. We climbed up the nine-meter ladder attached to the side of the pedestal to the crane driver's cabin. The view of the entire ship was impressive from that height.

Once we were back on the weather deck, we opened a manhole cover and climbed into the topside ballast tanks. These triangular tanks are located at the top of both sides of each hold and provide additional ballast capability to the ship. They are connected to the ship's primary ballast lines, and while a ship is loading or discharging, the volume of water in the topside tanks is continuously monitored and kept in equilibrium with cargo weight.

Ballast arrangements on board large bulk carriers are very important for several reasons. When a ship has no cargo on board and is proceeding to a load port, it will run too high in the water. Water ballast is used to submerge the propeller, aiding in propulsion efficiency and vessel maneuverability. While the ship is at sea, it consumes fuel, and ballast operations help compensate for this weight loss.

The last area we visited was the forecastle of the ship, which is an enclosed partial deck area located at the bow of the vessel. It houses various spares; the chain locker area, which holds the anchor chain cables; and the windlass, which is the winch used to lower and raise the ship's anchor. Our ships have port and starboard anchor chains that are twelve shackles in length, or about 325 meters.

As I write this chapter, the *STH Chiba* is en route to Iskenderun, Turkey, to discharge 51,148 tonnes of ammonium sulfate, which was loaded in Xiamen, China. Her routing has taken her through the Singapore Straits, past Sri Lanka, on her way to the Gulf of Aden, before proceeding into the Red Sea and transiting northbound through the Suez Canal. This route will take the *STH Chiba* through what is known as a **high-risk area** (HRA), specifically the Gulf of Aden, which is bordered by Yemen to the north, Somalia to the south, and Djibouti to the west. HRAs have grown increasingly dangerous in the past decade or so. When transiting HRAs, vessels must remain vigilant for piracy attacks, and when an STH ship passes through an HRA, we take added precautions against high-seas piracy.

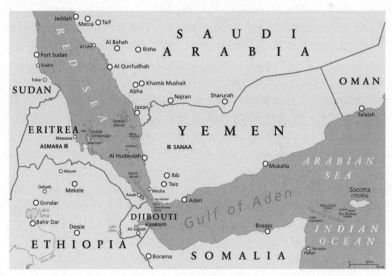

A map of the high-risk route via the Gulf of Aden taken by ships like the MV *STH Chiba*. Credit: Peter Hermes Furian / Alamy Stock Photo

Prior to one of our ships entering an HRA, we arrange to have a riding crew of three armed security personnel join the ship while en route. In the case of the *STH Chiba*, they boarded the ship from the *Grey Palm* transfer vessel, located about 480 kilometers south of Oman in the Arabian Sea. The men are equipped with automatic weapons to help dissuade any potential pirates from attacking our ship. They were disembarked at the *Golden Palm* transfer vessel, located about seventy-five kilometers off the coast of Eritrea in the Red Sea.

In addition to the security team, our crews are instructed to take further measures when transiting through HRAs. They place razor wire around the perimeter of the ship, and they also place high-pressure fire hoses in certain locations on the weather deck to help fight off any attackers. Various watertight doors leading into the ship's accommodation are bolted shut, and the windows on the bridge deck overlooking the weather deck are laminated with a temporary film of security glass.

All of these security measures, most of which are borne by our charterers but arranged by STH, are additional expenses we did not have in the earlier years of my career.

***

I have been very fortunate over the years to have attended numerous launchings and deliveries of new ships. Nevertheless, the traditional ritual continues to be just as thrilling as my first. It is a grand ceremonial event, dating back perhaps centuries. The ceremony usually takes place over about twenty-four hours, and perhaps no nation on the earth has perfected the launching ceremony better than Japan.

The launching of a massive vessel down a slipway is truly an incredible spectacle to behold, one of those sights you really cannot imagine unless seen. There are two primary methods of moving a large oceangoing vessel from a building site into the sea. By far, the most common is to have the ship built in a dry dock, and once completed, the dry dock is flooded and the ship is floated out to sea. The second method, which is increasingly rare, is to have the ship slide down a slipway, stern-first into the water. This method is still employed at Mitsui's Tamano Shipyard, located on the Inland Sea of Japan, a body of water surrounded by three of Japan's main islands: Honshū, Kyūshū, and Shikoku.

In Japan, it is customary for the owner of the ship to host a dinner the evening before the delivery, with a guest list of perhaps twenty to thirty people made up of shipyard executives, trading house representatives, bankers, Japanese classification society representatives, and, of course, the family and guests of the individual launching the ship.

For the dinner prior to the launching day of the MV *STH Oslo* at Tamano Shipyard, we requested everyone wear a *yukata*. As I explained earlier in the book, this is a casual version of the kimono, a robe usually made of cotton wrapped around the body and fastened with a sash. This made for a friendlier and less formal festive event. Everyone was seated Japanese-style on tatami mats, and we enjoyed a few special cultural presentations while the sake flowed liberally.

The traditional owner's dinner that my wife Jen and I hosted the night before the launching of MV *STH Oslo*. Credit: Mitsui Engineering & Shipbuilding

What made this launching extra special was that the sponsor of the ship was my wife, Jen, who christened her on May 16, 2018, sixteen years, almost to the day, after my mother launched the MV *Navios Meridian* at the same yard, down the same slipway. My children, their partners, and a few close friends also attended the *STH Oslo* ceremony with us.

The morning of a ship's delivery, before the ceremonies of cutting of the ribbon, breaking the champagne bottle on the hull, and naming of the ship, the shipyard executives and the owners meet in a conference room at the yard. It is all quite formal, with everyone dressed in their business best. There, all the principal parties sign the legal papers to record the delivery of the ship to the owners, including a protocol of delivery and the acceptance of spare parts inventories, stores and equipment delivered with the ship, and instructions for the release to the yard of the last installment of the agreed purchase price for the ship.

As the sponsor of the ship, Jen was brought to a private room, where a few personnel from the shipyard took her through the words she would speak to christen the ship and, most importantly, showed her how to manage the process of cutting the ribbon. In Japan, this process involves the sponsor using a large, heavy mallet to strike the top of a silver axe, which breaks the cord and releases the bottle of champagne. The silver axe is thought to bring good luck and scare evil spirits away from the ship. Following the ceremony, the mallet and axe are presented to the sponsor as a commemorative gift from the yard.

The launching itself is usually focused on the safety of the ship and the crew who will operate her as she sails away from the yard. All the shipyard workers and some of their family members who had been involved in the construction of the ship attend. For the launching of the STH Oslo, we also welcomed another thirty locals, including schoolchildren, to witness the event. The guests of honor normally stand on a dais facing the bow of the ship, perhaps ten to twelve meters above all the rest of the crowd and shipyard workers.

So, in total, there were perhaps one hundred people gathered as Jen read the following into a microphone on the dais: "I christen you STH Oslo, and I wish you and your crew and your owners every success. May God bless you and all who sail on you!" These words were followed by the ceremonial axe hammering, then the release of the bottle of champagne swinging down toward the bow of the ship, breaking apart as it hits the steel hull. Just as the bottle smashed against the ship, large sixty-foot-colored streamers exploded from casements located on the bow of the ship and unfurled to extend down the full length of the ship to the shipyard floor. The Japanese and American national anthems were played, and everyone was clapping and hollering as the ship slowly started to roll down the slipway into the Inland Sea.

It was undeniably a very proud moment for me.

CHAPTER 25

DECARBONIZATION: AN INFLECTION POINT FOR THE MARITIME INDUSTRY

"There are no passengers on Spaceship Earth. We are all crew."

MARSHALL MCLUHAN,
Canadian philosopher and author

M aritime transport has experienced several transitions in propulsion. A few millennia ago, from paddles and then oars, was a progression to sail; and then, in the nineteenth century, onto steam engines powered by coal. The last major maritime fuel transition occurred in 1912 when Winston Churchill, as the First Lord of the Admiralty, decided to switch the British Royal Navy from Welsh coal to Persian Gulf oil.

At the turn of the nineteenth century, the Royal Navy's fleet included warships burning both coal and oil for their propulsion systems. As the civilian head of the Royal Navy, Churchill established a commission to analyze how to go about making the change from coal to oil across the entire naval fleet. He instructed the commission's chairman, "to find the oil; to show how it can be stored cheaply; how it can be purchased regularly and cheaply in peace, and with absolute certainty during war." He did this because fuel oil, with a thermal content double that of coal, required much less storage capacity on a ship. In addition, it was a much easier fuel to manage on board ships. It could be pumped into holding tanks, as opposed to coal, which had to be handled and moved from storage on a ship to ensure that bunkers nearest the boiler were always full.

This pronouncement influenced the British government's decision in 1914 to buy a controlling stake in the Anglo-Persian Oil Company (one of the antecedents of the modern BP), because at the time, Great Britain had no proven oil reserves of its own.

When oil is refined, it produces distillates such as diesel, gasoline, naphtha, kerosene, and jet fuel, which are "cleaner" and therefore more expensive fuels. Heavy fuel oil—also known as bunker fuel—is the remnant from the distillation of crude oil in the production of petroleum products. It is the "bottom-of-the-barrel" oil. It has a tarlike consistency, and because it is the residue of the refining process, it is contaminated with several different compounds, making it more polluting than other sources of fuel. But it has one great advantage: It is cheaper than all other types of petroleum energy, which is why it has been the fuel of choice for the propulsion of large commercial ships since the early twentieth century.

Each of these propulsion evolutions took a few decades to complete, and we are now in the early transition of yet a new transformational change in maritime propulsion.

As Bill Gates notes in his book, *How to Avoid a Climate Disaster*, past transformations in fuel sources have come about because a new replacement fuel was cheaper or delivered more energy more efficiently. Today, transformational change is happening because of environmental pressures, something we have not seen before. It will therefore be a particularly challenging transition; and because it is not being driven by improved power designs or by economics, it will be expensive.

***

The International Maritime Organization (IMO), created in 1958, is a special United Nations agency originally tasked with responsibility for maritime safety and efficiency of navigation standards. IMO promulgates new rules for the industry regularly that all **flag state** nations around the world are obligated to enforce. Over the past few decades, its area of focus has increasingly been the prevention of marine pollution by ships. According to IMO, about 90 percent of global trade is transported by oceangoing vessels, and when one considers the value of the products carried, and alternative types of transport, ships provide the most economical and least environmentally damaging mode of global transport.

According to Oceana Europe, a philanthropic organization established by the Pew Charitable Trusts charged with protecting the oceans, about 2.5 percent of global carbon dioxide emissions come from ships trading around the world. Also, according to Pew, if ocean shipping were a country, it would be the sixth-largest producer of greenhouse gas (GHG) emissions after the United States, China, Russia, India, and Japan. Clarksons Research estimates that 1.8 percent of world GHG emissions (not just carbon dioxide) are emitted from the global fleet of ships.

If one defines carbon efficiency as a measurement of output that is produced with minimum carbon emissions relative to others in one's sector, then the maritime industry is far ahead of its transportation peers. According to Clarksons Research, the maritime sector's carbon efficiency is three times more effective than rail and nine times more effective than trucking. Nevertheless, as with most industries today, the maritime transport sector is very focused on new decarbonization regulations and initiatives, and our industry has made some significant improvements in the suppression of GHG emissions.

IMO promulgated new rules in the first decade of this century to address nitrogen oxide (NOx) emissions from large ships. IMO Tier I is a global exhaust emission level focused exclusively on NOx, which was applied to all ships built from 2000 onward. IMO Tier II, which represents a 20 percent reduction in NOx emissions over Tier I, went into effect for all ships built after 2011. IMO Tier III standards are now coming into effect for new ships, and this standard will represent a 70 percent reduction in permitted emissions from Tier I standards.

On January 1, 2020, new regulations—known as IMO 2020—came into effect that limit the sulfur content of fuel oil used on board commercial vessels. This has resulted in a significant decrease in sulfur oxide (SOx) emissions from ships. Before this new legislation was enacted, most large ships burned intermediate fuel oil (IFO), which is a blend of heavy fuel oil and gas oil. IFO is the fuel that goes into a ship's engine to create propulsion. It has a high level of viscosity (like that of peanut butter) and therefore must be heated to allow it to flow, burning even more energy to do so. It has a sulfur content of 3.5 percent. With the arrival of IMO 2020, ships have had to migrate away from burning IFO to burning very low sulfur fuel oil (VLSFO), which has a sulfur content of .5 percent, making it far less polluting.

In addition, IMO has established even stricter emission control areas, which have been adopted by certain nation states. Currently ships steaming into the Baltic Sea, the North Sea, the coasts of North America, certain areas of the Caribbean, parts of coastal China, and the major port areas of South Korea are only permitted to burn VLSFO with a maximum sulfur content of .1 percent, further limiting the release of SOx.

As I discussed earlier, shipyards have also begun to build ships with new hull designs, electronic eco engines, and various ESDs. Previously I pointed out that the STH ultramax ships burn on average about six tonnes per day less fuel than a similar-size non-eco vessel. Trafigura, a Swiss-based multinational commodity trading firm, estimates that for every tonne of VLSFO burned by a ship, there is a release of 3.15 tonnes of CO_2, another serious GHG, into the atmosphere. Our fleet of nine eco ships, which spends about 55 percent of its time at sea, emits about thirty-four thousand tonnes *less* CO_2 emissions per year, about a 20 percent improvement over ships with the mechanical engine. That is progress.

So contrary to what you might be reading in the press, the owners who control the world's fleets of ships are making efforts to reduce GHG emissions. But as is true with so many other industries, the pressure is building to move faster if we are to help in the universal effort to address global climate change. It seems a week does not go by now without some policy announcement or commentary from IMO, the EU, the Organization for Economic Co-operation and Development (OECD), commodity producers, shipowners, and cargo interests on how to get the maritime sector to improve the pace of its GHG initiatives.

***

In July 2021, the EU announced its plans to bring the maritime sector into their Emission Trading System (ETS), the first multicountry GHG emissions program, established in 2005. The maritime portion will be initiated in January 2023, with a phased-in approach over the next three years, so that all ships trading to EU ports will be required to buy allowances for CO_2 emissions by 2026.

There are a lot of moving parts to this new development, and so any estimates at this juncture are still somewhat academic. Nevertheless, Braemar ACM, a shipbrokering firm with headquarters in London and a global footprint, has estimated that at the current European emission allowances (EEA) futures price (about $70/ton), a typical panamax ship moving grain from South America into Europe would be required to purchase about $150,000 of carbon allowances, come 2026. That would translate into an additional freight cost of about $3 per ton of cargo, which will ultimately be passed on to the buyer and eventually to the general consumer.

The net effect of the EU ETS will be to increase pressure to scrap ships that burn more fuel and produce more CO_2 emissions because they will require the purchase of more EEA futures than the eco vessels.

There are several very early-stage initiatives being considered as alternatives to fuel oil that will help all industries to meet the climate change challenge. Some, such as liquefied natural gas (LNG), hydrogen, ammonia, atomic technology, and battery, are under active research today, but all of these are still at the early stages of development. I think it might be a decade, perhaps longer, before a new alternate fuel source of choice becomes mainstream for the maritime industry.

One of the major challenges to shifting the industry to more environmentally friendly fuels is the requirement for a new global infrastructure that can distribute, store, and refuel vessels with these new fuels. Ships need to be bunkered at various points on their voyages around the globe. It is relatively easy to convert the propulsion system from fuel oil to a combination of different biofuels on a ferry with a short, dedicated trade route. The same is true for container ships, because they tend to sail on regular schedules to designated ports of call. But tankers and dry bulk ships, which together account for about 75 percent of the global fleet of ships over ten thousand deadweight tonnes, operate as "tramps," an old term that characterized the nature of their routes—anywhere and everywhere, taking on cargo as needed. In order to shift over to any of these potential new fuels, ships will have to be bunkered at various points on their voyages around the globe. This is an overwhelming infrastructure challenge.

No one knows today what future regulations might be instituted that will require a complete redesign of propulsion systems at sea and **bunkering** installations on land. This could result in ships that are ordered now and delivered in 2025 through 2026 faced with technical obsolescence shortly after their delivery into an owner's fleet. Consequently, many dry bulk shipowners are currently delaying orders for newbuildings until there is more clarity around this issue.

There is a general consensus developing among the maritime community that the most effective method to decrease GHG emissions is for IMO to mandate a slow-speed regime throughout our industry to deal with GHG emissions. Speed optimization is *effective*, as it easily can be implemented; is *efficient*, because it reduces GHG emissions significantly by using less power; and is *immediate*, because it can be put in place quickly.

For instance, if the charterers of our STH ships reduced their ordered speed from fourteen knots to twelve knots, our consumption would drop to about sixteen tonnes of fuel burn a day, down from twenty-five tonnes. That is a 36 percent reduction in fuel consumed with an equivalent reduction in GHG emissions. Another benefit is a potential decrease in wait times at load ports and discharge ports. Ships quite often arrive at a port and wait a day or two or more to berth before the shoreside activity begins, wasting fuel and valuable time.

There is yet another benefit to enforcing speed optimization: It will reduce the supply of available ship days. A two-knot reduction across the non-eco dry bulk fleet effectively means a loss of about 6 percent of vessel capacity, as voyages will take longer to complete. The result of such a measure, assuming demand remains static, would be to increase *meaningfully* the daily earning capacity for the fleet.

Because of the potential higher earnings, a speed mandate would also allow the industry to enact a fuel tax of perhaps 25 percent, or about $150 per tonne, on all bunkering transactions. The effect would be to harvest an enormous sum of money which could be used to develop a "winner" for the new fuel propulsion system of the next generation of ships. Just as crucially, the funds could also be used to help build the global bunkering infrastructure required to support the new propulsion fuel.

***

In addition to the changes to the rapidly developing maritime fuel landscape, which I highlighted, there are other mounting third-party pressures that are serving to bring about fuel propulsion change through a focus on extensive reporting of maritime emissions.

A new global initiative in this area, established in 2019, is the Poseidon Principles, a group made up largely of thirty international banks that are very active in providing finance to the maritime industry. These institutions, which are focused on aligning their shipping portfolios with responsible environmental behavior, do so by assisting shipowners to finance the acquisition of fuel-efficient ships and newbuildings with alternative fuel capabilities, such as LNG, methanol, and battery power. Each institution is responsible for establishing a framework to report on the climate alignment of their shipping portfolios. More recently, we are learning of certain ship finance loan documentation that includes an interest rate margin adjustment mechanism based on a ship's carbon intensity rating, which provides an incentive for individual shipowners to reduce their ship's carbon footprint.

Sea Cargo Charter, which was established in 2020, serves as a vehicle for its corporate signatories to assess and disclose each company's maritime decarbonization footprint in relation to its stated climate goals. The major global grain traders, numerous large commodity trading firms, and a number of shipowning companies have signed on to this charter. The notion behind the Sea Cargo Charter is to create a global standard for analyzing emissions from ships as they move cargo around the world.

And these market pressures are having an impact. According to Clarksons Research, about 35 percent of all newbuilding ship orders in 2022 (dry bulk, tankers, and container ships) were contracted with alternative-fuel capabilities. This means, that in addition to burning VLSFO, these vessels' engines have been designed to cross over to certain alternative fuels for propulsion as these alternative fuels become proven and available.

I do not think shipowners and charterers of ships have yet to fully realize the effect this emerging new landscape might have on the dry bulk market. Collectively, these broad measures will create significant disruptions to the availability of ships, which could have a dramatic impact on vessel supply.

CHAPTER 26

DRY BULK: WHERE TO FROM HERE?

"Prediction is very difficult, especially if it's about the future."

NIELS BOHR,
Danish physicist

———————

There has been a steady upward trend in the growth of dry bulk trade for the past forty years (see Chart A, Chapter 1). Indeed, this growth began a few decades earlier with the rebuilding of Europe and Japan, following the Second World War. Except for occasional global economic impacts—such as the 1997 East Asian financial crisis, the 2008 through 2009 financial calamity, and the more recent COVID-19 pandemic—growth in seaborne dry bulk movements has continued uninterrupted for the past seventy years, propelled by three primary drivers.

By far, the most important driver in the growth of seaborne dry bulk commodities has been the globalization of trade among countries. Perhaps the key determinant of this development has been the level of international cooperation as countries endeavor to increase their export markets and source goods and commodities that are not available domestically. The World Trade Organization is the body responsible for instituting rules governing trade between its 164 member nations, and its stated goal is to "use trade as a means to improve the living standards of people across the globe." To paraphrase the Dartmouth economic historian Douglas Irwin, the creation of global trade policy has facilitated the rapid growth of world trade.

MV *STH Oslo* discharging a cargo of Chilean road salt in Three Rivers, Quebec. The backhoe is scraping up the last of the cargo into a pile so that the large grab bucket can continue the discharge. Credit: Author's Collection

The second driver of increasing commodity flows is the development of global commodity traders, who trade in oil, agricultural products, and various metals and commodities. The concept of comparative advantage encourages countries to produce or manufacture what they do best, which translates into more efficient use of resources and lowers the cost of goods. But these goods need to be moved, and it is the commodity traders acting as efficient middlemen who provide the pathways and conduits for the interchange of commodities across the globe. Their role effectively ensures a match between the sellers and buyers of an endless variety of cargoes. Companies involved in trading with a global footprint include, among many others, Glencore, Trafigura, Vitol, Gunvor, and Koch Industries, which were originally focused on oil but now trade a plethora of commodities; ADM, Bunge, Cargill, Louis Dreyfus, and COFCO, which trade agricultural products; and traders such as Wilmar and Olam, focused on sugar, rice, and palm oil.

The increasing flow of commodities across the globe has been aided by the explosive growth of China's industrial, manufacturing, and, more recently, consumer sectors. The nation's economic growth over the past forty years has created insatiable demand for both wet and dry bulk commodities.

The fragmentation thirty years ago of the former Soviet Union into numerous new countries also created fresh sources and avenues for the flow of commodities.

Maritime transport is the third leg—some would argue the backbone—of globalization. The development of larger and more sophisticated ships has led to improvements—not just in the volumes of cargoes carried across the oceans, but also in providing cost-effective transportation solutions. In addition, there has developed a robust infrastructure that surrounds maritime transport today. This includes not just IMO, but dozens of flag states, classification societies, international protection and indemnity clubs (independent, not-for-profit mutual insurance associations), and a well-developed body of maritime law, all of which serve to support global maritime transport.

***

The dramatic growth in seaborne dry bulk trade over the past thirty years has been driven by demand for three major commodities: iron ore, used in the fabrication of crude steel; thermal coal, used to generate electric power; and grains, produced to feed not just humans, but livestock as well. In 2022, these three commodities made up about 56 percent of total dry bulk volumes, and so they are considered to be the primary drivers of the dry bulk freight market.

There are a few significant takeaways from Chart B below. The first is that the dramatic rise in seaborne movements that commenced in the first decade of this century seems to correspond with China's entry into the WTO in 2001. The second is that the movement of thermal coal looks to be "peaking." Thermal coal imports into the EU have been in a decline for the past decade due to decarbonization initiatives by governments within this bloc. Unfortunately, these reductions are being offset by import increases in various Asian countries. (The current Russian-Ukrainian war will likely cause the import of thermal coal into Europe in the near term to reverse its downward trend, for Russian oil and gas supplies will become a strategic liability.) But to my way of thinking, the writing is on the wall: Global decarbonization initiatives are placing a ceiling on movements of thermal coal, and sometime within the next five to seven years, I believe we will see movements of this commodity on a declining trend.

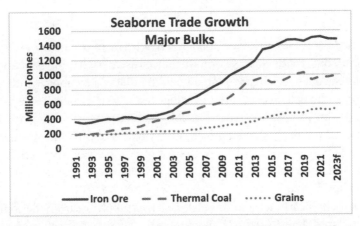

Chart B. Source: Clarksons Research Shipping Intelligence Network

The last takeaway is that almost all the growth in iron ore imports can be attributed to Chinese industrial development and urbanization over the past twenty years. As the Chinese economy matures, just as Japan did in the 1970s and 1980s and South Korea did in the 1980s and 1990s, its GDP growth rates will slow. In fact, we have already started to see this happen. Environmental pressures on steel-making capacity and the aging demographic of this country will also serve to hasten this change. This will eventually translate into a reduction in infrastructure development, thereby reducing the growth in crude steel production.

There is a thesis circulating today that India might very well replace China as the next global manufacturing hub, leading to rapid industrial development that will help propel the maritime markets to yet new highs. Its population demographic is a decade younger than that of China, the government of India is much less controversial from a geopolitical perspective, and labor wages in India are about one-quarter of those in China. But I believe these advantages are more than counterbalanced by one major disadvantage: Unlike China, India is a messy democracy. It is not able to benefit from a centrally planned autocracy, such as one finds in Beijing, which has been so instrumental in allowing China's rapid economic development.

The two main demand drivers of the dry bulk freight market could potentially be ending their thirty-year bull run sometime within the next five to seven years. This is not good news for those of us with investments in bulk carriers.

***

Now contrast what I have said about the steady rise of seaborne movements of commodities with Chart C. You might well ask what has happened to dry bulk rates. As I have already pointed out, the BDI is a composite index that represents the daily time charter earnings of the four principal-size categories of dry bulk ships. And what does this chart tell us? Given what I have just reviewed about the sustained growth in dry bulk seaborne movements, it is the oversupply of ships that has impacted global levels of maritime freight. The result? A ceiling creating low levels of freight rates that, as I write, are just beginning to recover.

One significant factor in this historical oversupply has been the commitment to build ships in Japan. This country has a very small natural resource base, and with urbanization and industrialization in the second half of the twentieth century, imports surged. The government increased shipbuilding capacity to support its growing domestic steel-making capabilities and provide much-needed employment. But more strategically, this new shipyard capacity provided an unprecedented supply of new ships, effectively guaranteeing an oversupply of vessels and, by extension, low levels of freight for Japanese commodity imports.

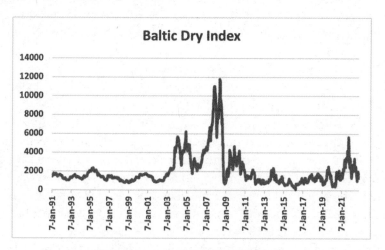

Chart C. Source: Baltic Shipping Exchange

And in the first decade of this century, China did the same. Because of the booming freight markets in 2004 through 2008, the government supported the development of massive shipyard capacity just at the time shipowners around the world thought our markets had entered a new "paradigm." They set about ordering a massive supply of new ships primarily from Chinese shipyards, which were delivered a few years later, effectively depressing the overall dry bulk market and reducing China's cost of importing dry bulk commodities.

***

Currently, newbuilding orders for dry bulk ships are at their lowest level in thirty years, which reflects several factors. Newbuilding prices remain high due to the increasing cost of steel plate, and increasing pressure for decarbonization, resulting in new, more environmentally friendly designs and the commensurate higher cost to build or retrofit ships up to new regulatory codes. There has been a significant reduction in the number of shipyards over the past decade, and a container ship ordering spree over the past three years has locked up the remaining shipyard capacity, well into 2025.

In addition, the current strong dry bulk market makes it more attractive to invest in existing "on-the-water" ships that provide a revenue-earning asset within months, as opposed to years with a newbuilding order. And maritime finance is much reduced due to fewer lending institutions and a focus on lending for eco ships.

I believe the new levels of regulatory legislation promulgated by IMO will, by necessity, cause slow-speed mandates to be established across a broad section of the fleet just at a time when newbuilding orders are very low. The resulting dearth of new orders and forced obsolescence due to new decarbonization pressures for dry bulk ships might lead our sector into unchartered waters.

It is conceivable that this new dynamic could help compensate for the possible demand disruption from reduced seaborne movements of iron ore and thermal coal that I have highlighted earlier.

It remains to be seen how these two potential offsetting developments will play out over the next few years. The decarbonization of the maritime industry presents those of us in the business with some enormous challenges. However, I firmly believe that for those companies and shipowners who have the foresight to position their companies appropriately, even greater opportunities will launch from these challenges.

CHAPTER 27

JUST GOOD BUSINESS
SENSE, REVISITED

"Ninety percent of selling is conviction
and 10 percent is persuasion."

SHIV KHERA,
Indian author of *You Can Win*

O n August 27, 2015, the MV *STH Athens* was the first of nine new-building ships to deliver into the STH fleet. The remaining eight newbuilding ships were all delivered from the shipyards between October 2015 and October 2018.

The spot market charter earnings of the ultramax category ship from September 2015 through to the end of 2020 averaged $9,450 per day. As the end of 2020 approached and we moved into 2021, the dry bulk markets started a steep ascent, and ultramax charter rates moved up from about $13,000 to about $40,000 per day. The average spot charter rate for an ultramax ship in 2021 was $30,906 per day, and for 2022, $25,569 per day (these numbers assume a 15 percent premium over the Baltic Supramax Index).

So, what had happened to the dry bulk market over the past twenty-four months? What accounted for this dramatic increase?

The last maritime dry bulk bull market occurred from 2003 through 2008. It was driven by elevated demand for dry bulk commodities in China, due to the enormous rates of Chinese urbanization and industrialization in the last decade of the twentieth century and the first decade of the twenty-first century. These demand drivers caused dry bulk market rates to soar to levels never before witnessed.

Today, we are in yet another surge in freight and time charter rates. It is not as pronounced as the last one, and the factors contributing to it are different.

The impact of the COVID-19 pandemic is principal among them. The global monetary and fiscal policies that countries across the world instituted to counteract the severe negative economic impacts of the pandemic caused global GDP growth to reach an impressive 5.8 percent in 2021. Although GDP growth figures for 2022 are expected to be more subdued, at the time of writing, the consensus is that it will be about 3 percent, which is the average rate of annual global GDP growth in the twenty-first century. High global GDP growth translates into increasing demand for commodities.

Over the past several years, the pandemic has created elevated levels of port congestion throughout the world. Most news reports have focused on queues of container ships waiting to load in China or discharge in the United States. But port congestion has also impacted the dry bulk sector, with a particular concentration on some countries that are very important to global trade, but it is not as widely reported. For example, in 2020 and 2021, Australia, a major exporter of iron ore and coal, instituted fourteen-day quarantines for vessels arriving at their ports. China, which is a major importer of all types of bulk commodities, instituted similar draconian quarantine measures. These actions detained ships in ports in these countries for extended periods, reducing the supply of available vessels for global trade. Although port congestion is currently declining, the aftereffects are still being felt. Fewer available ships increased the daily charter rates dramatically.

In addition, there have been vessel delays throughout the world caused by issues related to the crews that man them. Routinely, crews are changed or repatriated at various ports of call. However, throughout the pandemic, and, to some extent, as of this writing, policies concerning quarantine have impacted this process. STH has had crews arrive at certain ports, only to have one of the dozen crew members test positive for COVID-19. This resulted in the crew having to quarantine ashore, which prevented the scheduled crew change from proceeding. Other times, we have had to keep a ship at anchor for an additional three or four days awaiting logistical clearance of crews under ever-changing regulations.

Different national policies related to COVID-19 travel have meant that STH and other maritime companies have had to deviate our ships outside of their scheduled itineraries into ports where crew exchanges routinely took place without a problem. The Philippines is a major provider of ship's crews, and on more than one occasion, STH has deviated a vessel in ballast en route from north China to load at a port on the east coast of Australia to Manila for a crew change, resulting in perhaps three days of additional steaming time. These types of delays take vessel capacity out of the market and serve to tighten the available supply of ships.

Another factor affecting the dry bulk market is the current conflict in Ukraine, which has exacerbated the already tight dry bulk freight market. About 10 percent of global grain exports, or roughly 50 million tonnes, are exported out of Ukraine and Russia. The combined fertilizer exports (urea, potash, sulfur, etc.) from both countries are about 35 million tonnes. Ukraine also exports significant amounts of iron ore, 17 million tonnes in 2021.

Because of the disruptions to these exports due to the war, the importers of these commodities continue to be forced to search for new sources of supply. The substitute exporters they find often are located farther afield, resulting in greater **tonne-mile** demand. For instance, a large portion of Ukrainian grain is exported to the Middle East, North Africa, and Egypt. These importers have turned to the United States and South American grain markets for supply, which require more vessel time to transport an equivalent amount of commodity.

Perhaps the most dramatic impact of the Ukraine war has been its effect on the pricing of fossil fuels. Most EU countries have now cut or announced future cuts of imports of Russian oil. Russia has cut the supply of gas to certain European countries as well. This has caused several European nations to review, in the short term, their restrictive, climate-friendly policies on the burning of thermal coal for electricity production. The dry bulk market benefits from such plans as EU nations increase their imports of thermal coal to help offset the increased cost of oil and natural gas.

To add further fuel to the fire (pun intended), the underinvestment within the fossil fuel industry over the past decade due to lower per-barrel prices has created a serious supply issue leading to a dramatic increase in the cost of oil. The barrel price of crude oil averaged about $90 in 2022. This has caused the price of VLSFO, which in the second quarter of 2020 was selling for about $250 per tonne, to reach levels approaching $600 per tonne today.

All these disruptors have in aggregate reduced the available supply of ships at a time when the stream of newbuilding ships scheduled to deliver into the market in 2023 and 2024 is rapidly declining. There is a reluctance on the part of shipowners of generic dry bulk vessels to order new ships as they await further clarification on emission regulations. The result is that today the dry bulk forward order book of newbuildings, relative to the existing on-the-water fleet, is at its lowest point in over thirty years.

All these supply and demand transformations have not only impacted the freight market, but also encouraged rapidly rising ship values. Just as there is a daily freight rate market for a myriad of commodity movements across the globe, there is also a sale and purchase market for the price of ships. Although it is not as finely defined as the freight rate market, the sale and purchase market nevertheless fluctuates every few weeks. It is essentially a commodity market characterized by high volatility.

Several factors help to determine the underlying purchase price level of a ship. Age and the particular specifications of a vessel play an important role in determining value. The cost of a newbuilding and the time frame for delivery of such a ship versus the secondhand price of an on-the-water existing vessel are also significant elements in price valuation. Buyers and sellers will also be influenced by the ratio of the current price of a ship to its historical pricing. But perhaps the most essential determinant in the value proposition for a ship is the seller's and buyer's expectation of the forward freight market.

***

In the first quarter of 2016, the value of a five-year-old Japanese-built eco ultramax was about $18 million. In January 2022, a five-year-old unit was worth about $32 million.

When the STH newbuilding program was completed in 2018, I knew the company had a unique fleet. No one else in the international maritime markets had a fleet of nine modern, Japanese-built, eco ultramax ships. In addition, a few years after the delivery of our last ship, MES decided it would no longer build commercial ships. They chose to transition their two shipyards in Japan to the construction of naval ships for the Japan Self-Defense Forces. Although JMU, the other very large shipbuilding company, still builds commercial bulk carriers, it is no longer constructing ultramax vessels. The business decisions by these yards had made our fleet even more unique and sought after.

The general perception in the present dry bulk market is that the demand for the midsize ultramax category of ships makes them more attractive targets for investment and/or purchase than the larger kamsarmax and capesize ships. The latter categories of vessels have historically been dependent on the huge volumes of dry bulk imports into China, which have softened. The ultramax category of ships can service a wider variety of cargoes that are moved between a myriad of countries. These include, among others, commodities such as fertilizers, forestry products, alumina, nickel and manganese ores, scrap metal, cement, salt, and steel products, in addition to coal and grains.

Nothing highlights this more dramatically than comparing the recent capesize and ultramax daily earnings. In 2022, the average earnings of the capesize category of ship are $16,300, whereas the ultramax ship has earned $25,569. This is quite extraordinary when one considers that the newbuilding price of a capesize unit is normally about double that of the ultramax ship.

Assuming no dividends and conservative market assumptions for 2023, STH would have been a debt-free company by the end of that year and poised for a profitable future. However, despite positive demand projections, Robert and I were increasingly concerned about the elevated geopolitical and financial headwinds facing the global economy.

The Ukrainian war, which was originally expected to be a blitzkrieg that would last a week, was now looking to become a protracted engagement. Russia and China's increasingly close relations as trading partners could disrupt global trade, as well as the fate of Taiwan as an independent municipality. In addition, for the first time in its history, the democratic institutions of the United States were under fire: Major political figures were repudiating, without proof and for selfish political reasons, the validity of the election process at all levels of government; and laws were being promulgated that did not reflect the will of the majority of the population.

Inflation rates in the major economies around the globe were hitting multiple-decade highs, and central banks had commenced a tightening cycle of interest rates, which was bound to slow economic growth. It was particularly worrisome for developing economies with heavy U.S. dollar borrowings. Additionally, we were concerned with the rapid strengthening of the U.S. dollar. The commodity markets are dollar-denominated, and for countries and businesses holding nondollar currency, the cost of buying their imports has been increasing significantly. Most analysts expect the barrel price of oil to remain at elevated levels throughout 2023 and into 2024, which will be a tax on businesses and consumers throughout the world that will negatively impact economic growth.

Not only had hull values doubled, but similar to the sale of Navios in 2005, there was a perception that the dry bulk market had another few years of attractive runway ahead of it caused by a lack of forward newbuilding deliveries and the increasing decarbonization pressures that I have highlighted earlier. Any buyer would be able to lock in a positive earnings stream and, depending on how the buyer might structure an acquisition financially, it could provide a two-year cash-on-cash return of between 20 and 30 percent. For all these reasons, Robert and I felt the timing was good to explore the sale of the company, and following a few Zoom meetings with Anastassis David and George Mouskas to enlighten them on our thinking, we decided to sell.

We retained Evercore, a New York–based investment bank with a global footprint, to represent STH in the sale process and provide us with strategic advisory counsel. We targeted twenty-two possible buyer targets, fifteen of whom signed nondisclosure agreements and received our confidential offering memorandum. Six signatories were publicly listed maritime companies, another five were private ship-owning companies, and four were asset management firms with some exposure to the maritime sector. The potential buyers were given twenty-one days to provide bids.

Evercore developed a comparative analysis of the various bids that included, among other items, the bidder's ability to pay, an evaluation of the financial statements of the public companies, and the ability of an acquirer to get to the finish line in what was a large and unique acquisition opportunity. We narrowed the process down to a few potential buyers, but it soon became apparent that Diana Shipping Inc., a New York Stock Exchange–listed maritime entity headquartered in Athens, Greece, seemed to be the most motivated to get a deal done. Together with Evercore, we analyzed the performance of Diana's common stock, the company's financial results, its dividend policy, and the average daily trading volumes of the stock over the previous twelve quarters.

On August 11, 2022, we concluded an asset, as opposed to corporate, sale of the fleet for $330 million to Diana Shipping Inc. Two-thirds of the purchase price was cash, and the balance common stock, and it was the percentage relationship between these two elements that proved to be the most difficult aspect of the negotiation. We preferred an all-cash transaction, but the cash bidders were offering levels about 10 percent below the net asset value of our fleet based on the present market, whereas Diana was paying us a price 10 percent above our NAV.

The proceeds, both cash and stock, were be paid to us on a staggered basis as each of the nine ships redelivered back to STH at the end of their existing charters between October 2022 and January 2023, and then subsequently delivered to the buyers. The benefit for STH was that we managed to keep the profitable charters on our balance sheet for most of 2022.

There have been some negative press accounts concerning the sale of our fleet, focused on the price the buyers have paid for the ships. The financial analysts seem to be fixated on the fact that Diana paid us a premium to our fleet NAV and issued stock at about 18 percent below Diana's estimated common stock NAV. But there are some strong strategic reasons for the acquisition.

The dry bulk freight market was generally depressed in the three years leading up to 2020. In response, Diana initiated a stock buyback program. They acquired about $120 million of their stock at around $3.25 per share, and as part of the acquisition, they have now effectively reissued almost all of that stock to STH at $5.95 per share. A significant increase in valuation. In addition, the Diana fleet consisted primarily of kamsarmax up to capesize ships, and our nine ships provided the company exposure to the midsize category of dry bulk carriers. As I have highlighted earlier, these are less dependent on the Chinese market. Lastly, Diana acquired a fleet of nine ships with electronic engines, and an average age of five and a half years at the time of sale, which is about half the age of Diana's existing fleet. The STH ultramax ships are also viewed as premium units, because Japanese-built ships are generally considered better assets than similar-size ships built in China.

The parties to the transaction have come away satisfied that they have concluded the right deal for the right strategic reasons. That is simply good business.

CHAPTER 28

LESSONS LEARNED

"There are certain life lessons that you
can only learn in the struggle."

Idowu Koyenikan,
African and American business consultant

———————

I think it is important for any business leader to focus on a few fundamental truths that I believe are important when managing an international enterprise. So, at the risk of sounding a bit didactic, I would like to share with you a few lessons I have learned throughout my forty-eight years working in the maritime industry.

INTEGRITY

I am convinced that to succeed in business an organization must have an operating philosophy that reflects integrity. A business must establish an ethical code of conduct with an adherence to a framework of honesty and fairness. Without this, I do not believe a business will survive long-term. Most importantly, for a company to weave the thread of integrity into its fabric, the example must be set from the top of the organization.

Operating a global maritime transportation business in which one comes into contact with a variety of countries, each with its cultural norms and regulations, can present special challenges. It is imperative that a business leader stay informed on a wide variety of parameters and market forces that affect operations and profitability. These include "commissions" associated with business being concluded in some countries.

There are times when commissions, other than those that might be normal for an industry, may be requested when concluding a deal. They might be called a "facilitation fee" or an "introduction fee," but they are not the norm, and they are all too often simply a bribe, which might challenge the code of ethics established in a company.

In 1994, Sean Day and I were in Caracas putting the final touches on a new ten-year contract of affreightment with FMO. The existing contract was expiring at the end of that year, and we had been in talks with FMO for over twelve months to renew the contract for an additional ten years.

On the final day of our meetings, we met the former head of CVG, Leopoldo Sucre Figarella. He had oversight responsibilities for the industrial complex of the country; he had been a full cabinet member in government and had arguably been the second most powerful man in the country after the president. Although he had recently "retired," the seated official still looked to Sucre for guidance. He wielded considerable sway, although he was still very much operating behind the scenes. We were scheduled to meet with him as an act of good faith and respect.

We arrived midmorning to be greeted by one of his assistants, who walked us through an elegant set of offices to an anteroom, where we waited for the better part of forty minutes. Eventually we were ushered in to meet the man, who was sitting behind an enormous desk in a cavernous office with a large meeting table, separate dining and living room areas, and what looked to be a private washroom off to one side.

This was only the second time I had met the former minister, and it would be my last. As we walked into his office, he was seated behind his oversize desk wearing a baseball cap and sunglasses; he did not rise to greet us. Sean led the conversation while I listened and took notes. The terms for the contract renewal had been largely agreed by then, so the meeting was more about general pleasantries and a discussion about the long history of Navios's involvement in the movement of iron ore on the Orinoco River.

At one point, one of three aides standing off to the side approached and tapped me on the shoulder, indicating that I should follow him out of the meeting room. Standing in the adjacent anteroom, he gave me a slip of paper with the name of a Panamanian bank and an account number, and said, "The contract is yours, but we would like to see a one percent fee on the contract revenue transferred into this account each time Navios receives a payment for freight under the terms of the freight contract."

A few minutes later, Sean exited Sucre's office and we made our way directly to Simón Bolívar Airport, where we were catching the afternoon American Airlines flight back to New York. Sean was elated we had managed to conclude the new contract, because we had three or four competitors who were aggressively pursuing it. It was with some apprehension, then, that I showed him the note and explained to him what had happened with Sucre's aide. The flight home was somber. Not only did this business make up about 25 percent of our corporate revenue, but as you have read earlier, Navios was formed as a subsidiary of U.S. Steel in 1954, specifically to carry iron ore out of the Orinoco River. The company had been transporting this commodity ever since.

But it was on that flight home that I received one of the greatest lessons of integrity in my business career. Before we landed at JFK Airport, Sean made the decision that we should walk away from the contract. He did not want Navios paying a "side fee" to a Panamanian bank account. It was the most forceful lesson of integrity that I had witnessed up until then in my career—and one that never left me.

SEARCH FOR THE ACHILLES HEEL

A business may be growing successfully and producing a positive income stream, but there is always a vulnerability lurking somewhere within the depths of an organization. As businesses grow, it becomes more difficult to search out and find these potential problems, particularly if the financial metrics of the business all look good. But I think it is terribly important to keep an eye out and search for possible weaknesses and address them before they jump out and cause serious business reversals.

I spent most of my career in shipping involved in the commercial areas of the industry, but as I worked my way up the proverbial corporate ladder and became a senior executive, I became more in touch with other aspects of the business and how they affected the company as a whole. Whether it had to do with our cash management program, or operational facets of our business, or perhaps charter party contract details, or the company morale, or the performance of our managers and executives, I developed a laser like focus on what I would come to call the potential Achilles heel of the organization.

In 1985, on one of my trips to Argentina to help coordinate the joint venture for the Russian grain program, I decided to make time to "hop" over the River Plate to Uruguay to visit the Navios terminal operation. Even though at the time I was not responsible for general oversight of the terminal, I felt I might as well take advantage of my presence in the region to see for myself how the terminal operated.

After touring the facility for a day and watching grain being discharged from barges, I was struck by the fact that we had one old crane, dating back to 1955, mounted on one of our caissons that we used to discharge the barges. I went to bed that first night in Nueva Palmira and kept thinking about that crane.

The next day I rose early, drove to the terminal facility, and sat quietly on the embankment by myself, sipping a cup of coffee. I looked out at the dock, the overhead conveyor, and the crane. The barge train was gone and a panamax bulk carrier that had arrived during the night was docked alongside our caissons and was being loaded. And then it struck me: Why was our entire operation dependent on a piece of equipment that was thirty years old? It was the key vulnerability in our entire terminal operation.

Every time I went back to visit the terminal, I would be focused on that old crane. It took a few years of continued shoreside investments in the terminal before I was able to convince the Navios board of directors that we should be upgrading this one discharging crane with the construction of the new barge dock.

This was a great lesson for me, because as I gained responsibility for the entire company, I made a point of reviewing all our business segments from the perspective of their Achilles heels and the vulnerabilities they created. I evaluated not only existing business segments but, perhaps more notably, the potential problems of new ventures as well.

GET THE RIGHT PEOPLE ON THE BUS

People are the heart and soul of any organization. Whether you are an internet start-up, an investment bank, a manufacturing plant, a law firm, a hotel, a steel mill, or a far-flung maritime company—if you don't have the right team working with you, focused on shared goals, you will not succeed.

To move an organization in the direction you wish to see it proceed, you need to "get the right people on the bus" so that you can all move forward together. It sounds straightforward, but it can make for some gut-wrenching decision-making. It is quite easy to convince yourself that if things are going well, you don't need to rock the boat and you can follow the adage: "If it ain't broke, don't fix it."

But in business, you need to think outside the box, and sometimes the best way to achieve this is to hire someone from outside the box, which is precisely what I did with Robert Shaw. As a senior executive, he brought to the organization a new perspective and certain strengths that we lacked. His insights proved vital to moving the company forward.

Part of this process is looking at yourself in the mirror and having a deep sense of *your* professional strengths and, perhaps more importantly, *your* weaknesses. Once you have a firm understanding of these qualities, you will be better able to assess the kind of people you need to support you and the organization in the future.

FLATTEN THE ORGANIZATION

A streamlined organization that permits greater responsibility and self-determination will likely lead to a leaner, nimbler, and more efficient company. This will facilitate for those individuals running the business a better and larger perspective of what is going on. It will result in a more rapid—and I would stress *more effective*—decision-making process. It will also improve communication throughout the organization. In addition, it should achieve a reduction in administrative overhead costs, although this should not be the sole reason behind such an initiative.

Most businesses start small. STH is a good example of this: We had only two layers of management. It was easy to communicate, and mixed signals didn't occur. But as a company grows in scale, invariably new levels of management creep in and the process of managing becomes more cumbersome. Making decisions becomes more centralized, communication can become blurred, and organizational complexity leads to a slow system.

When I arrived at Navios in 1982, the company hierarchy included dozens of supervisors, managers, general managers, directors, senior directors, vice presidents, and a president—and probably one or two other positions that I have long since forgotten. Much of this management structure was inherited from Navios's time as a subsidiary of U.S. Steel. It was tedious to get a decision made, as there was always this chain of interconnected reporting steps—some vertical and some horizontal—that had to be ascended before an answer was given or a result was achieved.

By the time I left Navios, we had only seven senior executives and roughly the same number of general managers overseeing about 125 shore-side-based employees located in the Norwalk head office, the Uruguay terminal, and our Piraeus technical ship management office. Two layers, with perhaps a third layer in certain divisions.

Because the one constant in all businesses today is the pace of change, it is important for an organization to stay agile. Fewer management layers are one of the best ways to achieve this.

ENCOURAGE YOUNG PEOPLE IN YOUR ORGANIZATION

I have always enjoyed the mental stimulation that young people bring to an organization. Their thinking is less rigid, and they are generally motivated to learn. They always bring a fresh perspective to the table because they do not have years of experience that has left their thought processes "blinkered." And young people bring the tools and understanding of today's ever-changing new technologies with them that set them apart from the middle-aged workforce.

The greatest compliment I ever received while running Navios was that it was a remarkable training ground for someone who wanted to enter the world of maritime transport. The company was an owner of ships and a charterer of ships, and it also pursued an aggressive policy of controlling ocean freight and trading ocean freight derivatives.

This type of maritime operation involves a very different and much more complicated operating philosophy than the traditional owner who works his ships' spot around the globe, fixing time charters for short periods. The simultaneous chartering activity of going "long" and "short" on the market, on the same day, based on various positions we had around the globe, ensured that from both an operational and commercial perspective our young staff received a maritime education that was second to none.

Evidence of this superlative experience was that our youngest and brightest were routinely poached by other companies every year. While that was frustrating operationally, it forced us to hire new young recruits, often with virtually no business experience, maritime or otherwise, and a wide variety of educational backgrounds—not unlike me back in 1975, when I joined Fednav.

Our attitude was, "It's not what you know, but how you think." The idea was that the less they knew about our industry, the better, because they could bring a fresh perspective to the business. As in any training or teaching situation, the teacher can learn as much from his students as he teaches them.

FINANCIAL LEVERAGE

Perhaps the most important foundation of any business is its capital structure—the ratio of equity to various types of debt—and this is especially true in a business built on trading. I understand the benefit of using borrowed funds to enhance the returns on the equity capital one has invested in a business. However, I believe that too much financial leverage in a trading business can be a recipe for disaster. To properly manage a business that operates in such an environment, one needs to have an intense and unwavering focus on both its capital structure and exposure to market risk.

Take the example of D.K. Ludwig, the billionaire shipbuilder. He built ships in Japan against ten-year fixed-rate charters with companies like U.S. Steel, with little implied signature risk. He leveraged his deals to about 90 percent. Under these contracts, Ludwig had no technical ship management risk, because the ships were bareboat chartered, and he had no operating risk. Since he was not controlling the movement of the ships, and given the financial standing at that time of the counterparty, I would argue he had little or no credit risk. This was smart leverage.

In the twenty-first century, lenders to the maritime industry have reduced their advance rates to 55 to 60 percent. Although many shipowners have tried to fight this trend, I believe it is a healthy development for our industry. Why? Because today in our business, multiyear fixed-freight-rate contracts of affreightment, or long-term fixed-rate time charters, rarely exist. (The exception might be for specialized ships such as LNG carriers or belt self-unloading vessels.) In a spot market environment, the revenue stream from an asset is not guaranteed and, more significantly, it can fluctuate widely.

In a trading business, you must develop a strategy or business plan that focuses not only on the potential upside but, perhaps more crucially, on the downside risk and how your capital structure can withstand such risks. Whether it's a global financial crisis, like what we experienced in 2008, or a global pandemic like we are experiencing as I write, or some other type of

black swan event, a company must be structured on a sound financial footing that allows for these negative unforeseen events.

They will occur and they will impact your business in ways that you simply did not ever envision. It is why I believe firmly in the adage: "Plan low, pray high."

DO BUSINESS WITH PEOPLE YOU LIKE

My last lesson learned is one you think would be instinctive to most people: You should do business with individuals you like. After everything is said and done, people conclude deals with other people, not their businesses. So, it just makes sense. When businesspeople like one another, it leads to a level of communication that is elevated, which, in turn, creates trust, which is important in helping a business succeed.

I believe one of my strengths is an ability to size people up—to judge their character and qualities—very quickly. This has allowed me to conclude business with partners I respect and like—and to avoid concluding business with those I just don't like. I have seen business colleagues conclude deals with people they did not warm up to, because they felt the deal offered them a competitive advantage. In the short term that may work, but when the wheels start to come off the deal, the true character of those people you did not like tends to come out, and it can make life very difficult.

Before we concluded the Navios-Levant merger, I spent countless hours and had many visits with Anastassis David and his family. I came away respecting them for their high level of honesty and reliability. But for me, the most important element was that I came to like and trust Anastassis himself. This relationship became the bedrock of our business ventures over the years.

Life is too short to end up in business enterprises with people you do not like. Simple but true.

***

The lessons I have learned throughout my time in the maritime industry have served as a road map to help me address many of the obstacles I have encountered along the way. These lessons have provided me a sense of direction, not unlike the lighthouses that provided nineteenth-century ships with their bearings as they journeyed around the world.

Nevertheless, there is no doubt that luck can play a significant part in the success of any business, and I think most entrepreneurs would readily admit this. No matter how well you develop and then execute your strategies, ultimately there are events outside of your control that will impact your business.

Some colleagues and friends have told me that we were very fortunate to have sold NMH when we did. In other words, we got lucky. We were in the right place at the right time, during what was the very unusual event of enormous urbanization in China and the super-cycle dry bulk boom. I view it slightly differently.

Yes, we were in the right place at the right time, but that was the result of years of experience and much hard work to ensure the company was well positioned so that when our market did explode, we were able to find the best opportunities and run with them. To paraphrase a wise maxim of the ancient Romans: "Fortune favors the bold and the prepared."

AFTERWORD

The arrival of COVID-19 in Wuhan in December of 2019, and its rapid progression throughout the world, was a truly transformative experience for so many of us. It was something that none of us, except for a very few centenarians, had ever experienced. For me personally, it not only provided an opportunity to think about and write this book, but it also caused me to focus on just how interconnected we are with each other and with the global community at large.

At a micro level, COVID-19 disconnected us from our friends and relatives. We traveled less, or not at all. We spent huge amounts of time confined in our homes. We refrained from normal physical proximity with one another. Hugs and kisses were left by the wayside. Work life for many changed dramatically, with entire segments of the business community shifting from the routine 9-to-5 on-site paradigm to remote hybrid models.

On a macro level, COVID-19 made us understand just how interconnected the economies around the globe are, as many goods are not manufactured in their native countries, but, in numerous cases, half a world away. Factories, and in some cases entire industries, were shut down due to the ravages of the pandemic on their workforces, or the impact on the supply of the materials they needed to create their products. As I recounted earlier, when the economies started to reopen, surging demand for goods caused severe bottlenecks in the transportation infrastructure. For the very first time in my career, people across all segments of life were focused on maritime transport as a disrupter in their lives.

Trade between people and countries has been shrinking boundaries for a millennium, serving to bring people closer together. The business of maritime transport has allowed the movement of goods along the saltwater highway for thousands of years, helping to support the interconnectedness we all feel as humans. This interconnectivity between nations has become part of our reality. I believe it will continue to strengthen as people continue to reach out to people across borders. Possibly the greatest support for interconnectedness as we move further into the twenty-first century will be the efforts the human race must undertake to address global warming, which knows no borders.

Perhaps in August 1963, Martin Luther King Jr. said it best when he wrote in his "Letter from Birmingham Jail": "I am cognizant of the interrelatedness of all communities and states.... We are caught in an inescapable network of mutuality, tied in a single garment of destiny. Whatever affects one directly, affects all indirectly."

I am fortunate to have always had a sense of curiosity, which has helped me embrace a wide variety of interests and activities. However, maritime shipping has been, and will continue to be, an important part of my life. Whether or not I become involved in another maritime venture, I intend to keep a close eye on developments within this industry, one that has been such a stimulating and remarkable environment within which to have worked for so many years.

My journey has been fun, exciting, and in many ways a rewarding lifetime experience. I have traveled the globe and developed an understanding, knowledge, and appreciation for a wide variety of cultures. I have managed to cultivate friendships with individuals in countries scattered around the world. Most importantly, though, I have developed a diversity of perspectives, which I think is so essential in the increasingly interconnected world in which we live today.

Anthony R. Whitworth
Rowayton, Connecticut
September 2023

GLOSSARY

Address Commission: The fee paid by vessel owners to charterers. It is normally 3.75 percent of revenue. The charterer uses this fee to cover some of his commodity costs.

Auxiliary Boiler: A steam generator that draws high-pressure super-heated steam from the vessel's propulsion system that is then used to power other shipboard engines such as winches, pumps, or the freshwater evaporator.

Backhaul: A marine transportation carrier's return movement of cargo, usually opposite from the direction of its primary cargo distribution (which is known as the fronthaul, and has the highest cargo volumes).

Ballasted: Indicates a ship is proceeding without cargo, but has taken on weight (ballast) generally in the form of water to maintain stability and proper trim of a ship, and to ensure the propeller remains below water.

Ballast Water Treatment System (BWTS): The system used to destroy biological marine organisms from ballast water used to stabilize a ship, stopping the spread of invasive aquatic species being moved through the carriage of ballast water from one geographic area to another.

Baltic Dry Index (BDI): A composite index that measures the average spot (daily) rates for dry bulk freight, with a sector weighting of 40 percent capesize, 30 percent panamax, and 30 percent supramax. It is reported around the world as a proxy for dry bulk shipping stocks, as well as a general shipping market bellwether.

The category of contract for the lease of a vessel, generally for a number of years, where the vessel's owner places the vessel at the complete disposal of the charterer and pays only the capital costs to acquire the ship. The charterer has technical and commercial responsibility for the vessel and pays all operating costs, such as crew wages, victualing, maintenance/repairs, insurances, fuel, and port costs.

Beaufort Scale:
The method used to estimate wind speed based on the general condition of the surface of a large body of water for wind, waves, and swell.

Belt Self-Unloading/
Belt Self-Unloader:
Specialized ships that use gravity to release cargo through gates located along the bottom of a vessel's cargo holds onto conveyor belts that run along the entire length of the ship under the cargo hold. The cargo is transferred to an elevating system and moved on deck to a large discharging boom, with a conveyor belt that discharges the cargo to shore. Belt self-unloaders can discharge cargo much more rapidly than a conventional bulk carrier with cranes and grabs, and they require a minimum of shore-based labor and infrastructure.

Biomass Energy:
The energy produced from renewable sources such as wood and its products.

Black Swan Event:
The term coined by Nassim Taleb to define rare events that have catastrophic economic impacts when they do occur.

Boarding Clerk:
The person responsible for coordinating with the captain and port official's various aspects of a vessel's arrival and departure from a port.

Bollard:
A sturdy, short post used on a ship or a quay for mooring ships.

Break-Bulk:
Refers to goods that cannot be loaded in a container or in bulk, but must be stored and lashed separately in a vessel's hold or sometimes on deck.

Bridge Deck:	The upper deck from which the ship is controlled and constantly manned. This deck houses the electronics, navigational charts, the helm, and controls for the main engine, among many items.
Bunker Fuel:	Any fuel used on board a ship, usually to power engine propulsion or onboard generators.
Bunkering:	Stations at ports of call that supply fuel to oceangoing ships.
Caissons:	Large watertight retaining structure.
Capesize/ Capesize Ship:	A dry bulk carrier measuring anywhere from 250 to 280 meters in length, with a draft of about seventeen meters, with a carrying capacity of about 200,000 deadweight tonnes. Typical cargoes carried include iron ore, coal, and bauxite.
Charterers:	Companies that charter a ship.
Charter Party:	A maritime contract between the owner of a ship and the charterer for use in transporting cargo.
Clamshell Buckets:	Buckets with hinged jaws or teeth that are hung from cables on a crane and used to dig and pick up bulk materials.
Classification Society:	Establishes and maintains technical standards for construction and operation of marine vessels and offshore structures. It classifies and certifies marine vessels and structures on the basis of their structure, design, and safety standards.
Coke:	A commodity produced by heating coal at high temperatures for long periods. This high-carbon fuel is used in iron ore smelting.
Container Ship:	A cargo vessel that is designed to carry its load in truck-size intermodal containers.
Contract of Affreightment:	A contract between a shipowner and charterer in which the shipowner agrees to carry commodity in one or more vessels for the charterer at an agreed freight rate per tonne.

Cost/Insurance/ Freight (CIF):	The costs associated with transporting goods to the nearest port, loading the goods onto the ship, and paying freight for the goods to be delivered to a port chosen by the buyer. The price the buyer pays for the commodity includes all these costs.
Cumulative Annual Growth Rate (CAGR):	The geometric progression ratio that provides a constant rate of return over a specific period.
Deadweight:	A vessel's cargo-carrying capacity measured in tonnes.
Demurrage:	The fees charged to the charterer specified in a voyage charter by the shipowner, payable when the ship is loaded or unloaded in a time that is greater than stipulated in the charter party.
Derivative Contracts:	Financial contracts that allow shipowners, charterers, and speculators to hedge and trade against the volatility of a basket of standardized freight rates.
Derricks:	A lifting device that consists of a fixed, self-supporting post with a boom hinged at its base to provide articulation movement.
Draft:	The vertical distance between the waterline and the bottom of a ship's hull; the depth of water that a vessel requires to float freely.
Dry Bulk Carrier Ship:	Vessels ranging in size from 25,000 to 250,000 tonnes specially designed to transport large quantities of dry bulk material.
Dry Bulk Markets/ Shipping:	The movement of significant commodities carried in bulk—the so-called major bulks of iron ore, coal, and grain, together with ships carrying steel products (coils, plates, and rods); lumber or logs and other commodities such as bauxite, cement, fertilizer, forest products, and sugar are classified as the minor bulks.
Dunnage:	Dunnage is inexpensive waste material used to protect and secure cargo during transportation, such as wooden blocks, boards, and burlap.

Eurodollar Market:	U.S. dollars held in time deposit accounts in banks outside the United States; they are not subject to the legal jurisdiction of the U.S. Federal Reserve.
Fenders:	A safe interface between the hull of a ship docking and the berth structure itself.
Flag State:	The jurisdiction under whose laws a vessel is registered and whose nationality the ship is deemed to be.
Forward Freight Agreements (FFAs):	Forward financial contracts that allow shipowners, charterers, and speculators to manage financial risk by hedging against the volatility of freight rates. The agreements are derived from the underlying maritime shipping routes.
Free on Board (FOB):	The term used to indicate that the seller of the commodity is responsible for placing the cargo into the ship, and the buyer assumes the cost and risk of transporting the commodity to its destination.
Funnel:	The smokestack, or chimney, of a ship through which exhaust gases are expelled.
Geared/gearless:	Terms used for vessels equipped with onboard cranes, or without cranes.
Gross Registered Tonnes:	The total permanently enclosed capacity of a vessel by volume, including spaces that are not available for the carriage of commodity, such as the engine room, fuel tanks, and crew quarters.
Handysize/ Handymax:	Geared dry bulk carriers of between 20,000 and 45,000 deadweight tonnes.
Hatch Coaming:	A raised section of deck plating around a cargo hold designed to prevent water ingress.
High-Risk Area (HRA):	An industry designation to indicate the passage of a ship through waters considered high risk for piracy attacks.

Hopper:	A large container for bulk cargoes such as coal or grain or aggregates that tapers downward (like a funnel) and is able to discharge its contents onto a conveyor belt.
Inert Gas Systems:	The system, used in vessels that transport cargo such as crude oil that produces flammable gases, to prevent fire or explosion by pumping into the cargo holds inert gas containing insufficient oxygen to support ignition.
Landed Cost:	The sum of expenses associated with shipping a product to its final destination.
Laytime:	The amount of time in a voyage charter allowed by a shipowner to have his vessel loaded and discharged.
Lay Up/Layup:	Taking a ship temporarily out of service to await better markets.
Lifting(s):	Industry term for cargo(es)
Lightweight:	The actual weight of a ship with no fuel, water, or cargo on board.
Liner Services:	Ships that operate within a schedule and have a fixed port rotation, with published dates of calls at the advertised ports.
Marine Pilots:	Trained seamen with knowledge of a specific port or restricted waterway hired to assist in the maneuvering of a vessel.
Newbuilding:	A term used in the industry to describe new ships that have been ordered by owners at shipyards.
Off Hire:	The time when the obligation of a charterer to pay hire to an owner is exempted due to specific reasons tabled in a charter party contract, such as a breakdown of hull and machinery, arrest of the ship by creditors, or any other cause preventing the full working of the ship.
Panamax:	Dry bulk carriers of between 72,000 and 85,000 deadweight tonnes.

Pedestal Cranes:	Steel crane house bolted to elevated pedestals via the slew bearing; winches, electrical cabinets, and/or power units are located inside the crane house to protect it from the harsh marine environment.
Petcoke (Petroleum Coke):	A carbon-intensive fuel created during oil refining
Product Tankers:	Tankers between 50,000 and 75,000 deadweight tonnes, with coated tanks used to carry refined oil products such as aviation fuel or gasoline.
Radial Telescopic Ship Loader:	A method of loading ships using a belt conveyor that, because of the radial and telescopic features, allows the operator to load multiple holds of a ship from one feeding position.
Rollers:	Long, powerful waves.
Roll-on/Roll-off (roro):	A vessel designed to carry wheeled vehicles such as cars and trucks.
Rudder:	A primary control surface that is used to steer a ship by deflecting water flow. It is located at the stern of a vessel just aft of the propeller.
SHEX:	Calculation of laytime excluding Sundays and holidays, even if loading/discharging work is carried out.
SHINC:	Calculation of laytime including Sundays and holidays.
Shipping Agent/ Agency:	A company retained by cargo interests, shipowners, and charterers of ships in ports around the world to represent their interests when loading or discharging a ship.
Shipbrokers:	Companies that assist shipowners in finding employment for their ships and serves as a liaison between them and charterers or vessel operators or other shipowners who may require tonnage. They are used as a source of market research and information.

Sinking Fund:	A fund containing money set aside or saved to pay off a debt or a bond.
Special Survey Dry Dock:	Ships undergo a full dry-docking every five years during which all of the equipment is inspected, the hull is painted, and all class certificates are surveyed and renewed.
Spot Market:	Time charter rates and voyage freight rates quoted daily.
Superstructure:	The part of the ship that rises above the main deck at the aft end of the ship. It typically houses crew and officer quarters, the galley, and the bridge deck, from where the ship is controlled.
Supramax:	Craned dry bulk carrier of between 52,000 and 58,000 deadweight tonnes.
Tailings Dam:	A large earth-filled embankment used to store the by-products of mining operations, in liquid, solid, or slurry.
Take or Pay:	A contract in which a charterer agrees to pay for any shortfall in the cargo volumes stipulated in the agreement, regardless of reason. Also known as a "hell or high water" contract.
Tank Top:	The floor of a vessel's hold.
Technical Ship Management:	The service rendered to operate and maintain ships. It includes such things as arranging for crews, victualing, equipment and stores, repairs and maintenance, insurance, dry docks, etc.
Thermal Coal:	Coal used to create steam to power large turbines to generate electricity.
Time Charter:	The hiring of a vessel for a specific period. The owner still manages and crews the vessel, but the charterer selects the ports and directs the vessel where to go. The charterer pays for all fuel the vessel consumes, port charges, commissions, and a daily rate of hire to the owner of the vessel.

Tonnes:

Metric units of mass that is equal to 1,000 kilograms. It is the equivalent of about 2,204 pounds, which is one long ton.

Tonne-Mile:

A measurement that reflects both volumes shipped (tonnes) and distance shipped (miles). Tonne-mile provides a more precise figure of demand for commodity.

Tween Deck:

An extra deck with cargo hatches located between the tank top and the main deck of a ship.

Ultramax:

Craned dry bulk carrier of between 60,000 and 65,000 deadweight tonnes.

Warped:

A manner of moving a boat alongside a dock face by hauling on lines attached to dock bollards.

Weather Deck:

An exposed deck open to the elements.

REFERENCES AND CITATIONS FOR SOURCES USED

- "The Yeoman Story – A review by Kurt Lawson FIQ," Agg-Net, https://www.agg-net.com/resources/articles/business-finance/the-yeoman-story.
- "'There is no wealth to distribute': Venezuela poverty rate surges," Al Jazeera, July 8, 2020, https://www.aljazeera.com/economy/2020/7/8/there-is-no-wealth-to-distribute-venezuela-poverty-rate-surges.
- Kimberly Amadeo, "Causes of the 2008 Global Financial Crisis," The Balance, last modified December 13, 2022, https://www.thebalancemoney.com/what-caused-2008-global-financial-crisis-3306176.
- Biomass Energy Systems: "Florida Eucalyptus Energy Farm," 1982
- Claude Couture, "Quebec," The Canadian Encyclopedia, last modified March 30, 2021, https://www.thecanadianencyclopedia.ca/en/article/quebec.
- James H. Marsh, "Quebec Bridge Disaster," The Canadian Encyclopedia, last modified March 4, 2015, https://www.thecanadianencyclopedia.ca/en/article/quebec-bridge-disaster-feature.
- Paul-André Linteau, "Quebec Since Confederation," The Canadian Encyclopedia, last modified March 4, 2015, https://www.thecanadianencyclopedia.ca/en/article/quebec-since-confederation
- "Galley," Cayman Islands Seafarers Association, http://www.caymanseafarers.ky/gallery.

- Mark Munson, "Coal to Oil and the Great Green Fleet," Center for International Maritime Security, May 7, 2013, https://cimsec.org/coal-to-oil-and-the-great-green-fleet/.

- Amelia Cheatham, Diana Roy, and Rocio Cara Labrador, "Venezuela: The Rise and Fall of a Petrostate," Council on Foreign Relations, last modified March 10, 2023, https://www.cfr.org/backgrounder/venezuela-crisis.

- Lindsay Maizland and Eleanor Albert, "The Chinese Communist Party," Council on Foreign Relations,, last modified October 6, 2022, https://www.cfr.org/backgrounder/chinese-communist-party.

- Miguel Tinker Salas, *The Enduring Legacy: Oil, Culture, and Society in Venezuela* (Durham: Duke University Press, 2009).

- "The State of Food Security and Nutrition in the World," Food and Agricultural Organization of the United Nations, https://www.fao.org/publications/sofi/2022/en/.

- Great Lakes St. Lawrence Seaway System, https://greatlakes-seaway.com/en/.

- *Hansard: UK Commons Sitting*, vol. 4, no. 2, (1821).

- Bill Gates, *How to Avoid a Climate Disaster: The Solutions We Have and the Breakthroughs We Need* (New York: Knopf Doubleday Publishing, 2021).

- Ignacio Rodríguez-Iturbe, "A Modern Statistical Study of Monthly Levels of the Orinoco River," *International Association of Scientific Hydrology*, vol. 13, no. 4 (1968): 25-41.

- "Uruguay," International Monetary Fund, https://www.imf.org/en/Countries/URY.

- International Rivers Network, https://www.irn.org/.

- Brian Beers, "How the Federal Reserve Devises Monetary Policy," Investopedia, last modified November 30, 2022, https://www.investopedia.com/investing/federal-reserve-monetary-policy/.

- James Chen, "What Is The Dutch Disease? Origin of Term and Examples," Investopedia, last modified October 31, 2021, https://www.investopedia.com/terms/d/dutchdisease.asp.

- "Israel Science & Technology: Oil & Natural Gas ," Jewish Virtual Library, https://www.jewishvirtuallibrary.org/oil-and-natural-gas-in-israel.
- League of Nations Data for Oil Production
- Liverpool Ships, http://www.liverpoolships.org/.
- Soumaya Chakraborty, "Understanding Design of Bulk Carriers," Marine Insight, September 26, 2019, https://www.marineinsight.com/naval-architecture/understanding-design-bulk-carriers/.
- "The Top Ten Zinc Producing Mines in the World," Mining.com, October 8, 2018, https://www.mining.com/top-ten-zinc-producing-mines-world/.
- *Montreal Gazette*: Various articles 1977–1988.
- Vegard Bye, *Nationalization of Oil in Venezuela*, vol. 16, no. 1 (1979).
- New Geography, http://www.newgeography.com/.
- Michael C. Jensen, "Soviet Grain Deal Is Called a Coup," *New York Times*, September 29, 1972, https://www.nytimes.com/1972/09/29/archives/soviet-grain-deal-is-called-a-coup-capitalistic-skill-surprised.html.
- "Climate Change: Shipping Pollution," Oceana Europe, https://europe.oceana.org/shipping-pollution/
- Rachel Chenven Powers, "The 'Great Grain Robbery' of 1972," Oceanic Engineering Society,, October 28, 2015, https://earthzine.org/the-great-grain-robbery-of-1972/.
- Max Roser, Hannah Ritchie, Esteban Ortiz-Ospina, and Lucas Rodés-Guirao, "World Population Growth," Our World in Data, https://ourworldindata.org/world-population-growth.
- Sophia Murphy, David Burch, and Jennifer Clapp, "Cereal Secrets: The world's largest grain traders and global agriculture," Oxfam Research Reports, August 3, 2012, https://www.oxfam.org/en/research/cereal-secrets-worlds-largest-grain-traders-and-global-agriculture.
- Canal de Panamá, https://pancanal.com/.
- Tom Bergin, "The Great Greek Shipping Myth," Reuters Investigates, November 25, 2015, https://www.reuters.com/investigates/special-report/eurozone-greece-shipping/.

- David E. Bloom, David Canning, and Günther Fink, "Urbanization and the Wealth of Nations," *Science*, vol. 319, no. 5864 (2008): 772-775, https://www.science.org/doi/abs/10.1126/science.1153057.

- "Ore Carriers," *ScienceDirect*, https://www.sciencedirect.com/topics/engineering/ore-carriers.

- Ivan Diaz-Rainey, Gbenga Ibikunle, and Anne-Laure Mention, "The technological transformation of capital markets," *Technological Forecasting and Social Change*, vol. 99, (2015): 277-284, https://www.sciencedirect.com/science/article/abs/pii/S0040162515002528.

- Eileen Reid Marcil, *Tall Ships and Tankers: The History of the Davie Shipbuilders* (Toronto: McClelland & Stewart, 1997).

- "World Urbanization Prospects, 2018 Revision," United Nations, https://www.un.org/development/desa/pd/content/world-urbanization-prospects-2018-revision.

- U. S. House Resolution 5660 (H.R.5660, 106th Congress): Commodity Futures Modernization Act of 2000

- "Best Countries Ranking," *U.S. News & World Report*, April 2021, https://www.usnews.com/media/best-countries/overall-rankings-2021.pdf

- "Canadian name," Wikipedia, last modified March 7, 2023, https://en.wikipedia.org/wiki/Canadian_name.

- "Daniel K. Ludwig," Wikipedia, last modified November 30, 2022, https://en.wikipedia.org/wiki/Daniel_K._Ludwig.

- "General Agreement on Tariffs and Trade," Wikipedia, last modified February 6, 2023, https://en.wikipedia.org/wiki/General_Agreement_on_Tariffs_and_Trade.

- "Greek shipping," Wikipedia, last modified March 13, 2023, https://en.wikipedia.org/wiki/Greek_shipping.

- "Orinoco," Wikipedia, last modified January 7, 2023, https://en.wikipedia.org/wiki/Orinoco.

- "Security (finance)," Wikipedia, last modified March 6, 2023, https://en.wikipedia.org/wiki/Security_(finance).

- "1989 Tiananmen Square protests and massacre," Wikipedia, last modified March 12, 2023, https://en.wikipedia.org/wiki/1989_Tiananmen_Square_protests_and_massacre.

- "Venezuela," Wikipedia, last modified March 13, 2023, https://en.wikipedia.org/wiki/Venezuela.
- Geoffrey Migiro, "Countries With The Most Natural Resources," *World Atlas*, August 29, 2018, https://www.worldatlas.com/articles/countries-with-the-most-natural-resources.html.
- "Latin America and Caribbean—Southern Cone Inland Waterways Transportation Study: The Paraguay-Paraná Hidrovía: Its Role in the Regional Economy and Impact on Climate Change," World Bank, 2010, https://openknowledge.worldbank.org/entities/publication/40663fb1-aef1-52b4-b08e-61ec919f6f10.
- Javier Blas and Jack Farchy, *The World for Sale: Money, Power, and the Traders Who Barter the Earth's Resources* (Oxford: Oxford University Press, 2021).

ACKNOWLEDGMENTS

Michael Bell, a former executive vice president of Fednav, was my primary mentor. He had the most direct influence on my career development during my formative years in maritime shipping. I met him a few months after I joined the company. He was a larger-than-life individual whose outgoing personality and physical size made him a presence felt at all times by all people. He encouraged, criticized, taught, reprimanded, and directed me. Although I did not realize it at the time, he guided my career from 1976 until 1988, and for that, I will be forever indebted. Sadly, he will not be able to read this book, as he passed away in 2020.

I have generally avoided developing close personal friendships within my industry. I was wary of a personal relationship affecting my judgment, and I never wanted to find myself in the position of having to terminate the employment of a friend. Perhaps most importantly, I wanted my time away from the industry to be with friends who would not draw me into discussing business issues during my leisure time. Nevertheless, I have enjoyed a few business relationships that matured into close friendships, three of which I would like to take a moment to mention.

Perhaps the most significant is with Robert Shaw, whom I first met in 1999, and with whom I continue to work, even as I write these words. We have developed a close, collaborative working relationship over nearly two and a half decades that has matured into a strong personal bond.

Robert is many things that I am not: He is an erudite individual, whereas I am more of a man with, I like to think, a good deal of common sense. He has a remarkably strong understanding of the complexities of the written word, whereas I am more numerate. He is multilingual, whereas I am bilingual. He has an amazing ability to grind down into the details, whereas I generally view things from a macro perspective. He is an unflagging networker who is constantly reaching out to connect with others, while I am perhaps more of an individualist. He loves the stimulation of city living (and has withdrawal symptoms if he is away from a city for much longer than a fortnight!), whereas I love the peace and quiet of the country. In essence, many of Robert's character traits complement my own, and vice versa, which possibly explains why we have been successful in our endeavors together.

Shigeki Nakagawa was for many years the president of Fednav Asia, responsible for much of that company's activity in Japan. We first met in 1984 on one of my initial trips to Japan, and we developed a strong rapport built upon his familiarizing me with the unique business customs of this remarkable country.

But as the years moved by, we became good friends as he introduced me to the Japanese culture: etiquette, food, domestic travel, and, of course, Japanese golf. Even though we remain physically half a world apart, and have not done business together for over twenty years, we find time to communicate regularly by telephone. Of course, anytime I am in Japan on business or a personal trip, or he is back in Canada visiting Fednav, we always spend time together. He has been a wonderful guiding hand over the years.

Pablo Soler was responsible for managing the Navios dry bulk terminal in Uruguay, and we share many memories of travels undertaken together over close to twenty years, not just in Uruguay, but also throughout South America. We were strategically able to develop the terminal in Nueva Palmira into a globally recognized port facility that became synonymous with professionalism and efficiency. We have developed a close rapport that continues today.

I thank each of them for their unwavering support and friendship through the decades.

***

Many people have provided me with guidance, information, and memories throughout the past twenty-four months that have helped me tremendously in the process of writing this book.

Robert Shaw kindly agreed to read early drafts and offered me not only editorial comment, but also ideas as to themes, structure, and form, which resulted in a better manuscript.

Dave Carlucci and Sandy Levinson read an early draft and offered me some useful suggestions and comments from the perspective of readers who are not in the maritime industry. I thank them both for taking the time to plow through the manuscript of a novice writer.

Several retired Navios employees provided me color, context, and information on various activities of the group. Most interviews were conducted by FaceTime, and with certain colleagues I had multiple exchanges.

- Frank Caviglia was particularly helpful in providing me with details of the Navios-owned fleet in the 1960s through 1980s.
- Sean Day helped to refresh my memory of the difficult early years at Navios following Fednav's initial investment in the company.
- Ennio Distefano was able to brief me on his time working in both the Orinoco and Plate Rivers, as well as his time spent up at Kivalina, Alaska.
- David Elsy was kind enough to review with me the development of Navios's self-unloading business in the 1980s and 1990s, as well as freight initiatives with U.S. Steel over the years.
- Chris Kitsos shared some of the Navios Ship Agencies' history with me.
- Michael McClure kindly offered me insights into his time working for Navios in the Bahamas, the Navios office move to New York, and Navios's involvement in the movement of Russian grain in the 1980s.
- Ted Petrone provided me with guidance on Navios's time-chartered fleet in the early 1980s.
- Geoff Riches offered me colorful details of both the Glensanda and Red Dog operational start-ups.
- John Weale was most helpful in providing me with information on strategic Navios initiatives in the early 1980s.

I am also grateful to Theyre Smith and John Peacock, who worked at Fednav for many years and who provided me with some invaluable perspective.

To all of the above, I offer my sincere thanks.

One of the difficulties of writing a book of this nature is that various individuals have differing recollections of past events, some of which reconfirmed my own thinking and others that did not. Consequently, there were occasions when I had to make a judgmental decision as to the accuracy of past events. I am therefore fully accountable for any inconsistencies, errors, or omissions that some may find in this manuscript. The fog created by the passing of time is my only excuse.

Paul Dinas courageously agreed to take on the task of editing the manuscript of a novice writer. He assisted me in redrafting the structure of the manuscript from an initial seventeen to twenty-eight chapters. In addition, he suggested intelligent edits, offered me plenty of thought-provoking questions, and was always a source of encouragement when things got tedious. The manuscript in its current form is largely a reflection of his input. For his efforts, I am truly thankful.

Stephanie Finnegan proved to be invaluable as a copy editor. She reviewed the final draft of the manuscript and made many spelling, grammar, and punctuation edits. She also addressed a number of changes to the citations in the text.

And, finally, a special thanks to my wife, Jen, who has stood by and watched me work on this manuscript over the past thirty-six months at odd hours of the day and night. She read the manuscript at various times during the writing process and was a sounding board when I shared thoughts with her of what I was contemplating writing or not writing into the text. My work has interrupted many of our daily routines, and I offer her my apologies. It is not an exaggeration to say that without her emotional support and love, I simply could not have completed this effort.